D0500280

The

NEW AMERICAN
REVOLUTION

THE MAKING OF A POPULIST MOVEMENT

Kayleigh McEnany

THRESHOLD EDITIONS

New York   London   Toronto   Sydney   New Delhi

An Imprint of Simon & Schuster, Inc.
1230 Avenue of the Americas
New York, NY 10020

First Threshold Editions hardcover edition January 2018

THRESHOLD EDITIONS and colophon are trademarks of Simon & Schuster, Inc.

For information about special discounts for bulk purchases, please contact
Simon & Schuster Special Sales at 1-866-506-1949 or business@simonandschuster.com.

The Simon & Schuster Speakers Bureau can bring authors to your live event.
For more information, or to book an event, contact the Simon & Schuster Speakers
Bureau at 1-866-248-3049 or visit our website at www.simonspeakers.com.

Interior design by Joy O'Meara

Manufactured in the United States of America

10 9 8 7 6 5 4 3 2 1

Library of Congress Cataloging-in-Publication Data is available.

ISBN 978-1-5011-7968-6
ISBN 978-1-5011-7970-9 (ebook)

For the American people—this is your story.

And for Megan Carpenter and Rachel Joy Scott—
two women whose lives will always inspire mine.

CONTENTS

FOREWORD

By Sean Hannity

"How did you see it—this movement of the people that elected Donald Trump as president?" It's a question I'm asked often, and the answer might lie in my past. I was a paperboy at eight, a dishwasher at twelve, a cook at thirteen, a busboy at fourteen, a waiter at fifteen, and a bartender at seventeen. Then I started painting houses, hanging wallpaper, laying tile, and framing roofs. That's how I spent two decades of my life, and despite a long career as a prime-time host at Fox News and a syndicated radio host, I never lost touch with my blue-collar roots. It's who I am at my core.

While CNN was already heralding the "passing of the torch" from Barack Obama to Hillary Clinton the night before the election, I offered a reality check on the eve of Trump's victory, saying this: "Now the liberal-loving Clinton media—the mainstream media—you know, the ones colluding with the campaign? They've declared this election over before your votes have even been cast or counted. Now they say it's impossible for Donald Trump to win. I disagree. I don't think they could be further from the truth."

If the Destroy Trump Media had left the ivory tower echo chamber of Manhattan and DC and listened to the American people, maybe they would have seen it too. During Election 2016, I was on the road with these candidates—talking to the people, observing the crowds. You could feel this movement continually building behind President Trump. As the media lavished praise on the Obama presidency, I made a conscious decision to acknowledge the struggles of the people, not the so-called successes of a failed president. Every day I told my viewers about the 95 million Americans out of work, the 50 million in poverty, the 13 million on food stamps, and the fifty-one-year low in homeowners. These were the forgotten men and women whom President Trump spoke of. They are the story of Election 2016.

The plight of the people is something you rarely heard on CNN, and if you did, it was probably coming from my former intern and frequent guest on my Fox News show, Kayleigh McEnany. Kayleigh and her CNN coworker Jeffrey Lord were the two lone conservatives on CNN panels chock-full of liberal Democrats. Outnumbered 8-to-1 or, if she was lucky, 7-to-2, Kayleigh never backed down in fighting for the conservative movement supporting Donald Trump. My first Fox show, *Hannity & Colmes*, was her training ground as a young college student, which prepared her to fight for our president in the Destroy Trump Media. Now, my program *Hannity* is her welcome home after leaving CNN to become RNC spokesperson.

In *The New American Revolution*, Kayleigh puts a face on the struggles of the American people. These Americans—plagued by terrorism, criminal wrongdoing, economic hardship, and so much more—together formed the unstoppable movement of the people. Kayleigh traveled the country and profiled the lives of these Americans in moving detail—a mother in Lakeway, Texas, who lost her only child and husband to terrorism; a wife in McBee, South Carolina, whose husband died on an Obama-era VA waitlist; and a mother in Mineral Springs, Arkansas, whose son was killed in a tragic encounter with an illegal immigrant. You won't find these stories in the mainstream media, but you will find them here in the pages ahead. Why did Donald Trump win the presidency? Well, it's because of Americans like these, left behind by the federal government but resolutely determined to take their country back.

There's a painting that says it better than words ever could. It's a painting that I purchased called *The Forgotten Man* by Jon McNaughton. In it, a man in jeans, a flannel shirt, and a zip-down sweatshirt sits on a bench with his head cast down and his hands on his knees in apparent frustration. Behind him stands President Barack Obama with his foot on the Constitution, surrounded by the presidents who came before him. The White House glows in the far-off distance. Supposed to be America's house, it is now inaccessible to the exasperated citizen planted on a secluded bench. The painting's message is simple: Why are we not taking care of this guy who doesn't have a job, who's in poverty, who's out of work? In *The New American Revolution*, Kayleigh tells his story, the story of the forgotten man and woman who Donald Trump promised would be forgotten no longer.

INTRODUCTION

February 23, 2016. It was the night of the Nevada Republican caucuses and my first time appearing on one of those infamous CNN election night panels as the lone conservative Trump supporter stacked against seven anti-Trump panelists. You know the ones I'm talking about. Anderson Cooper in front of a glistening red, white, and blue set between two glass tables with four news personalities on either side of him. Well, I was one of those panelists, sitting just to the left of Anderson. I was that blond girl passionately advocating for then candidate Donald Trump, proudly wearing my gold cross and often seen sparring with the likes of Van Jones through the primaries, the debates, the conventions, and ultimately election night—a night no one will ever forget.

"I think Donald Trump is, at this point, the inevitable nominee," I said to my colleagues that night of the Nevada caucuses, several months before Trump would go on to clinch the Republican nomination. "He's restored hope in the American people." My liberal co-panelists at CNN were less than enthused by my optimistic Trump projections, but— much to their dismay—they would realize on November 8, 2016, that Donald Trump was indeed on an unstoppable path to the White House. As it turned out, conservative icons such as Sean Hannity, Rush Limbaugh, Laura Ingraham, and Mark Levin had a far better read on the American people than the Hollywood and media elite.

During my path through the heights of academia—Harvard, Georgetown, and Oxford—I had supplemented my curriculum with the work of conservative thought leaders like these. They often provided common sense that was woefully lacking on my liberal campuses, and their well-formed opinions equipped me to battle for President Trump in the bowels of the mainstream media.

As a young girl, I grew up listening to Rush Limbaugh in my dad's truck—a nostalgic memory that I was honored to share with Rush in person at the 2017 Media Research Center Gala. And as a teenage college student, I served as an intern for Fox News's *Hannity & Colmes*, where I learned from Sean Hannity, a valiant, bold, thoughtful conservative leader and one of the few television hosts with the foresight to see Donald Trump's victory on the horizon. Sean's occasional notes of encouragement throughout the 2016 election would rejuvenate my embattled spirit as I fought back against false and misleading stories aimed at taking down Donald Trump. His show, *Hannity*, now serves as a haven of truth for conservatives everywhere.

My internship with *Hannity & Colmes* eventually turned into a job at Fox News as a producer with *The Mike Huckabee Show*. Governor Mike Huckabee, a man of unparalleled integrity and Christian faith, opened my young eyes to the many exasperating aspects of Washington that Donald Trump would go on to describe as "the swamp"—the petty political games, the broken promises, the corruption, and betrayal. I took notice of Governor Huckabee's earnest demeanor and love for everyday Americans—attributes found rarely in the political class.

My work at Fox News with these two great conservatives undoubtedly prepared me for my role as a rare Trump supporter at CNN, but I would be remiss if I did not mention my liberal mentor and friend whom I miss deeply—the late Alan Colmes.

When I was just a no-name college student, Alan took the time to recommend me for an internship. It didn't matter that I was conservative or a millennial; Alan wanted to help me because helping was in his DNA. For the next ten years of my career and last ten years of Alan's life, he would periodically reach out to check in or provide words of support. "You maintained your composure and dignity, and that is key," he wrote to me after a particularly hostile CNN segment.

All throughout the election, conservatives—and even some liberals—would stop me and ask "How do you keep your cool on those outnumbered panels?" Well, the wise words of a man lost too soon are the answer. "[Y]ou don't fight fire with fire, you fight it with water," Alan shared with me. Faced with attacks that got far too personal, I would continually remind myself of those words. They gave me serenity. Another Alan truism always seemed to come in handy: "Don't pay attention to any critics."

My very public role at CNN as Trump supporter made me a target throughout 2016—a target for the left, for *Saturday Night Live*, and for Twitter. Just like any TV commentator, I received all kinds of hateful messages and calls. I laughed most of them off, but one always got to me. It's one I received just one day before that first CNN election night panel: "I believe you may want to tuck your cross in when showing support for someone who goes against so many things that the Bible teaches."

I found the sarcastic suggestion to be entirely wrongheaded. None of us are perfect—not me, no politician, and certainly not the judgmental author of that criticism. None of us are deserving of wearing a cross. And yet, therein lies the beauty of that symbol around my neck: the perfect God nailed to the cross so that humanity might have a chance at a salvation that we do not deserve.

Van Jones, my far left colleague at CNN, had no idea about that message I received one day before the Nevada election night panel. In fact, until that evening, Van and I had never even met. When I arrived at CNN's DC bureau, I was escorted upstairs to the greenroom. As I rounded the corner in anxious anticipation, I saw a room packed with political pundits. Before I could even introduce myself, I heard a voice confidently ring out from the crowd, "I love your cross." It was Van Jones, a man whom at the time I knew as Obama's radical left-wing green czar but whom I would come to know as a devout Christian and kind-spirited colleague.

I felt it was important to share the life of Alan Colmes and the words of Van Jones with you, especially now. It's no secret we live in highly partisan times, but we are more alike than we think. Left or right. Conservative or liberal. Lively dialogue and dissenting thought animate the

American spirit, but love of country and countryman defines the American heart.

If you picked up this book because you recognized my name or my picture, you likely know about my passionate advocacy for Donald Trump, a man who I believe is draining the Washington swamp and changing it for the better. You might love my viewpoint or maybe you hate it. Either way, I think it's important that we come to know one another as people, not just as political partisans. Though some may sum me up as "that girl on TV," I'm really just a small-town girl from the world's strawberry capital.

Yes, I've spent the past decade of my life walking the halls of some of the world's most elite institutions: the twisting stairwells of Oxford University's Gothic spires, the old brick roads of Georgetown University and Harvard Law School, the checkered floors of the Old Executive Office Building (where the offices of most of the White House staff are located), and the bustling, illuminating sets of New York City newsrooms. But these venerable institutions always felt distant from the place I call home.

For the first sixteen years of my life, I grew up in a small town called Plant City, in the heart of Florida. The quaint agricultural town was truly idyllic, iconic small-town America, where you treated your neighbors as friends, where the weekend revolved around Little League games at the ballpark, and where every Sunday you occupied the pews of the local church. With a dad who built a roofing company from the ground up and a mom who was a teacher turned stay-at-home mom, I learned the values of faith, family, and a good day's work.

As I left the comfort of my tiny all-girls Catholic school and the pews of my Southern Baptist church for the soaring confines of academia, it became clear that there was not just a misunderstanding of the worldview of small-town America but an outright disdain for it. My neighbors were the first responders, teachers, and local business leaders. They were not "deplorable" or "irredeemable"; rather, they were the forgotten men and women who Donald Trump vowed would be "forgotten no longer."

Just after Donald Trump was inaugurated as the forty-fifth president

Me and a spontaneous group of Trump voters at a University of Florida football game. *Courtesy of Author's Collection*

of the United States, I endeavored to tell the stories of the faceless Trump voters. There are many books that profile the president, but this would profile the people. I would of course set out to interview many in the Trump world: Ivanka Trump, Jared Kushner, Lara Trump, Ben Carson, Mike Huckabee, Sarah Huckabee Sanders, and several others in the campaign and administration. Their stories are inseparable from the story of the 2016 election and are included in this book. But there is a story beyond the public faces we all know. It is the untold story of the nearly 63 million Americans who sent Trump to 1600 Pennsylvania Avenue.

As I traveled the country in search of the unknown Trump voter, what I found was anger toward the governing elite that defied party lines. Millions of Americans had been left behind by a government purporting to represent them. These people are the backbone of American society, and these are their stories—the stories of the men and women who have been trampled beneath the polished shoes of the elite. They are good, hardworking citizens who just wanted a shot at the American Dream. Instead, they found themselves up against a rigged system.

In the beginning, I aimed to capture the anger that motivated a distrustful, change-oriented electorate, but instead, what I encountered were tears—the tears of a mother who lost her only son and husband in a heinous act of terrorism; the tears of a wife who lost her other half to incompetent medical care; the tears of a family who lost their brave loved one in a valiant act of heroism; and so many others. Tucked away in a charming, family-built log cabin in Wadsworth, Ohio, and sequestered in the corner of a barbecue restaurant in Texarkana, Texas, I heard deeply moving stories of loss that burdened my heart and moistened my eyes.

I found Americans who were plagued by the greatest issues of our time: terrorism, crime, health care, immigration, and poisoned water in Flint. But amid tragedy, I recognized breathtaking signs of strength and hope that forever changed me. Remarkably, when faced with various crises, their solution was consistent: God, not government. Though these men and women might have cast a ballot for a presidential candidate, their ultimate hope rested not in the elaborate promises of a politician but in the eternal ones of a savior—a savior who saw them through the unimaginable and lifted them up in a way government never could. It was a journey through the soul of America, and a life-changing one at that.

As the great Americans whose stories fill these pages welcomed me into their homes and communities and opened their hearts to me, a beautiful quote by C. S. Lewis consistently came to mind: "God whispers to us in our pleasures, speaks in our conscience, but shouts in our pain: it is His megaphone to rouse a deaf world." For it was amid struggle and hardship that the men and women I interviewed heard God in the most miraculous of ways. They had profound faith, boundless hope, and contagious optimism as they confronted what many would see as a dismal future. But this isn't just a story of their struggle—it's a story of their triumph, an account of their hard-fought battle and eventual victory on the day people dethroned the elite and took their country back.

As you proceed through the pages that follow, you will encounter a wide array of great Americans. Their stories will touch your heart. It's the story of Election 2016, yes. But more than that, it's the story of the American people—their struggle, their triumph, their resilience, and their heart.

★ PART ONE ★

The People

On that unforgettable Tuesday night, I sat on CNN's illuminated election set watching one of the greatest political moments in modern history take place right before my very eyes. With Van Jones and Paul Begala on one side and Jeffrey Lord and Anderson Cooper on the other, our usually chatty eight-person CNN panel remained silently transfixed on Wolf Blitzer in the center of the room, where he announced the election results as state by state trickled in for Donald Trump.

Just after 11:00 p.m., it became clear that Trump would carry the state of Florida and likely become our next president. With more than 13 million Americans watching, the CNN cameras swung to our side of the room for comment. Anderson Cooper asked me for my thoughts, and I repeated what I had often said over the past year and a half: "[The American people] want their government back. This is supposed to be a government of, by, and for the people. It's increasingly become one of, by, and for the elite. This is the people rising up saying, 'It's time to listen to us' . . . Donald Trump ran against Republicans, he ran against Democrats, he ran against the elite, he ran against the government, he ran against the media, but he was an unmistakable voice for the people."

That, in a nutshell, explains Election 2016. Intended to be a government "of the people, by the people, for the people," many Americans felt it had become a government *despite* the people. Even though the Declaration of Independence promises every American "life, liberty, and the pursuit of happiness," these unalienable rights guaranteed to all seemed to have fallen away for so many. Lives lost, property confiscated, jobs outsourced. Whether on the left or the right, there was severe disenchantment with the Washington political class. It's what animated the rise of outsiders like Donald Trump and Bernie Sanders on both sides of the political spectrum.

The chapters that follow in Part I, "The People," tell the stories of great American heroes, many of whom have encountered more hurt, pain, and struggle than most encounter in a lifetime. Some voted for Donald Trump. Some did not. But their hurt and their loss are reflective of the emotions that fueled a frustrated electorate. As I wrote these pages, I was often driven to tears as I reflected on the many broken hearts I had met. But as I sat across from the men and women whose life stories I am about to relate, I recognized an abounding, almost inexplicable peace. Where government might have failed them, faith filled the gap.

Life

TWO BRIGHT LIGHTS

Terrorism

"And we know that in all things God works for the good of those who love him, who have been called according to his purpose."
—ROMANS 8:28

On the night of July 14, 2016, in Nice, France, there was one question that Sean Copeland asked over and over again until he took his last breath on this earth: "Is Brodie OK?"

He asked "Is Brodie OK?" as he struggled to overcome his injuries and follow his son's lifeless body into the hotel. He asked "Is Brodie OK?" as his daughter loaded Sean's broken frame into a stranger's car. And he asked "Is Brodie OK?" repeatedly during the doctors' hour-long attempt to revive him.

Sean asked if Brodie, his eleven-year-old son, was OK until the moment Sean passed away. Right before Sean drew his final breath, he looked up at his daughter, Maegan, and stated with assurance, "Brodie is dead."

I got chills as Kim shared her husband's last words with me. Marveling at what she had managed to tell me through her tears, I said, "From all accounts I've read, when you die and go to heaven, the first thing you see is your family greeting you."

"Yes," she replied, "I think Sean saw Brodie, and Brodie was, like, 'Daddy, come be with me.'" Despite having gone through unspeakable tragedy, Kim felt a peaceful assurance—assurance that her son and husband entered heaven that evening together after an act of evil cost them their earthly lives. "Sean knew he was joining his baby boy in heaven . . . I know that, and I would've done the same thing," Kim said. "I would've been, like, 'OK, I'm going with you.'"

The way Sean's persistent question changed to certainty in an instant was truly inexplicable. Brodie's body was more than a mile away with his mom, Kim, and his brother, Austin. Sean had no way of knowing Brodie's status, since Maegan's phone had died—and yet he did in that final transition from earth to heaven. Sean's seeing his son matches the myriad

Brodie and Sean. *Courtesy of J. West*

near-death experiences described in popular books like Don Piper and Cecil Murphey's *90 Minutes in Heaven: A True Story of Death and Life* and Todd Burpo and Lynn Vincent's *Heaven Is for Real: A Little Boy's Astounding Story of His Trip to Heaven and Back*. In these nonfiction accounts, people who briefly died but were revived describe meeting relatives who had passed before them—just as Sean did.

Sean's parting words are a spring of hope for Kim, who lost her son and her husband in the span of an hour in Nice, France, during which the world watched and mourned together.

"Mom, I'm scared," said Brodie Copeland, looking up at his mother with his bright blue eyes and freckle-dusted nose.

"Why are you scared?" Kim asked as she, Brodie, and the three other members of the Copeland family walked out of the Hard Rock Cafe and into a joyful beachside celebration along the spectacular palm-tree-dotted promenade of Nice, France.

"What does ISIS look like?" he inquired back.

"What do you mean? There's no look." It was a curious question from a characteristically carefree blond-haired boy—a boy whom they called the "Copeland Crush" because of his athletic prowess on the baseball field.

"There's a man in there," Brodie replied, referring to the bathroom of the Hard Rock. "He's sitting on the floor with a backpack, and he's digging through all of his stuff. And it made me scared, Mom. I want to know what ISIS looks like."

When Kim had taken Brodie to the bathroom after dinner, she noticed a security guard positioned just outside of the men's bathroom. *What is going on?* she thought at the time. The guard told Brodie it was safe to enter, but as any protective mom would do, Kim looked at her son and said, "Go with me to the women's restroom." And just as any strong-willed fifth-grade boy would reply, Brodie said, "No way! I'm not going to the girl's bathroom!" Kim waited outside as Brodie encountered the man who had prompted his line of questioning.

"ISIS has no look," Kim repeated to Brodie, who continued to inquire about ISIS as the Copelands prepared for a once-in-a-lifetime French fireworks show. "We're fine. We are all together," she gently assured her son.

"Just enjoy it," Austin and Maegan told their younger brother.

"He was freaked out," Kim told me. "It was so crazy. He had this intuition, and we were all, like, 'Brodie, it's fine.'" The picture-perfect Texas family had spent the whole day together on the third stop of what Kim described as their "dream vacation." Tired of foreign cuisine, Brodie and his dad, Sean, wanted to start the evening with a good old-fashioned hamburger and french fries, which was why they had chosen the Hard Rock Cafe. Brodie had satisfied his craving for American cuisine even earlier than the rest of his family, starting his morning with a warm piece of apple pie. He had quite the healthy, boyish sweet tooth and a dazzling personality to accompany it. Born on April Fools' Day,

Kim soon realized "just how fitting that birthday was for . . . her little bundle of joy."[1]

Leaving their safe little slice of Americana that night, the Copelands continued toward the Promenade des Anglais, an eleven-mile sprawling walkway set along the azure blue waters of the Mediterranean Sea. It was one of the last times they would walk together as a family of five. Though night had obscured the beauty of the rocky pebble beach, the festivities—fireworks, music—nevertheless persisted as thirty thousand attendees got ready to commemorate the French national holiday of Bastille Day.

For the Copelands, the jubilant event was the next stop in their celebration-filled vacation. Austin was turning twenty-two. Kim was turning forty. And a first-ever tour of Europe seemed like the perfect idea. Sean would kick off the trip by completing one of the highest items on his bucket list: running with the bulls in the small, quaint town of Pamplona, Spain. Then it was off to the bustling beaches of Barcelona and the sparkling waters of Nice, nestled in the heart of the French Riviera. "We chose Nice for Bastille Day because we thought it would be a safer place than Paris," Kim told me. The trip was set to end in Paris, celebrating Kim's birthday with dinner in the Eiffel Tower. The final stop was one that the family would never make.

When the Copelands reached the rocky shores of the Mediterranean on that warm July evening, they sat atop stones that lined the beach as glistening fireworks shot up before them. Appearing to emerge straight from the ocean floor, pops of color launched from barges, filling the dead of night with shimmering strips of sparkles. But as the thousands of onlookers around Kim reveled at the majestic sight before them, Brodie's anxious demeanor began to worry her. This was an uncommon disposition for Brodie Copeland, who usually had a smile on his face and whose lively personality never failed to get those around him laughing.[2]

"I was kind of a nervous wreck during the fireworks show," Kim remembered. As the Copelands ate dinner on the second floor of the Hard Rock overlooking the promenade that evening, Kim observed armed guards dressed in camouflage with military-style berets. Brandishing machine guns, they walked up and down the street in lockstep, peering

Guards whom Kim observed during dinner. *Courtesy of Kim Copeland*

from side to side. "It was very intimidating," she recalled. Something in Kim prompted her to take a picture of the guards on patrol. The photograph shows weapon-clad Frenchmen marching in front of a red and yellow children's candy stand—the same candy stand where Kim's life would forever change.

As the Copeland family watched the elaborate fireworks display, Kim wondered, *Is something going to happen?* When the show ended, Kim's nerves subsided. *OK, we're good now,* she thought, seeing the throngs of revelers as a source of communal comfort.

The Bastille Day festivities were historically tranquil, family friendly, and statistically much safer than the Copeland boys' earlier feat on vacation: running with the bulls in Pamplona. The running of the bulls takes place during the festival of Sanfermines, commemorating the martyrdom of Pamplona's patron saint, Saint Fermín. Fences line the ancient cobblestone streets, boards shield windowed storefronts, and spectators hover over the balconies of multicolored buildings in anxious anticipation.[3] Kim, Maegan, and Brodie Copeland were among the eager onlookers leaning over a balcony and waiting for Sean and Austin to charge down the street.

At 8:00 a.m., a rocket would be fired, signaling Sean and Austin along with hundreds of others to race toward an arena a half-mile away. A second rocket would sound as a pack of rowdy bulls was unleashed behind them.[4] It is not uncommon for the raucous animals to trample runners or even gore them with their horns. Each year, fifty to one hundred runners are injured during the running of the bulls.[5] In 2015 an American student was among the injured as cameras captured a vicious bull thrusting its sixteen-inch horns into the young male. The runner was fortunate enough to survive the violent encounter, but fifteen others have not been so lucky.[6]

Worried about the array of potential dangers—goring, a pileup, trampling—Kim woke up in tears at 2:00 a.m. the night before the run. Feeling apprehensive, she woke her husband and pleaded with him, "Please don't do this. You're fifty years old. I'm scared, and I don't think it's going to be OK."

In his compassionate but fearless way, Sean calmed her fears. "It's fine," he said, "I've got you and three kids to take care of. I'm not going to put myself in harm's way. Everything will be OK. I've lived a full life. I'm not worried about me, but I am worried about Austin."

The next morning, before the run, Sean pulled his oldest son, Austin, into another room. "I have everything I could want in my life, but my main worry is you. You're just twenty-two years old. You have your whole life ahead," Sean said. "If you don't want to do it, we won't run. But if we decide to do it, we will do it together."

"Dad, this is why we came to Europe," Austin replied. "We have to do it."

So Sean and Austin together joined the crowd in the narrow streets of Pamplona and ran as a herd of bulls chased behind them. "I will never forget the joy on his face that day," Austin said at his father and

Austin and Sean after running with the bulls in Pamplona, Spain. *Courtesy of Kim Copeland*

brother's memorial weeks later.[7] Kim, wanting to capture her husband's giant smile, snapped a photo from the balcony as Sean looked up with his arm around Austin. Both wore the traditional white shirts with red handkerchiefs, the red symbolizing the martyrdom of Saint Fermín. The irony of the image is noteworthy: Sean wearing that red handkerchief honoring a man who gave his life for his faith. Just days later, Sean would sacrifice his own life in heroic fashion. "Our family is so grateful for those photos we took that day," Austin noted at the memorial service. "Him looking the proudest, happiest version of himself that I've ever seen, beaming from ear to ear. My dad gave us so much happiness, but this was his moment."[8]

The Copeland boys had made it through the running of the bulls, but the real danger lay ahead. As the fireworks show concluded, the Copelands prepared to head to the promenade, departing from the beach

Sean and Brodie on the beach in Nice, France. *Courtesy of Kim Copeland*

where they had already made so many memories. After arriving in Nice, they rented beach chairs and grew accustomed to the stony French shoreline, so different from the sandy American beaches. The wind whipping along the Mediterranean coast created huge waves, so large that tourists were barred from the water. But Sean and Brodie, with their adventurous and lively spirits, ran right up to the edge to stick their feet in. Father and son sat on the shore, identically postured: legs extended, hands slightly behind them, and feet just barely touching the water. Sean in his white hat, and Brodie in his camouflage Hill Country Reds baseball hat. "They were two peas in a pod," Kim reminisced. "They did everything together . . . he was that dad that, as soon as he would get home from work, would change clothes and go out and throw the ball with Brodie."

Recalling that windy day in Nice, Kim explained, "Brodie and Sean didn't like to sit. They couldn't just sit on the beach and relax." So after Brodie had a ball get sucked into the waves and after Sean chased down his hat that flew away, recovering it with the aid of a stranger, they rented scooters, something Brodie had been begging to do the entire trip. When the two returned, Kim asked if they had fun. "It was fun," Brodie replied, "except that Dad is so big that his wouldn't go very fast, so I had to wait for him." Kim and I laughed together as she imagined Sean dragging behind as Brodie urged him forward, but she also gently wiped a tear from her face as she shared with me those final memories of her husband and son.

Brodie eventually grew bored of the rocky beach, so with his characteristically inventive nature he came up with "his next big idea," in Maegan's words: a beach massage business. Brodie gathered an assortment of perfectly smooth stones that were just right. "This is a good stone," he would say. Maegan was lying on the beach when Brodie decided to try out his first business pitch. "Let me give you a massage. It's the special stone premium backrub," he bragged. "Only after the massage did he mention it was $5 for five minutes," Meagan laughingly recalled two weeks later.[9] "I thought that was too much, but Brodie drove a hard bargain." When it was time to leave the beach, Brodie quickly informed the family, "We can't leave yet. Business is booming!"

With a collection of beachside memories forever imprinted in their minds, the Copelands left the beach together one last time on July 14, 2016. The promenade, which had been shut down all day and closed to traffic, was now filled with stages featuring all kinds of music. After listening to some of the bands, the Copelands decided to head back toward the hotel. On the way, Brodie saw a candy stand and gravitated toward it as if it were a magnet. "The line is too long. There will be another one. Let's get closer to the hotel," his family told him. But upon spotting a second candy stand along the sidewalk, Brodie made a beeline for it. "It was just a mere seconds later that our lives were changed forever," Maegan said.[10]

Brodie picked up a small brown paper bag and gleefully filled it with all different types of candy. Sean, Kim, Austin, and Maegan watched from behind as he made his way around the stand, surrounded by other children. "Turn around for a picture," Kim said as she snapped a photo, the last picture she would take of her son: Brodie's left hand clutching the paper bag while his right shoveled into a pile of red and yellow gummy candies, grinning from ear to ear as he prepared his bag of treats.

Brodie continued to pick out his candy until an abrupt word of warning filled the air. "Watch out!" Sean yelled. Kim snapped her head to the right to find a large white semi truck barreling straight for them. "Austin, get Kim and Maegan!" Sean shouted. Jumping into action mode, Austin picked up his sister and grabbed Kim by her arm, thrusting the three of them backward. Meanwhile, Sean ran forward directly into the pathway of the rapidly approaching semi to grab Brodie. But before Sean could return his son to safety, the nineteen-ton refrigerator truck struck them both and dozens of others at a rate of fifty-six miles per hour.

The very last picture taken of Brodie. *Courtesy of Kim Copeland*

Chaos ensued.

Screaming victims. Spectators briskly fleeing the scene. The zigzagging truck continuing on its murderous path. Almost instantaneously, the terrifying popping of crisscrossing gunfire rang out. Fearing that the shots might be part of a coordinated attack, Kim instructed Austin to get Brodie back to their hotel, which was nearby. Austin ran forward to find his younger brother, whose Hill Country Reds baseball hat was lost in the collision. Scooping Brodie's body into his arms, Austin darted toward the hotel with Kim following closely behind. Still able to hobble with the assistance of a bystander, Sean and his daughter trailed their family, with Sean asking what would become his persistent question, "Is Brodie OK? How is he? Tell me if Brodie is all right." Sean collapsed just before the entryway, unable to make it all the way back.

Holding Brodie close to his chest, Austin entered the hotel lobby overlooking the Mediterranean—the Bay of Angels, by no small coincidence—and gently laid his brother on the floor. Kim and Austin hovered around their eleven-year-old loved one in anguish. "I knew that he was gone," Kim said.[11] So, too, were his hopes and dreams. Brodie was going to be a baseball player then a sitcom actor and then president of the United States. His exuberant and lively nature made him perfectly suited for starring in *Annie* as Daddy Warbucks and in *Peter Pan* as Michael Darling, the youngest Darling sibling who flies off to the whimsical Neverland, where boys are never forced to grow up. Before Brodie's grandmother watched him act in his first play, Brodie confidently looked at her and coolly commented, "Grannie Annie, prepare to be impressed." Though baseball and acting were Brodie's two passions, he did everything: drums, voice lessons, golf, football. Just weeks earlier, after completing fifth grade, Brodie's teacher told him, "When you get your Academy Award, I hope you remember me." That day would never come. Though Kim knew in her heart that Brodie was gone, two strangers rushed over and began performing CPR, desperate to save his life if they possibly could.

Kim glanced up from her son and out of the glass entryway. The automatic doors opened and closed, and each time they opened, she caught a glimpse of her husband lying on the ground outside. Kim had met Sean when Austin was just four years old. Fresh out of college, Kim had taken a job as a preschool teacher. "I was on the playground and in walks this handsome single man," she said. "One day he came to pick Austin up and asked me for a date, and I said no." But Kim always regretted that, and before the end of the school year she put a note in Austin's backpack, leaving her phone number and asking for updates on Austin's soccer game the next year. She hoped Sean would call, and sure enough, he did. On their first date, Kim and Sean spent six hours talking.

"Conversation was so easy with him," she said. And one of the main things that attracted Kim to Sean was that he was such a good dad, proof of which was right in front of her as she looked out at her husband, battered after throwing himself in front of a truck in an effort to save his son. Kim attempted to walk out the doors to go see Sean, but she physically could not move. Her legs were frozen like cement blocks, preventing her from leaving her son to comfort her husband. It was from that vantage point that Kim viewed her husband of twelve years alive for the last time.

While Kim and Austin tended to Brodie, Maegan went into survival mode, urgently searching for a means of transportation. Since the scene along the promenade was still chaotic, no first responders were allowed to dispatch. Determined to get her dad to the hospital, Maegan screamed and demanded that someone transport her father. Her efforts ultimately proved successful. Maegan found a resident willing to help load Sean into a car and carry him to the hospital.

Meanwhile, after performing CPR on Brodie for a long time, the two strangers looked at Kim and said, "No, he's gone." Kim would later find out that Brodie had died immediately upon impact. With no ambulances dispatched, there was nowhere to take Brodie's broken body. The hotel had no choice but to resort to a closet. As they picked up Brodie's motionless body, Kim began to vomit. "[It] was the night my world was turned upside down," Kim said.[12]

Since the hotel was on lockdown, Kim and Austin were not permitted to return to their rooms. "Austin was beside himself," Kim remembers. "He had blood all over him." Austin implored the hotel attendants to let him go change. "I can't be in these clothes," he said. They finally consented, taking Austin through a back hallway and up to the room. For almost four hours the hotel barred anyone from entering, leaving, or moving around the building, forcing Kim and Austin to stay downstairs in a private banquet room, just the two of them. The pair frantically tried to call Maegan, but her phone had died. As Kim waited for news of her husband's whereabouts and status, she dropped to her knees and began pleading with God. "Please don't take my husband," she prayed. "I just lost my son. I can't do this without my husband. Please."

"I was just on my knees begging," she told me as she began to choke up, remembering her desperation. And then, after a seemingly endless wait, she got the call.

"How's he doing?" Kim asked nervously.

"He didn't make it," Maegan replied.

THE NEW AMERICAN REVOLUTION   25

Sean had died from internal bleeding because of a tear in his aorta. He died in a tremendous act of heroism. "So Sean lost his life saving his son and saving you guys?" I asked her.

In a low and sad voice, she said yes.

"So he was a hero in every sense of the word," I said.

"Every sense of it," she proudly replied.

Because the entire city was shut down, Maegan was stuck at the hospital alone to mourn the death of her father. "I'm getting you back to your family," a nurse said to her in a resolute voice. The two of them drove back toward the hotel, Maegan staying on the phone with Kim and Austin the whole way. As they drove down the road, two police officers stopped the car and put guns to the heads of Maegan and the nurse. "Oh my gosh, they have a gun to my head. I've got to go," Maegan said before swiftly dropping the phone. Kim and Austin were hysterical at the thought of a third member of the family in danger. Unaware of what was going on, they were relieved when Maegan finally made it back to the hotel safely to rejoin the surviving members of her family.

The Copelands' dream vacation—the "trip of a lifetime" that Sean had hoped for—had quickly spiraled into a nightmare. The earthly family of three—still an eternal family of five—was left to pick up the broken pieces of their life, nearly six thousand miles away from their Lakeway, Texas, home.

★　★　★　★

I still remember where I was standing that afternoon, packing for the Republican National Convention in eager anticipation of the four days that lay ahead. Bopping around the house and trying on dresses, I stopped in my tracks when I heard the news. "We are just getting initial word of breaking news coming out of Nice, France . . . dozens of people dead after a truck crashed into a crowd celebrating Bastille Day."[13] Horrifying images soon filled the screen. People running. Flashing police lights. A massive truck with dozens of bullet holes scattered across the front window. My anxious preparation ceased and my excited spirit deflated as I took in the scene. "There are a lot of details we don't know right now," the anchor cautioned. "Was this an accident? Was it something more sinister?"[14] Something more sinister? Yes. This was certainly another in a long line of terrorist attacks.

The very next day, the French president announced that the horrific attack was indeed an act of terrorism. "France as a whole is under the threat of Islamist terrorism," he warned.[15] Eighty-six people had died and approximately two hundred were injured at that Bastille Day celebration when Mohamed Lahouaiej Bouhlel accelerated a cargo truck in a weaving path, mowing down innocent bystanders over a one-mile stretch.[16] The collective heartbreak of our nation for our Western European ally only increased when news emerged that at least two Americans were among the dead.

Almost everyone has seen that memorable black-and-white image of father and son standing on a baseball mound that was broadcast across national news. Brodie is looking up admiringly into his father's eyes, glove in hand. His father is gazing down proudly at his son as their shadows cast across the mound. And then came one of those final pictures of Brodie Copeland, taken just two days before the attack: Brodie,

One of Brodie's last pictures. *Courtesy of Kim Copeland*

halfway in a breaking wave on the shoreline of the Mediterranean, smiling with that tiny gap in between his two front teeth. He was the picture of innocence, extinguished by evil—an evil that he intuitively felt was on the horizon that evening when he encountered a man hurriedly digging through a backpack in the Hard Rock Cafe bathroom. According to Reuters, Mohamed's brother claims that his murderous sibling sent a picture of himself laughing while standing among a crowd at the promenade just hours before the attack.[17] Whether the man Brodie encountered was Mohamed or one of his several accomplices, we may never know.

As details of the attack emerged, French authorities forced Kim, Austin, and Maegan to remain in Nice for several days. Sean's brothers flew to France to support the family through those first days of loss. An ambulance moved Brodie's body to join his father's at the hospital, which had become a makeshift morgue. In between interviews with the police, mouth swabbing to confirm identities, and mounds of paperwork, the three Copelands clung tightly to one another. "They gave us two suites," Kim recalled. "But the three of us stayed in one bed—like, all together for days—and didn't move. We didn't leave each other's sides." They held on to one another and faced the unimaginable. "We were all on our phones the whole time . . . We read all of the comments, and the outpouring of support, and prayers," Kim said.

Meanwhile, across the Atlantic, their Texas community held the Copeland family in their hearts. Hill Country Baseball, a second family to the Copelands, met at Mount Bonnell to embrace one another and remember Brodie and Sean.[18] Throngs of mourners packed into Lake Hills Church for a candlelight vigil. A mother sat with her arm tightly wrapped around her little girl. "Join me as we bow our heads," the preacher told his congregation. Another mom lightly rubbed her son's back, proudly displaying the number 8, Brodie's baseball number. Speaking to God, the preacher prayed, "Bring peace to the Copeland family. Give us your amazing grace to forgive that man that took Sean and Brodie."

"That's really what got me through those first days," Kim said. "Just knowing that the world has me." The world truly did have Kim.

Memorials were arranged all along the Nice promenade where the attack occurred. Just in front of a picture of Sean and Brodie on the mound, an American flag stood tall. A Sharpie and a pile of smooth stones from Nice's beach—the same type Brodie had used for his massage business—lay adjacent to a bed of flowers. All sorts of messages of love and support quickly filled the stones. "Business is booming," wrote Maegan on one—those funny words Brodie had uttered just days before. "Psalm 23" was written on another: "Even though I walk through the valley of the shadow of death, I will fear no evil, for you are with me." They were the same words spoken by President George W. Bush to a broken nation the night of the September 11, 2001, attacks.

After remaining in Nice for more than a week, authorities finally cleared the Copeland family to return to America. Just before heading home, authorities told Kim that Sean's and Brodie's bodies would not be ready for two more days. "We're not leaving without them," they all agreed. "We came as a family of five. We are leaving as a family of five." Unwilling to leave their two loved ones behind, the family stayed until they could leave as one on a connecting flight to Dover Air Force Base in Delaware.

Together as one family unit, Kim, Austin, and Maegan flew to Paris on the same flight as Brodie and Sean, their two bodies stored below. Everywhere the Copelands went, FBI escorts accompanied them, taking them through back hallways and putting them on flights before the other passengers. During a one-night layover, Kim grew worried that the bodies of her son and husband might be left behind. The pilot learned of her fears and came over to the family. "I heard you're nervous," he said. "I'm going down below in the plane and will personally lay my eyes on the caskets and let you know." He returned to assure Kim that her entire family was on board. "You're good. I've got you," the kind man told her. Kim and her family finally made it to Dover Air Force Base, the same base where so many American families have gone to meet their fallen loved ones who perished in battle while making the ultimate sacrifice for our freedoms. Back in the States, the FBI conducted autopsies and interviews before permitting the Copelands to make their final journey home to Texas.

When Kim, Austin, and Maegan arrived back in Lakeway, the whole town was decorated in red and black. Red and black ribbons were affixed to street signs, trees, and lampposts. Red and black banners and posters. The same red and black of Brodie's Hill Country Reds baseball team. Although there were visible signs of collective support everywhere, it could not change the hardest part: the house. "This house that we built together—that we wanted to live in forever—is empty," Kim said.[19]

Beyond dealing with a silent home, once filled with life, Kim had to plan a funeral. She searched for her husband's burial instructions, "something I never thought I would be doing at the age of forty," she said. But in the place of instructions for interment, Kim found something much different: words that would carry her through the rest of her life. "Please do not be too sad with my passing," Sean wrote. "I have had a great life and the best kids ever. Enjoy the rest of your lives and live life to the fullest. Live happy. Live fun. Live strong. I will see you in heaven."

★　★　★　★

Sean's instructions—"Live happy. Live fun. Live strong"—and Kim's faith in Jesus Christ have carried her through the inconceivable. They got her through the Celebration of Life memorial service, the funeral, and the many difficult days to follow: her fortieth birthday, when she was supposed to be dining in the Eiffel Tower but instead was left to collect her family's remains; Sean's birthday, when she drank a Dr Pepper and a Crown and Seven for him; the first day of school, when she couldn't bear to see that bus pull up without Brodie on it; and the hardest day of all, what would have been Brodie's twelfth birthday.

I asked Kim if she was ever angry with God. "Oh, yeah," she said. In addition to losing her son and husband, Kim's mom died of melanoma when Kim was just nine years old. Since Kim's dad was a football coach who worked long hours, the family moved in with her grandmother, Maw-Maw. Later in life Maw-Maw was diagnosed with Alzheimer's. The disease ravaged her, leaving her unable to attend Kim's wedding. "Maw-Maw quickly became a shell of the strong woman we once knew," Kim said. "She kept hanging on longer than any doctor could even imagine, even though we were praying for the Lord to take her home." [20]

"This is the hand I was dealt," Kim told me. She has experienced more loss than most do in a lifetime: a son, a husband, and a mother who perished all too soon and a grandmother devastated by an awful disease. Kim had reason to be angry, and in the aftermath of Nice she was. "What did I do, God?" she would ask. "What did I do to deserve this?" When Kim met her pastor to plan Sean and Brodie's funeral, he provided words of wisdom. "You're going to hear some crazy stuff, Kim. People are going to tell you this was God's plan. This was not God's plan. He did not plan this to happen. He allowed it, but he did not plan for your life to be this way."

Kim had a realization. God did not plan for evil to extinguish innocence on that day in Nice or for cancer and Alzheimer's to steal the lives of her mom and Maw-Maw. Evil and subsequent hurt are a result of human sin, not part of God's outline for Kim's life. "You have to figure out what you're going to do on this side of it," Kim's pastor advised. After hearing those words, Kim had a choice: to let the anger consume her or fall into the arms of her loving heavenly father. She chose the latter.

Kim's strength is embedded in the loving assurances God gives her daily and in the knowledge that she will be reunited with her family in their heavenly home. In August of 2005, when Kim became pregnant with Brodie and she saw that positive test result, she excitedly shared the news with her dad over the phone. Her excitement turned to sadness when in that very same phone call he informed her that Maw-Maw had finally passed. But there was a certain beauty in that bittersweet exchange of news. "On the same day that I found out I was pregnant," Kim recalled, "I was able to tell my dad that he was going to be a grandpa for the very first time . . . I truly believed Maw-Maw and Brodie crossed paths that day." [21]

Maw-Maw, Kim's mom, Brodie, and Sean are all together again, awaiting Kim's company. In the meantime Kim starts every morning with quiet time, immersed in her Bible. Sitting at her kitchen table, where a big vase of Mediterranean stones from Sean and Brodie's memorial reside, she talks to God and her deceased husband and son. She gets little signs in return, namely through dragonflies and coins. On the day of the funeral, as the pastor gave the graveside speech, fifty dragonflies circled above their heads. And when her sister got in a bad car crash, when she was crying and scared, two dragonflies flew through the pouring rain, bringing her peace.

Ever since Kim returned from Nice, she's been finding coins in the strangest of places. When she got home, she went in the laundry room and for some reason there were coins scattered everywhere. *That's weird,* she thought as she picked them up to prepare for visitors. When she left the room, she looked around and there was nothing there—no coins, all clean. But when she came back a little later, there were coins sprinkled everywhere! She now collects these coins in a jar; they are pennies from heaven.

Kim told me that she had another coin encounter the day before we met as she prepared to view Sean and Brodie's headstones for the first time. She leaned over to show me the picture: black headstones, lily-white flowers, and the perfectly suited engraved words on each. "Live happy. Live fun. Live strong," read Sean's, with Brodie lying in eternal peace right beside him. "I can fly. I can fly. I can fly," read Brodie's—the words he so passionately and effectively delivered when he played Michael Darling in *Peter Pan*. Just before Kim left to view the memorials, a dime flew out of her purse, seemingly from nowhere. Another coin from heaven.

★　　★　　★　　★

While Kim's ultimate hope is in God, she still looks to her earthly leaders for commonsense change. In the aftermath of the Bastille Day attack, Kim received a call from President Barack Obama. The leader of the free world was on the other end of the phone—an unimaginable interaction just a few days earlier. In a brief discussion, the commander-in-chief said he was sorry for her loss. Kim hung up the phone a bit disappointed. "It was as if the phone call was a duty for him, not an empathetic outreach," she remembers. "He was just going through the motions."

By contrast, when Kim returned to Texas, she randomly received a phone call from President George W. Bush's representative. "The former president would like to meet you," the woman said. Kim, Austin, and Maegan traveled to an event in Dallas where President Bush was speaking. Whisked away into a back room, just she and her two kids met one-on-one with the former president. He wrapped up Kim in a warm hug, leaving his arm around her the entire time they spoke. President Bush asked the Copeland family all about Sean and Brodie. He really wanted to know who they were as people. With his arm still around Kim, she nervously tried to scoot away. "Get back over here!" he said with that slight Texas twang and infectious smile. He kept his arm there the whole time. "He was amazing," Kim said.

I asked Kim which candidate, Hillary Clinton or Donald Trump, had the better answer to terrorism in the 2016 election. "Trump had the answer," she said without hesitation. She explained that terrorism is one of those things you take for granted. *OK, terrorism is happening,* you think, but then Nice made everyone realize it could happen to anybody. "Here we are. Here's a father and a son in Nice, France, the South of France, where the rich and famous go to vacation," she said. "[We're] on a dream vacation . . . [I]t can happen to anyone, anywhere."

The very month that Sean and Brodie lost their lives in Nice, Intel-Center released a study, confirmed by CNN, revealing that "there has been a significant attack directed or inspired by ISIS every 84 hours since June 8 in cities outside the war zones . . ."[22] It is a study I would constantly reference throughout the 2016 election in support of Trump's practical tactics to fighting terrorism. That summer the terror attacks seemed to be endless. Forty-nine dead at the Pulse nightclub. Twenty-three killed in a Bangladesh bakery, many of them butchered to death, including three beautiful young American students.[23] An eighty-four-year-old French priest heinously forced to his knees on the altar of his church in northern France and his throat cut during Mass as *"Allahu Akbar"* rang out.[24] These are just a few of the attacks motivated by radical Islam.

In many cases, the attacker was known to authorities. Adel Kermiche, the nineteen-year-old radicalized man who, with another attacker, killed the French priest, sat in jail just four months earlier.[25] Kermiche had attempted to travel to Syria two times, making it all the way to Turkey in the second attempt before being sent back to France. After Kermiche spent less than a year in a French jail, authorities released the man known to be friends with a terrorist featured in an ISIS beheading video. House arrest and the electronic monitor he wore failed to stop him from wreaking deadly havoc that day, four months after being released from jail.

Being known to authorities appears to be a trend among ISIS terrorists. A neighbor claims to have reported the June 2017 London Bridge attackers after they tried to radicalize her children.[26] One of the terrorists even appeared in a documentary called *Jihadis Next Door*, in which he can be seen arguing furiously with police over an "ISIS-looking flag" that he had displayed in a park.[27] The London Bridge attack killed eight innocents. Even Mohamed Lahouaiej Bouhlel, the Nice attacker, while not known to the intelligence community, was known to local authorities for his slew of criminal convictions for theft, violence, and drug use.[28]

Even though President Trump's strict approach to terrorism was demonized, twisted, and taken out of context by the mainstream media, Americans saw through the misrepresentation and recognized common sense. In an August 2016 terrorism speech, then-candidate Trump highlighted the warning signs missed in our own country: the Orlando shooter, who allegedly celebrated in a classroom on 9/11; the Fort Hood terrorist, who proclaimed "We love death more than you love life!" to a roomful of mental health experts; and the suspicious signs at the home of the San Bernardino shooters that a neighbor noticed but failed to report.[29] "These warning signs were ignored because political correctness has replaced common sense in our society," Trump concluded before offering to create a commission dedicated to identifying these indications of possible violence.[30]

Trump also acknowledged the connection between some immigration and terrorism. Though most immigrants come hoping to make valuable contributions to our country, a small group seeks to use our immigration process and cause destruction, as Obama's own intelligence chiefs warned.[31] Trump ordered a temporary freeze on immigration from terror hotbed countries, not in an effort to target a religion, but in response to congressional data revealing that 65 percent of individuals convicted of terrorism in the U.S. are foreign born.[32] This pause in immigration from countries where significant terror organizations are known to operate—not a permanent ban, as the media suggested—also came on the heels of a foreign-born woman entering the U.S. on a K-1 fiancée visa and joining her husband in killing fourteen innocent Americans in San Bernardino, California.[33]

Trump also proposed limiting the number of incoming refugees, not because of a lack of empathy for refugees, but as a solution to warnings by Obama's CIA director and director of national intelligence about ISIS's attempt to infiltrate our refugee population and the former NATO commander's acknowledgment that 1,500 ISIS fighters had already entered Europe.[34] Meanwhile, Trump's opponent, Hillary Clinton, proposed to increase Syrian refugee numbers by more than 500 percent despite the FBI director's warning of the difficulty in vetting this group of immigrants.[35]

Voters recognized that, while catching every red flag is impossible, we must be vigilant and bold in reporting abnormal behavior because of the danger in failing to heed warning signs. Americans understood that, while most immigrants are good, hardworking people, it's inexcusable when a twenty-nine-year-old Pakistani woman comes to the U.S. on a fiancée visa and assists in killing fourteen people at a San Bernardino Christmas party. Ultimately, Americans agreed that more can be done to prevent radical Islamic terrorism from striking their loved ones, and they sent an unmistakable message on November 8, 2016, in the election of Donald Trump.

★   ★   ★   ★

On July 14, 2016, Mohamed Lahouaiej Bouhlel set out with the goal to destroy—to diminish faith, to decimate family, to eclipse good with evil. He failed. Kim's faith is stronger than ever and her family is closer because of the tragedy. Kim told her pastor that "an act that was intended to tear us apart has brought us together closer than we ever have been before."

After Kim and I first sat down at McArthur's for lunch, a vibrant local sports pub in the heart of Texas, our conversation almost instantly turned to Romans 8:28. It was the second time I had heard that verse in the span of a week. Just a few days earlier, I had encountered Romans 8:28 five states over in the tiny little town of McBee, South Carolina, where "8:28" has served as a lifelong

With Kim at McArthur's in Lakeway, Texas. *Courtesy of author's collection*

source of strength for a mother and wife whom you will meet later. I noticed Kim's Facebook likewise referenced Romans 8:28: "And we know that in all things God works for the good of those who love him, who have been called according to his purpose." Kim has seen this manifested in her own life as God has turned evil to good.

Although the one-year anniversary of Sean and Brodie's death has not even passed at the time I write these words, Kim has already used her loss to bless others. Sean's bucket list hangs on Kim's refrigerator as she tries to complete items on his behalf. "In the typical Sean Copeland fashion, this bucket list [is] an Excel spreadsheet that was highlighted, prioritized, crossed out, you name it," Austin described at the memorial service.[36] Kim was able to cross out running with the bulls in Pamplona,

Brodie and Sean. *Courtesy of Kim Copeland*

one of the top items on the list, and has since crossed out several others. There are some that she cannot complete but there are many she can. One of Sean's dreams was to throw out the first pitch at a baseball game. Austin did it for him. In memory of his father and brother, Austin threw out the first pitch at the minor-league Round Rock Express team's opening day as Kim and Maegan looked on in support. Kim also presented an award to a Texas Rangers player in July of 2017 for "Hometown Heroes Day" just days before Sean and Brodie's first anniversary in heaven.

While some of Sean's bucket list items are thrilling and action-filled, most are selfless and other-oriented, like leaving a $100 tip on a $20 bill, an item that Kim has already fulfilled. Or putting a smile on a kid's face, something Sean himself completed when he dressed up like a teddy bear and went to a children's hospital. Kim is already hard at work on one of the big ones: starting a charity.

About a year and a half before the Nice attack, Sean wrote to the Texas Baseball coaching staff about his son, describing him as "full of personality . . . [and] tremendous energy."[37] He wrote, "He plays football like his older brother, but Brodie loves baseball. He thinks he will win the Golden Spikes and Heisman in college before starting his career as an actor in a sitcom." Sure of his son's talent, Sean emphatically continued, "Knowing him, he may very well do it." So moved by the letter, the Longhorns director of baseball operations organized a practice visit for Brodie. In came eleven-year-old Brodie like a full-grown, college-age baseball recruit, touring the weight room and meeting the players. "He had those big eyes," his mom remembered.[38] Brodie never got to hit his first home run—although he came very close—but Kim said, "He got to experience all of that. Now I look back, and I thank God for that. He got a 'recruiting' trip."[39]

That Texas Longhorns recruiting trip came full circle when Kim partnered with the team to create the Sean & Brodie Copeland Memorial Endowment Fund, a project to help players in memory of Brodie. One player each year who embodies the spirit of Sean and Brodie Copeland will receive an annual scholarship, with one condition: they wear the number 8, Brodie's number, on the back of their jersey. "I want it to be someone who has to work hard for what they've accomplished in life. Someone who will appreciate the story and honor that . . ." Kim said.[40]

She found that person in the first recipient of the scholarship, Andrés Sosa, who had ironically already switched to number 8 during his junior year in high school after wearing the number 21 his whole life. "I changed my number not knowing the reason why," Andrés told CBS Austin.[41] "Now I know . . . A lot of people call it a coincidence, but I saw it was God."[42] Andrés came to the United States from Mexico. He didn't know any English and yet worked his way through school and into college baseball. He has become an accomplished young man and person of faith. "I recently went to my first retreat, and it was meant to be," he said.[43] "I didn't want to go. But I experienced something amazing—my first encounter with my Lord and Savior—and it truly changed my life forever."[44]

As Kim gives back through her pain, she has found that she is blessed in return. When she came back to visit the UT baseball team, who remembered her and Brodie from the recruiting visit, all the players came to her with tears in their eyes to offer their support. While Kim maintains her Hill Country Baseball family, she has gained a new one in Texas Longhorns Baseball. On Mother's Day, Andrés called her and left a message. "I'm thinking about you today," Kim remembers him saying. "I love you, and you gained a son in me and I gained a mom in you. I will be in your life forever." Through Andrés, Kim has continued to get those little signs that God is watching down on her. When Andrés got his first hit as a college baseball player, it was brought to his attention that it was March 8, after his eighth at bat, while wearing the number 8. "Sean and Brodie are looking after me," Andrés marveled.[45]

★　★　★　★

At that colorful candy stand tucked away in the inviting promenade of Nice France, the Copeland family—five bright lights in this world—came face-to-face with darkness. It was a darkness Brodie felt and recognized in the lead-up to the attack, and one that Kim feared as she watched the fireworks along the beach that night. But the beauty of light is that, if shined brightly enough, it will inevitably pierce through the darkness.

The lives and legacy of Brodie and Sean Copeland shine like a bright light through Kim, Austin, and Maegan. Kim's goal in this life is to live a good life, carry on in their memory, and make them proud. She will aim to make others smile, just as her son and husband did. "It's who they were. Two peas in a pod who loved to make others smile," Kim said. As for a lifetime without her husband and son, she and the kids always say that this life is like one little drop of water in an entire ocean.

"Did I ever expect to have lost my mother, husband, and son all before the age of forty? No," she told me. "But it's the hand I was dealt, and I can let it destroy me or make me stronger, and I choose stronger." Kim chooses stronger, but she realizes what enables her to make that decision. As she told her pastor while planning to lay her son and husband to eternal rest, "It's God who's giving me strength, because I could never do this on my own."

THE WINNER

Veterans' Affairs

"Courage is almost a contradiction in terms.
It means a strong desire to live taking the form of a readiness to die."
—G. K. CHESTERTON

"This nation will remain the land of the free
only so long as it is the home of the brave."
—ELMER DAVIS

That fateful moment had arrived—the one that forty-six-year-old Barry Lynn Coates faithfully called "his burden to carry." The 30-degree chill that filled McBee, South Carolina, on that winter morning was unavoidable; but the departure of an angel on earth to his heavenly home was not. And that is what Donna Coates, Barry Lynn's wife, says is the hardest part: it was needless and preventable, if not for the callous indifference of a few.

In the months before her husband was bedridden, Donna would wake up each morning to find Barry Lynn roaming around the backyard, "praying the word," in Donna's words. "Lord, if this burden is meant for me to carry, you let me carry it," he would say, "but you set my feet on the path in which you've chosen for me to walk, and don't you let me stray from that path." It was reminiscent of the exquisite and pained prayer of Jesus Christ in the Garden of Gethsemane the night before his crucifixion: "My Father, if it is possible, may this cup be taken from me. Yet not as I will, but as you will."

The week leading up to Saturday, January 23, 2016, was a difficult one. Barry Lynn had been very ill. He was in extreme pain, and the end seemed near. The preacher anointed Barry Lynn's head with oils, and on Tuesday, Barry Lynn—who went by Barry and Lynn as well as the combined Barry Lynn—asked the hospice nurse, "Can the doctor just put me to sleep and let me go on?"

"No doctor will order that for you," the nurse replied.

"It's not fair for me to know in my mind what's going on with my body," he said in languish.

Although the nurse had nothing to offer him, God apparently did. When Donna woke up Wednesday morning and looked over at Lynn, he was unconscious—not by medicine but by the grace of God. "It was like the lights were on but no one was home," she recalled.

Over the next few days, Lynn would be lucid one moment and gone in the next. At night Donna slept on a blow-up mattress at the foot of Lynn's hospital bed. "I would hear him talk all night long," she remembered. One night, Barry Lynn rode trucks with his brother, Randall. Another night he was selling mobile homes in a job he had previously worked. All the episodes from Lynn's life were playing out once more.

But he was conscious as could be on Friday morning when Donna looked over at him and said, "You know what today is?"

Donna and Barry Lynn. *Courtesy of Donna Coates*

Lynn answered, "Poo's birthday." Shaney Poo or just plain old Shane was one of Lynn's five children and father to one of Barry Lynn's seven grandbabies. Lynn stayed alert enough to have breakfast with Donna and wish Shane a happy birthday before pointing to a piece of paper on the floor that he hallucinated and then falling right to sleep.

Although the week was undoubtedly a painful one for Donna, it was nevertheless proof of "how God answers prayers," she told me. God heard Barry Lynn's worrisome plea to his nurse and helped his faithful child rest in peaceful slumber as the end drew near.

Donna awoke on that Saturday, dutifully curled up at the end of Lynn's bed. As was her practice, she always got Lynn dressed before herself.

She gently walked to the edge of his bed and whispered, "We got to go take a bath. You know why?"

"No," Lynn replied.

"Because you're stinky," she said jokingly, tapping him softly on the nose.

"I don't stink!" Lynn retorted.

"Yes, you do!" She tapped his nose again, one last time.

"I love you, Pooky Butt," Lynn said, just as he always did.

"I love you too, Lynn."

Donna got Lynn off the bed by sitting with her back to his and joining arms. Shuffling along the floors of the warm home they had built, Donna and Barry Lynn danced back-to-back all the way to the bathroom, a last manifestation of Barry Lynn's infectious sense of humor. Then Donna gently guided her soul mate into the bathtub. As Donna turned to say, "Move your feet, honey, so I can shut the door," she gazed into Barry Lynn Coates's big green eyes one final time.

"If you ever experience that in life, you'll understand what I mean when I say that I literally seen his soul leave his body," she told me. "He was eye to eye with me the entire time until he drew his last breath on the face of this earth . . . and that's something you'll never, ever remove from your mind." As Donna always did, she held Barry Lynn's hands and loved him until the very last moment he left this earth for the inviting pearly gates of heaven.

Barry Lynn and Donna holding hands. *Courtesy of Donna Coates*

★ ★ ★ ★

Perhaps Barry Lynn Coates had a wide variety of names—Daddy and Papaw in addition to Barry, Lynn, and Barry Lynn—because he meant so much to so many. Donna's mom, Diane, told me if she had to rank Barry Lynn's priorities, it would be "love for his savior, love for his family, and love for his country."

"And in that order," Donna added.

"He called me Mama," Diane said, beaming. She explained that Lynn's grandparents had raised him. His granddaddy was "tough as a lighter knot," Donna recalled, referring to the hard resinous core of a pine tree. Remembering his childhood, Lynn would say, "Papa didn't call me but one time. If he had to call me twice, I knew what was waiting on me when I got to the house."

"They instilled in him strong faith. And he had it," Mama told me. "He loved witnessing to other people. That was Lynn's goal."

Mama said she would go into Donna's salon, Salon 828, and ask, "Where's Lynn?"

"He's at the post office," Donna would reply. "He and Mrs. Ruby's having church this morning."

"That's right. He would be in one place or another praying with people and witnessing," Mama reminisced. Lynn's grandparents raised him in the church. Sunday morning. Sunday night. Wednesday night. "Church was not an option. It was a requirement. Then, when it became an option for him as an adult, it was still a requirement. Do you understand what I'm saying?" Donna asked me.

"Absolutely," I replied as I explained to Donna and Mama that my mom was raised in a strict but loving Southern Baptist

With Donna and Mama at Sam Kendall's in Hartsville, South Carolina. *Courtesy of author's collection*

home in a tiny back-road town called Green Cove Springs, Florida. I described how my mom had to sit in the bleachers during her high school dance, since dancing was strictly prohibited in the old-time Southern Baptist way.

"Aha," Mama said. "My parents were Pentecostals," otherwise known as the Church of God, a strict, conservative Protestant denomination. "We weren't allowed to carry purses, wear pants, wear shorts." She remembered when Papa came to her ball game. "Daddy came and got me off the ball court. He had never been to one of my games, and he came in and saw me in a pair of shorts . . . He made my coach promise he would let me wear longer shorts. And I did at home games." A mischievous smile crossed Mama's face. "But I didn't at away games!" Mama let out a warm chuckle. "You never knew when Daddy was going to show up."

In line with the family tradition, Donna was raised in a strict home full of faith. "I had a Marine Corps daddy and a Church of God mommy," Donna shared. "Mama carried me to church before I could carry myself."

When our food arrived at Sam Kendall's in the cozy town of Hartsville, South Carolina, Donna turned to Diane and said, "Mama, you want to say the blessing?" Diane, a sweet woman with an inviting spirit, bowed her head and began to pray over our beautiful lunch and accompanying sweet teas: "God, gracious heavenly father, we're so thankful to be able to come out today." Her prayer's focus quickly turned to me, her welcome guest. "Bless Kayleigh's hands, her mind, her thoughts, as she bears witness to Lynn and so many other peoples' lives. Lord, may she be able to help another person along the way. Lynn would love that with all of his heart." Over the next three hours, it became very clear to me, Lynn had been more than just a valiant veteran; he had been a father, a son, and an angel who took joy in helping others.

Donna met Lynn when she was only fifteen and he was eighteen. He had grown up just five miles down the road. What drew Donna to Barry Lynn? "He had the prettiest green eyes that God laid on any man in this entire world," she said. Mama was worried about the budding adolescent romance: they were just too young. She separated the couple, a move she now regrets, since Donna and Barry Lynn did not reconnect until later in life. They got married as adults in 2011 and merged their two existing families to become a modern version of the Brady Bunch.

Like Donna's dad, Barry Lynn's grandfather was a veteran too—a prisoner of war in World War II. Because of his grandfather, "Lynn was very, very patriotic," Mama noted, which prompted him to join ROTC in high school and eventually the United States Army. After his military service, Barry had a wide array of jobs: in the mill, in pawnshops, selling used cars and mobile homes.[1] But the worst was yet to come. The Coateses and Donna's family, the Catoes, both pledged their lives and their loyalty to their country—a country that would ultimately betray them.

★　★　★　★

The writing was on the wall for an entire year: rectal bleeding, excruciating pain, oddly shaped stools—all highly unusual symptoms for a man in his forties. Citing severe abdominal pain, Barry Lynn went to his local VA medical center in Hartsville, South Carolina, in November of 2010.[2] Although his lungs and liver looked normal, the ER doctor noticed blood in Lynn's stool and recommended he get a colonoscopy. At the follow-up appointment two months later with a different doctor at a different clinic, Lynn was not given a colonoscopy or even a simple rectal exam. "Just keep taking the medication," the doctor told him.

But the pain got worse and worse, causing Barry Lynn to pick up the phone in late February and request to see a GI specialist. Instead, he received a March 3 appointment with the same doctor who had told him to just take the medication. Barry Lynn reminded this doctor that the initial ER doctor had recommended a colonoscopy. Rather than taking Lynn's request seriously, she said a colonoscopy "might be needed" and sent him on his way with hemorrhoid suppositories. A colonoscopy consultation was never set up, and as the symptoms got worse, Lynn kept calling and calling and calling, pleading with the VA to give him the recommended colonoscopy.

In June of that year, Lynn took it upon himself to go to a different clinic. The third doctor immediately gave him narcotics and stool softener, a remedy that the doctor was surprised had not been given already. The third doctor concurred that a colonoscopy was necessary and scheduled a GI consult that did not take place until August—a full ten months after Lynn's pain began. At the consult, Barry Lynn told his fourth doctor about his yearlong pain, rectal bleeding, and constipation. She gave no colonoscopy referral and merely advised him to return in two months. The reasons for not making a colonoscopy referral were completely unknown to him at the time. "If you were in as much pain as I am, you would not wait another two months to see what's going on. You would probably do it this week," he told the doctor after experiencing increasing pain for six months.[3]

"You know, this may sound crude, and I don't mean it to be," Mama told me. "Barry would say, 'Mama, my stool is flat when it comes out' . . . [T]he only relief that he could get was to sit in a tub of hot water, almost hot enough to burn him." In September, Lynn wrote all of his symptoms in a message to one of his many doctors. The doctor simply replied with the familiar "You may need to be considered for a colonoscopy" and now "may need to see a surgeon" too. In October Lynn described to his fourth doctor that his stools were bright red in color. She finally agreed to a colonoscopy consultation in April—a full six months away and a year and a half after his struggles began. Mama grew concerned and told Donna, "I think Barry Lynn may have cancer."

"Mama, don't you say that," Donna snapped.

Lynn continued to call the VA incessantly, pleading to have a consultation scheduled, and on November 30, 2011, he received one, followed by a December 9, 2011, colonoscopy. Lynn was sedated for fewer than five minutes at Fort Jackson Hospital when the doctor immediately came out and said he had discovered a tumor the size of a baseball in Lynn's rectum. Lynn was swiftly diagnosed with stage 4 colon cancer and faced less than a 5 percent chance of living another five years. "I don't understand how in the world they missed this," Lynn's oncologist later told him. "I can feel the palpitation of the tumor on my fingertip."

Days later, Lynn had a chance to confront one of the doctors who dithered over giving him a colonoscopy. He showed her Fort Jackson's findings of a gigantic tumor and explained that she should listen to her patients.[4]

"I listen to my patients," she curtly replied.

"No, ma'am, you do not listen to your patients," Lynn told the doctor. "If you did, I would have been checked a long time ago."

"It was the only time I've ever seen him get really upset," Mama said.

Because the tumor was so large, Lynn had an inverted colostomy on December 16, returning home just two days before Christmas. The upcoming year would be a hard one for Barry Lynn: chemotherapy and twenty-six radiation treatments followed by a fourteen-hour surgery in July. "They cut me at my belly button, stopped at my woody woodpecker . . . and then split me up my backside," Lynn used to say in his characteristically good spirit.

Lynn was given a permanent colostomy, in which a contraption is installed to divert excrement through the abdomen and into a bag that hangs outside the body. Lynn had to change bags multiple times a day, a daunting task that he managed to turn into a comical one. Barry Lynn named his colostomy bag "Fred." Mama was lying on a couch, relaxing during a beachside vacation, when Lynn said he had to go to the bathroom and change Fred. Lynn decided in his usual good humor to play one of his jokes on Mama. He came back with a bag full of brown goo that he laid on Mama's chest. She screamed and jumped up as the mushy substance flew everywhere, completely unaware that it was just a bag full of peanut butter. Ever since that day, Lynn would joke, "Mama, you want some peanut butter with that?" "No!" she would shout.

"He played right up to the end," Mama said, laughing. Lynn walked out sporting Donna's dress before his son's wedding, and he paraded around wearing Donna's nightcap during their trip to the mountains. When Mama's bed collapsed in the middle of the night, Lynn thought that it was a hoot. "That tickled Lynn good," Mama remembered. "It made his day."

His personality was infectious. "You couldn't be around Lynn without him making you his friend," Donna said. One of Lynn's VA oncologists had a very formal demeanor, maintaining a professional distance from her patients. "Not with Lynn Coates you didn't," said Donna. "You're going to be my friend," he told the oncologist. After Lynn passed, the hospital reached out to tell Donna that Lynn had been one of their favorite patients.

Lynn kept his sense of humor despite his waning quality of life. In addition to the chemo and radiation, he had to insert a catheter into his urinary tract several times daily to relieve himself. He became both impotent and incontinent. The chemo caused neuropathy damage to his hands and feet, causing extreme pain.[5] But there were at least a few silver linings. When he first started chemo, he didn't lose all of his hair. People would comment, "Lynn, you don't even look like you're sick." "That's how good God is," Lynn would reply. And despite how bad it got, "Lynn Coates never once threw up. He would get tired and he would get weak, but he never once threw up," Donna noted. "Strongest man I ever knew."

Battling cancer was hard not only for Lynn but for Donna as well.

In the beginning she was working twelve hours days before leaving her salon in the hands of her cousin. The what-ifs were difficult to accept. "Sometimes I can just kick myself," she told Lynn. "If I took five minutes and just googled, I would have known." In Lynn's sweet, calm demeanor, he replied with words of wisdom, "Don't you ever, ever do that to yourself. It's the plan that God had for my life. It worked out his way, not your way, and you can't blame yourself for that."

Barry Lynn. *Courtesy of Donna Coates*

As Lynn continued to struggle, McBee, South Carolina—"a small little country town where love still abounds," as Donna describes it—rallied around the Coates family. Barry Lynn's cancer-ridden lungs had a hard time breathing when smoke coming off the family's woodstove filled the room. Recognizing this, the Coateses' tiny little Southern Baptist church stepped up, organizing a fund-raiser so that Lynn and Donna could buy a heating and air-conditioning unit.

"It's a good little town," Mama affirmed.

"Just good country folk people that just love each other," Donna chimed in. "When somebody's heart hurts, everybody's heart hurts . . . We rejoice together. We cry together. We mourn together. We do all those things together."

That's how it's done in the South, no matter the tragedy, no matter the circumstance. Donna pointed out that when the Charleston church shooting happened, leaving nine dead at Emanuel African Methodist Episcopal Church, the whole state of South Carolina stepped up. "We will be Charleston strong," she said.

Donna and Mama resent how some northerners caricature the South, including their sweet little town of McBee, which wrapped its arms around Lynn. "A lot of northerners think southerners are stupid," Mama said. "We are laid-back, but we know a lot more than northern people give us credit for." That laid-back culture manifests itself in big ways and in small. I told Mama and Donna how I was shocked that I never once got beeped at during my two-hour drive from Charlotte to Hartsville, even though I blocked two lanes of traffic at one point when I struggled to get into the far right lane at a stoplight in an effort to make my turn.

"In New York City, they are beeping at you before the light ever turns green," I said, laughing.

"It's southern hospitality," Donna explained. "It's not a difference of the Mason-Dixon Line but a difference of culture. It's still 'Yes, ma'am,' 'No, ma'am,' 'Yes, sir,' 'No, sir.' Manners and respect. You put someone first before yourself. Put Jesus first, then others, then yourself."

And that is exactly what Barry Lynn did right up until the very end. His daunting circumstances never managed to change his selfless attitude, always putting others first. His grandbaby, Karlie Ann, was turning one, and nothing—not even chemotherapy—would stop Lynn from making it to her birthday party. "If it had something to do with those babies, he was there," Mama said. He would go to events for his grandchildren even if he knew that he wasn't supposed to, due to his health. Donna showed me a picture of Lynn evidently in misery but proudly wearing a pink feathery crown for his sweet granddaughter. "No greater love hath Papaw than to show up at grandbaby's birthday just a few days after chemo," she wrote beneath the picture.

Lynn showed the same devotion to Donna even when he was in pain. Two days before he died, Donna had a broken tooth fixed. The very last text she has from her husband reads, *Are you OK?* "The man's dying," Donna said with emphasis. "And he's asking me if I'm OK—over a tooth. It was the sweetest thing in this world. He cared about my tooth." And when Donna had a hysterectomy, Lynn visited her each day even though it took everything in him to make it to her hospital bed. He would stay as long as he could and then say, "I can't stay any longer, but I want to let you know I love you."

In the aftermath of that operation, Donna's wise father said to his

Barry Lynn at Karlie Ann's birthday party. *Courtesy of Donna Coates*

daughter, "I need you to understand something, baby. Sometimes heal-ing comes on the other side, not this side. Do you understand what I'm saying?"

"Yes, sir," Donna answered.

As Lynn's battle against cancer continued, another battle was brew-ing on the horizon: a battle against the federal government. Donna's local news station, News Channel 10, reported that $1.02 million in funding for colonoscopies to the William Jennings Bryan Dorn VA Center had been mismanaged.[6] With ten thousand men in line for colo-noscopies, the money was intended to reduce backlogs but instead was used for other purposes. Only one-third of the $1.02 million was used for improving access to care. That money could have saved Barry Lynn's life had the money been properly utilized; instead, he languished on a VA waiting list. Infuriated, Donna wrote a letter to the news station, which picked up Lynn's story.

Shortly after, CNN called Lynn, asking him to share his story with a wider audience. In a January 30, 2014, story titled "Veterans Dying Because of Health Care Delays," CNN told the world about Barry Lynn

Coates.[7] A growing sense of wrongdoing at the VA prompted a broader, six-month-long CNN investigation, culminating in the April 2014 revelation that "at least 40 U.S. veterans died waiting for appointments at the Phoenix Veterans Affairs Health Care system, many of whom were placed on a secret waiting list."[8] The rightfully outraged headlines quickly followed:

"Arizona VA Boss Accused of Covering Up Veterans' Deaths . . ."[9]

" 'Don't Let Me Die': Veteran's Tearful Plea Before He Succumbed to Cancer . . ."[10]

"VA Director at Phoenix Hospital Got $9K Bonus."[11]

The VA waiting list scandal was upon us, and Barry Lynn Coates was at the very center of it, in the national spotlight.

★   ★   ★   ★

Barry Lynn always used to say, "God gave me cancer for a reason. It was my burden to bear and my story to tell. And I thank God that he did that for me." Donna found that strange at the time: here was her husband essentially thanking God for cancer. In hindsight, she understands exactly what he meant.

Just as the VA scandal gained traction, Barry Lynn's cancer got worse. With Lynn's CT scan results in her hand, Donna nervously glanced down and saw the words "metastasized to the liver and lungs." Stunned, she dropped the paper on the floor and began to cry. "I knew it," she told me. She knew that meant that her husband was going to die. "Donna, what does it say?" Barry Lynn asked. In lieu of a doctor delivering the news, Donna explained to her husband that his days were numbered. Donna went back to the oncology department—agitated at the lack of attentiveness—and said to the chief, "We don't have a diagnosis or a prognosis. I'm not here to be anyone's friend. I am here for my husband to get well."

Lynn was given a different oncologist, one of the only doctors at the VA he grew to know and love. When Lynn approached one of his original negligent doctors to show her that the cancer had metastasized, the dismissive doctor finally dropped her callousness for compassion. "I'm so sorry," she lamented, far too late. "I have a new policy where I send everyone over for a colonoscopy immediately."

Donna said, "That should have been her policy from day one ... Barry Lynn shouldn't have had to sacrifice his life to get it." Lynn's new doctor ordered an MRI to see if Lynn's cancer had spread to his brain, in addition to a new round of chemotherapy. But before Barry Lynn could take these next steps, he was given a surprising opportunity: a chance to testify before the United States Congress.

Faced with a choice of continuing his time-sensitive and badly needed treatment or sharing his story, Lynn chose the latter, putting chemo off for a full two weeks. "It may not help me, but it will help someone coming behind me," he told Donna. So Barry Lynn and Donna set aside Lynn's health for the moment and drove to our nation's capital. Sitting before a panel of our elected leaders in April of 2014, Lynn shared his story.

"My name is Barry Lynn Coates and due to the inadequate and lack of follow-up care I received through the VA system, I stand before you terminally ill today." [12] Lynn then proceeded to lay out the VA's inexcusable incompetence in excruciating detail: the neglected pain, the missed symptoms, the misdiagnoses, and the horrible mismanagement. "Men and women across this country volunteer every day to serve in the armed forces ... Other nations have to force service in order to maintain a strong military," Lynn pointed out to the lawmakers looking down at him from their comfortable perches. [13] "The very least this country should do is to ensure that those volunteers are taken care of after they have made sacrifices to take care of our country." He left the elected officials before him with a pointed question. "So I ask you today, how many more vets will be allowed to suffer and die before someone is held accountable?" [14]

Following hours of congressional testimony, Lynn and his family met their South Carolina representatives face-to-face. Though some politicians seemed uninterested in hearing Lynn's story, at least a few showed that they cared. Remembering that day, Donna said, "Jeff Miller—I think the world of him. Tom Rice—love him. Tim Scott—love him ..." Congressman Miller sent Lynn home with a daily devotional book of prayers that he signed with the message "God bless you." Congressman Rice sat down with Lynn for a very long time and just fell in love with the cheery veteran. When Lynn passed, Miller mailed Donna a heartfelt letter, and Rice sent Donna "this big old huge beautiful flower from his office," she said. "I'm so sorry for your loss, on behalf of my wife and my staff," the message read.

"It was personal to him," Donna noted.

Senator Tim Scott rose before Congress and honored Barry Lynn. "We will never forget his sacrifice," Scott vowed.[15]

"Sometimes that makes a world of difference, and the politicians don't realize that," Mama pointed out. While so many of our politicians know how to put on a good face for the cameras, you really grow to know them through the eyes of their constituents who know them personally.

After sharing his story and confronting his leaders, Lynn returned home to his regrettable reality. Chemotherapy and radiation were accompanied by hope-filled trials. The Coates couple used football as a distraction. Donna was a Clemson fan, proudly wearing her purple and orange for Saturday games. Lynn, however, rooted for rival South Carolina.

"That was the only division in that house. He was Carolina," Mama recalled.

"But it made for some fun Saturdays," Donna reminisced. "He was very competitive. 'You've gotta root for the home team,' he would say." Donna would retort, "I am. It just happens to be the upstate home team."

"That was our break," Donna said. "That's what college football became for us. It was a day we didn't have to study chemo and radiation. It was about Carolina and Clemson . . . our escape time from this world." Their little grandson, Trenton Samuel, would run around the house, through the kitchen, and into the living room, yelling, "Run, Deshaun, run!" It didn't matter who was playing: "Run, Deshaun, run!" would ring through the house as Trenton shouted encouragement to Clemson Tigers quarterback Deshaun Watson. Lynn would say, "No, Sam-*u*-el," with a heavy emphasis on the *u*, "it's 'Go, Gamecocks!'"

Barry Lynn and Donna. *Courtesy of Donna Coates*

Trenton was "Papaw's boy." Donna's daughter, Brianna, didn't think she could have a child, so she prayed, "Lord, if you give me a child, I will give him back to you all the days of his life." She did just that when she named her firstborn Trenton Samuel. Samuel was the long-awaited child of Hannah, and the name means "heart of the Lord." While the rest of the family called Trenton Samuel "Trenton," Barry Lynn insisted on "Sam-*u*-el." "Boy, I see many spankings in your future. You as rotten as you can be," Barry Lynn would joke.

Eventually, Donna and Lynn moved permanently to their condo in Myrtle Beach to be closer to their doctors in Charleston. "It's funny how God makes provisions, because when we got the condo, we had no idea we would need it for Charleston," Donna said. Barry Lynn just loved being at the beach. He would go through chemotherapy and then head straight outside and float atop the water, trying to forget about his cancer. One day, as Lynn and Donna swam in the pool, Donna said, "Lynn, what we going to do if this trial doesn't work?"

"Why are you worried about things you cannot change?" he asked. "You cannot change this. This is God's path which he's laid for me. Honey, nothing stays the same. Everything changes from day to day."

"Well, Lynn, I can't do this."

"You're stronger than you've ever given yourself credit for being. I know you can do it."

In those last few months, a potential source of hope turned to despair. A brand-new drug called Lonsurf had hit the market. Donna pleaded with the VA to get Lynn the new medicine. Lonsurf was FDA-approved and available in the private market, but the VA was dragging its feet in negotiating the price. Sixty minuscule white-and-pink tablets for a whopping $10,000—it seemed crazy. "[But] it doesn't make any difference to you when it's your husband that needs the medicine and they need it now," Donna said.

Donna remembers the day those four expensive little packets arrived on her doorstep. Lynn was the first to get it from the VA after they finally stopped haggling over the price. When the pills arrived, Barry Lynn was at an appointment—only the second one Donna had missed in five years. She texted Lynn: *Honey, your medicine is here.* She still remembers that it was December 2 when she got her hands on that medicine. "The day I put my hand on this medicine was the day that the doctor looked at Lynn and said, 'There is nothing we can do for you.' If they had given him this medicine one month ago, two months ago . . . he would have had a chance."

"It was a chance," Mama chimed in.

At this point, though, Barry Lynn was too far gone. His bilirubin count was too high, indicating liver problems and signaling that he was no longer strong enough to take the medicine. The end was nearing.

Lynn wanted to go home to McBee for his last days on earth, so he and Donna left Myrtle Beach for the last time. In Lynn's final days the tumors growing in his body began to form blood clots. One of the clots would break free, ultimately taking his life almost a year from the day that Lynn's grandmother died of lung cancer. Donna reminds herself of Lynn's confidence in her strength every time an anniversary or Christmas or Easter rolls around. "He believed in me when I didn't believe in myself," Donna said. He wanted her to keep fighting for the veterans, as she has done.

After Lynn's death, CNN called Donna and asked if she would participate in a town hall meeting where she would have the opportunity to confront President Barack Obama. Although Donna's attorneys did not want her to go, she remembered what Lynn had always told her: "If you can help anyone, help them." And so that's what Donna did. At a town hall in Fort Lee, Virginia, Donna stood tall, clutching her husband's folded flag, and looked the world's most powerful man directly in the eye.

"Mr. President, I stand before you today with my husband's flag," she said.[16] "Two years ago, Barry Lynn testified in front of Congress, and we heard a lot of promises about reform and accountability, but still nothing's changed. In fact, the contracted doctor that misdiagnosed my husband is still treating our veterans at the same VA clinic."[17] Remembering Mama's sage advice, Donna decided to provide some to the president. "My mama's always told me that if you stop talking about stuff and do it, then you don't have to talk about it any longer. So when are we going to actually start holding these contracted doctors and the VA employees accountable? For it's the difference between life and death. And families like mine, they're tired of waiting."[18] As President Obama looked at Donna with a disaffected stare, slightly nodding, Donna stated with a shaky voice, "And the only true change that's come since we began talking was that I am now a widow. And my family, we won't ever be the same."[19]

As Donna described this confrontation, she told me that President Obama promised to find out why Lynn's doctor was never fired or even reprimanded. To her knowledge, the president never did that. "It's on camera," she told me, pulling up the video on her phone. Sure enough, after providing an excuse for inaction at the VA, Obama looked at Donna and said, "I don't know the particular case of this individual doctor, but you can bet I'll find out after this meeting."[20] And off camera, Donna remembers Obama telling her, "I want you to know that your husband's story will not go unheard." Obama never did follow up, Donna told me, and the incompetent doctor is still treating our veterans today.

"She gets up every morning. She still goes to her jobs. She lives in her multimillion-dollar home. How's her life changed?" Donna asked, frustrated. "She doesn't know what it's like to start over. She doesn't know what it's like to have lost half of who you are . . . She don't understand that pain and that hurt." Donna, on the other hand, will deal with the life-changing consequences of that VA doctor's actions. "My grandchildren lost their Papaw. My children have lost their daddy. I've lost my husband. We've lost the person who held our family together. What's she lost?" Donna asked.

"Nothing," we both said in unison.

★ ★ ★ ★

At that Fort Lee, Virginia, town hall meeting, Donna shared a little slice of her reality with President Obama. But the magnitude of Donna's pain and the gravity of the betrayal was something Barack Obama could never fully understand. "The love of her life died that day," Mama said, and Donna was left alone to pick up the pieces.

One of the hardest moments was 2:00 p.m. on Wednesday, January 27, 2016. Donna wearily got out of the car with the help of her six-foot-two-inch brother Darren, nicknamed "Bubba," and walked with his assistance to the tiny redbrick Baptist church with its tall white steeple—the church Mama had raised her in, the church she had attended with her husband, and the church where Barry Lynn would be laid to rest. Donna dragged her body up the steps, through the four columns, and up to the white double doors with her head buried in her brother's chest the whole way. Donna had called her brother the morning Barry Lynn passed away. Darren picked up the phone, and Donna said, "Bubba." Immediately recognizing that something was wrong, he replied, "I'm on my way." He rushed to his car and drove twenty hours from Corpus Christi, Texas, to get home. "We used to fight like cats and dogs when we were little," Donna recalled. Darren would jokingly tease her with names like "Ms. Piggy," "Ms. Hoggy," and "Fluffy," but now here was Darren, her tall source of strength.

As Donna tried to walk through the church door that day to stand before her husband's body for the last time, she looked over at her brother and said, "I can't do it, Bubba."

"You've got to," he said.

"I can't do it," she insisted, standing motionless.

"You've got to," Bubba repeated.

"The hardest steps I've ever had to take was putting my foot on the steps of that church," Donna told me. Bubba sat beside her the entire time as Donna kept her head firmly nestled in his chest. When they left the building and walked to the church cemetery, Bubba kept saying to his sister, "Breathe, Donna. Just breathe. Breathe."

Barry Lynn was buried in the church graveyard, just behind the worship building. His body rests in eternal peace beneath a marker that reads "True Love Never Dies." "I want to be buried next to you," Lynn told his wife. Just behind Timrod Baptist Church, the plots are all lined up: "My granddaddy, my grandmother, Kennedy, me, Barry Lynn, Mama, and then Daddy," Donna told me.

Kennedy Paige, buried right beside Donna's plot, was the beautiful granddaughter whom Donna lost when her daughter Amber's cervix opened up just after Barry Lynn got diagnosed with cancer. "That was one of the worst periods in my entire life," Donna remembered. But Donna made it through, just like she would make it through the dark year that followed Barry Lynn's death, in large part thanks to the support of those around her.

The day Lynn passed away, wise old Aunt Betty came over. Aunt Betty had overcome more suffering than most humans could take, losing her husband and two children in a house fire. "He was my leaning post," Aunt Betty would say of her husband. "He was the one who held me up. We fought this life together." Aunt Betty wrapped her niece in a warm motherly hug and looked her straight in the eyes.

"Donna," she said.

"Yes, ma'am?"

"Today's hard," she said. "There's days that are going to be harder to come."

"Yes, ma'am."

"But I know one thing."

"What's that?" Donna asked.

"You can get through this," she assured her broken loved one.

"Why?" Donna asked in disbelief.

"Because you my niece," Aunt Betty said. "And if I can live through what I've lived through, you can get through this too."

Aunt Betty has since passed, but her guidance lives on in Donna's heart as she tries to make it through each painful day. "It's still horrible," Donna said about a year and a half later. "Some days are better than other days. Some days are worse than other days."

Donna's grandmother lost a husband and two children, one to cancer and one in an accident. People would always offer Granny that age-old saying "Time heals all wounds." But Granny told Donna, "I'm here to tell you, that's a lie." Donna then shared with me a truth that Granny had passed along to her: time doesn't heal all wounds; it puts a scab on top of them. Every once in a while, something will come along and knock the scab right off. "It will hurt just as bad as the day it happened, and it will heal over again," Donna told me. And the cycle would continue until the very end of one's life. "And Granny never lied," Donna added. "That's the truth."

Granny was right. "I have moments where I cry all day after a year and a half out," Donna said. On those days she clings tightly to Lynn's boot camp jacket. Lynn got that jacket in 1991. He would wear it in the yard, all tattered from age. "It's precious to me," Donna explained. "It was the one thing I absolutely refused to give away . . . I'll pick it up and wear it sometimes. You know, to keep him near to me. I love that thing. It's just raggedy and worn and in pieces, but it's his."

In addition to emotional pain, Donna has incurred financial pain as well. There were telephone and utility bills, groceries, and the costs of day-to-day life. "There's a limit to what Mommy and Daddy could do when you're country people and retired," Mama injected. "You live on a fixed income." During Lynn's sickness, Donna had to quit managing her salon. *OK, God, I have a choice,* she thought. *My salon will be here when I come back, but Barry Lynn may not be.* "So I chose him," she said. She had worked really hard to build Salon 828, giving a lot of her life to that business. It was her baby, and she loved it. Because Donna stepped away from the salon, she lost most of the clientele she had spent her life building. "I've had to start completely over," she said.

But Salon 828 was appropriately named. "My salon name is Salon 828. You know why?" Donna said. "I always say I've been through things that are designed to kill folks, and I'm still here . . . I've buried a lot of people in my life." And during those times, Donna always looked to Romans 8:28, the same verse that has given Kim Copeland so much hope after losing her husband and son: "And we know that in all things God works for the good of those who love him, who have been called according to his purpose." That simple but salient verse is embroidered and hung in Donna's salon. "I know you're still working everything to my good," she says to her savior.

And Donna's financial hardship has indeed been alleviated. Lynn had the foresight to sell the Myrtle Beach condo just before he passed. "That's what kept her going. She couldn't have made it financially," Mama said. And Donna is rebuilding her customer base at the salon. "I always say, there isn't a day when I haven't had a biscuit to my lips. The good Lord's been good to me. He's been good to me," Donna emphasized.

In the aftermath of Barry Lynn's death, Donna's faith was challenged. "Donna got angry," Mama told me. "But I got angry." Mama would ask, "Why, God? We did everything that you asked us to do. We prayed for healings. We know you can heal. Why didn't you heal him? Why did you let him die?" One day, Mama was driving along the road asking those very questions. "You could've healed him," she told God. "You didn't answer my prayer." Like a clear voice from heaven, God responded, "But I answered his."

"Wow, and you felt God saying that to you?" I asked Mama. "Oh, yeah," she said confidently. God had answered Barry Lynn's persistent prayer of conforming his life to God's will: "Lord, put my feet on the path you have chosen for me, and don't let me stray from that."

★   ★   ★   ★

I was sitting on a CNN set in Washington, DC, when a story broke that made the consequences of the 2016 election painfully clear. "A new report [came] out moments ago with a rather scathing indictment of the scandal-plagued VA hospital in Phoenix," the anchor said.[21] "This coming two years after a massive overhaul."[22] Thirty-eight thousand delayed appointments—in just one hospital. The sixth report by the inspector general showing persistent mismanagement at the VA. According to one of those reports, as many as 307,000 veterans might have been waiting for care when they died, although the exact number is impossible to know due to "data limitations."[23] And yet, for two years nothing meaningful had been done. Our veterans still suffered at the hands of inexcusable incompetence.

"Nothing's changed," Donna said regretfully as we talked over a plate of cheesecake. When Donna and her boyfriend, Mike, searched for a new home in May of 2016, Donna took notice of the "100% Veterans" tag on her real estate agent's car. Donna shared Barry Lynn's story with the agent, who countered with her own sad story. The agent's husband went to the VA with a big knot on his neck. "If I send you over for tests, I'm going to look silly," the doctor replied, seeming to suggest that the knot was nothing serious. After an entire year of inaction, the man finally consulted an outside physician, who immediately sent him for tests. Lymphoma had been growing in the neglected veteran for an entire year. One VA oncologist was honest enough to tell the patient, "The best thing you can do is use outside insurance. If you wait to get a referral here, you will be dead." And when the veteran sought out a patient advocate at the VA to share his story, the so-called advocate was useless, telling him, "If you don't like what we have to say, I would suggest you find an attorney."

Donna says that many veterans did not discuss the problems with the VA publicly because they feared that their compensation would be taken away. "It's literally taking on the federal government when you take on the VA. It's taking on the whole huge monstrosity of the federal government, and that's daunting to a lot of people," she said. She feels more distrust than fear based on a history of verifiable government betrayal. In addition to losing her husband due to government mismanagement, Donna's father was subjected to poisonous water when he served at Marine Corp Base Camp Lejeune in Jacksonville, North Carolina.[24] He now suffers from fibromyalgia and carpal tunnel syndrome. Although the government provides disability benefits, Donna said, "No one's seen a penny. Daddy hasn't seen a dime in compensation."

Donna distrusts government for good reason, but she did place her trust in President Donald Trump during the 2016 election. "I have more trust in him than I do [Hillary Clinton], and I'm going to tell you why," Donna explained. "Benghazi—that, to me, was a deal breaker."

"He's more of a man of action, he really is," Mama added. "Sometimes he needs to watch his tongue, but at least he's honest . . . and she definitely wasn't for the vets. You could tell by the way she talked that she wasn't interested in them."

Mama's disdain for the way Hillary talked about the problems at the VA was understandable. In October of 2015, MSNBC's Rachel Maddow asked Clinton about the VA scandal noting, "You can't find a person in politics who doesn't say we shouldn't do right by our veterans. But for some reason, this can't get fixed fast enough."[25]

"Yeah, I don't understand that. You know, I don't understand why we have such a problem, because there have been a number of surveys of veterans, and overall, veterans who do get treated are satisfied with their treatment . . ." Clinton replied, seeming to marginalize the VA scandal.[26]

Her out-of-touch response came just one month after that IG report revealed that as many as 307,000 veterans might have died waiting for care. But Clinton nevertheless complained about "the constant berating of the VA that comes from Republicans" during her interview, leading the liberal Maddow to retort, "But in part because there has been real scandal."[27]

Clinton, not willing to acknowledge the true gravity of the VA scandal, replied, "There has been . . . [but] it's not been as widespread as it has been made out to be."[28]

Senator John McCain and several congressmen rebuked Clinton's comments, with McCain saying, "I don't know what Hillary Clinton's view of what 'widespread' is but the facts are stubborn things. The VA Deputy Secretary Sloan Gibson recently admitted that there are nearly 500,000 appointments with extended wait times . . . The VA Inspector General said there are 800,000 records stalled . . . If that's not quote 'widespread,' I would like to know what Hillary Clinton's definition of 'widespread' is."[29] Florida congressman David Jolly plainly stated that Clinton "trying to downplay this atrocity is inexcusable and outright insulting."[30]

Clinton, who constantly spoke of the plight of the illegal immigrant, seemed to have little understanding of the plight of our own veterans, the men and women who risked their lives for our country's safety. Pointing to this important truth, Trump said, "The media and my opponent discuss one thing and only one thing, the needs of people living here illegally. In many cases, by the way, they're treated better than our vets."[31] Veterans, who voted for Trump by a 26-point margin, recognized Clinton's disinterest and Trump's repeated calls for a fix to the VA's mismanagement.[32]

As for the solution, Donna says that throwing money at the VA will never solve the problem. During Obama's Fort Lee town hall meeting, Donna remembers the president touting that "we have increased the VA budget by 85%. No president has increased the VA budget faster and more aggressively than I have . . ."[33] However, this biggest-ever increase appears to have done little to solve the problem. According to Donna, the answers are "accountability and responsibility"—something we saw very little of in the wake of the waiting list scandal. Although Secretary of Veterans Affairs Eric Shinseki did resign in May of 2014, many of the doctors who displayed callous ineptitude are still in their positions. And in the wake of the scandal, the department rewarded its executives and employees with more than $142 million in bonuses.[34] As our veterans suffered, the VA employees were well taken care of.

"They have to stop *talking* about it and *be* about it," Donna said. Just a few days after our interview, Donna sent me a Facebook message: "A win for us on Capitol Hill today," she wrote. President Trump had signed into law the VA Accountability and Whistleblower Protection Act, legislation that protected whistleblowers and made it easier to fire VA employees. "Hallelujah. Thank you, Jesus. It's at least a start," Donna said.

It was a big victory for our veterans, a victory that received little coverage from the mainstream media, which opts instead to obsess over salacious gossip and innuendo. "I wish right now they'd leave Trump alone and let him do his job," Mama said. "All of them have done wrong in their life, every one of them. He was elected to the office by the people. They need to sit down and shut up." The media engenders division and distraction at a time when Donna recognizes that we must come together to solve our nation's problems. Although she was frustrated with Obama never following through on his promise, she said, "It doesn't matter who's in office. God instructs in his word that we are supposed to pray for those people . . . How stupid are we to pray that he falls? Because if he falls, we all fall."

★   ★   ★   ★

Just before I traveled to McBee, South Carolina, Donna sent me a message. She asked me to call Barry Lynn's chapter of the book "Winner Either Way." Winner either way? Barry Lynn was dealt what seems to most a very bad hand in life. The average person who was betrayed by the federal government, ravaged by cancer, and dead before the age of fifty would not label him- or herself a "winner" in this life. But Barry Lynn Coates was far from average.

"I'm a winner either way," Barry Lynn would always say to Donna. "If I get to stay here and God heals my body on this side, I will be with y'all. And if I don't, then I get to go home and be with the Lord."

"But *I* don't win, Lynn," Donna would reply. "It's not a win for *me*."

"But we'll get to be together," Lynn would say without missing a beat.

A year and a half later Donna Coates can say "We'll be together" with all the confidence that Barry Lynn did, because God has given her little signs amid her pain.

For almost a year after Lynn passed away, Trenton Samuel would continue to traverse the house screaming "Papaw!" But this time he was met with silence instead of Lynn's typical jovial response of "Sam-*u*-el!" After Papaw passed, God brought Mike, a new boyfriend and soon-to-be husband, into Donna's life. Mike hadn't been to church in fifteen years, but with Donna's prodding he went. Now he won't miss

Barry Lynn with Trenton Samuel, dressing up as Santa during his illness. *Courtesy of Donna Coates*

a Sunday and even brings his sister along with him. One day Mike was Facetiming with Trenton, and Trenton said, "Hey, Papaw." It shocked Mike, and it shocked Donna too. No one had told Trenton to call Mike by that name, a name solely reserved for Barry Lynn. Sitting on the porch in a rocking chair, Trenton's mom said to him, "Who told you that was Papaw Mike?" Trenton looked up at her and said, "Papaw." Trenton had received permission from his grandpa in heaven to pass along the name.

Karlie Ann, Donna's other grandchild, had a Papaw encounter too. Standing at the door of the house, Karlie eagerly said to her mom, "Mama, Mama, there's Papaw! Papaw!" With a beaming smile, the blond-haired girl repeatedly asked her mother, "Mama, do you see Papaw?" Curious, her mom walked to the door and looked outside but saw no one. Karlie, meanwhile, still stood there with that huge smile on her face. As Donna recounted the story, she cried so hard that she could barely get the words out, "So, yeah, I do. I think that Barry Lynn's still around, and he watches us."

"You're definitely going to see him again, and you know he's in heaven," I assured her.

"Oh, yeah, and that makes heaven that much sweeter," Donna said with satisfaction.

THE TRANSFORMATION

Immigration

"He will wipe every tear from their eyes. There will be no more death or mourning or crying or pain, for the old order of things has passed away."
—REVELATION 21:4

As Sabine Durden walked toward the car beneath the yellow hue of a glowing Waffle House sign, she suddenly lost all power in her body. Slumping forward, her fiancé, Anthony, came to her side and helped her into the rental vehicle.

What in the world is going on? I've never experienced jet lag like this, she thought.

It was 8:45 a.m. when Sabine's body unexplainably collapsed in Atlanta, Georgia. Meanwhile, in Moreno Valley, California, the clock read 5:45 a.m.—a time that Sabine would never forget.

"My body knew, I didn't," she said to me as her big green eyes peered through a waterfall of tears.

Sabine and Anthony left the Waffle House to arrive at a soaring mansion. Eager to finally meet Anthony's family, Sabine's anticipation spiraled into an odd burdening achiness. She changed into her pajamas, expecting to be enveloped in restful slumber. But as Sabine relaxed, her phone buzzed.

I'm not going to answer, she thought. *These are women from the gym wanting the late-night advice of their trainer. They can gain some weight and we'll work it out when I get back.* But her phone lit up again and again and again.

Sabine finally glanced at her illuminated device to find a flurry of frantic messages. "Please call me. This is Elaina, Dominic's best friend." An endless list of names with urgent pleas invaded her home screen—all the names of Dominic's friends from the 911 dispatch office he worked at in Moreno Valley. Suddenly awake, Sabine attempted to play the voice mails, but none of them would play.

"God protected me. I know that," she stated without hesitation. "If I would have heard those voice mails and what happened, I would have grabbed that rental car and taken off over a cliff."

Bewildered and confused, she ran upstairs and through the unfamiliar halls of a home she had never been in to find Anthony, who still remembers the look of Sabine's eyes, "huge and full of fear."

"Something has happened to Dominic!" she cried. The couple called Dominic's dispatch office, and when the woman on the other end heard it was Sabine, her voice abruptly changed.

"Ma'am, can you please hold."

"Listen, just let me speak to Dominic," Sabine urged.

"Just wait for the supervisor."

Sabine looked at Anthony and quipped, "That boy done crashed his bike and is probably in the hospital in a body cast. I'm going to hurt him when I get home!"

"The supervisor got on," Sabine recounted. "And that sentence that you hear on TV." She paused as her voice took a painful, lower tone. "It's forever engraved: I'm so sorry to inform you that Dominic was killed this morning."

Sabine clutched the phone and screamed as members of Anthony's family began flooding into the room. Sabine and Anthony both fell to the floor, wailing in despair, as Sabine tried to comprehend the death of "[her] only child, [her] best friend, and the love of [her] life."[1]

"That's the biggest bullshit I ever heard. It's a lie . . . If that's one of his pranks . . . I'm never going to talk to him again," she stated in disbelief.

The phone let out another harrowing ring. This time it was the police chief.

Several of Dom's friends had already identified the body, and Sabine needed to call the coroner. Panicked and in disbelief, Sabine and Anthony rushed back to the airport. The rental car agent casually re-marked, "Hey, you guys were here this morning," but then he saw the look on Sabine's face. "Oh my God."

Sabine and Anthony dragged their weary bodies onto the plane, and the stewardess brought the couple a big bottle of water and a towel. Their howling cries filled the entirety of the six-hour flight. "We cried loudly, and we didn't care," Sabine recalled.

When Sabine arrived at Ontario California International Airport, she had settled into confident denial. "We're going to wake up. This did not happen. No way."

Less than twenty-four hours earlier, Dominic, Anthony, and Sabine had eaten dinner together before Dom drove them to the airport. As Dom took Sabine's bag out of his truck, Sabine fell forward, right into his arms. Like a big, warm teddy bear, Dom wrapped Sabine in his lov-ing embrace, swirled her around, and kissed her.

"Now, we will be back in a week," she joked. "I have hidden cameras all over the house, so watch out."

"I took them down, don't worry. Go have a party," Anthony chimed in.

The three of them shared a final laugh together.

Sabine remembered, "He hugged me and kissed me, and I still see him walk to his truck. The one I drive now." She paused for several sec-onds and her voice began to shake. "And he just stood there and smiled at me and said 'I love you' because we always [did] that. We knew we didn't have to but we said and showed it."

"Have a safe trip," Dominic instructed her.

"You be safe too," replied Sabine.

"Always, Mom."

"And that was the last time I saw and heard him," Sabine told me.

Less than a day earlier, Sabine had happily departed from the bus-tling San Bernardino County airport, anxiously prepared to meet new family. But now Sabine had returned to a nightmare.

As Sabine exited the terminal, she gazed down the stairs and saw the distressed faces of Dominic's three best friends.

Sabine's body hit the floor as she lost consciousness. It was real.

★ ★ ★ ★

Just before 5:45 a.m. on July 12, 2012, Dominic left for work at the sheriff's department on his black and chrome motorcycle as he did on any ordinary day. But on this July morning Dominic would cross paths with someone who was not even supposed to be here in the United States. The encounter would cost him his life.

Dominic had a booming laugh and a desire to help others. He worked as a 911 dispatcher and flew small planes in his spare time, but his dream was to become a helicopter pilot for the police department. As a dispatcher "he was the calming voice, the rock who everybody looked to for strength," according to his coworker.[2]

Dom was the kind of guy who would volunteer to work on Thanksgiving and Christmas because he wanted the employees with children to be home with their kids. Beloved by all, he was "everyone's plus-one."[3] In his spare time he worked tirelessly in service of other people. He worked as a volunteer firefighter and, in 2002, was named Moreno Valley Volunteer of the Year for performing more than one thousand service hours. In short, Dominic was a model citizen.

Dom was also a prankster, known for his lighthearted jokes. He and his mom would exchange gag gifts at Christmas, aiming to outdo each other with silly wrapping paper and unpredictable shenanigans.

Dom always knew how to get a good laugh, like the time when he arranged for the police to pull him over with his friend in the car. He pulled out a big wad of money and had the officers

Dominic. *Courtesy of Sabine Durden*

pretend to arrest him as they proclaimed to Dom's wide-eyed friend, "You didn't know that Dom was the best-known male prostitute in town?" Sabine remembers Dom crawling into the house with his big, booming laugh as his friend looked white as a sheet. "I will never be able to hear my son laugh again," Sabine lamented.

Dom called himself "a proud mama's boy." "We were never apart longer than two weeks," Sabine proudly boasted. "People tell me now that he would always talk about his mom and how proud he was . . . and how much he enjoyed hanging out." One time Sabine crashed her motorcycle, and Dom ran over to her with huge, tearful eyes.

"You almost made my worst nightmare come true," he exclaimed.

"Nah, nah, nah. [The] worst nightmare would be something happening to you," Sabine replied.

Six months later, something did happen to Dom.

Dom rode his motorcycle down Pigeon Pass Road on his familiar route to work through California's sparse green foliage and red dirt mountains. He was sitting in the left lane while he waited at a light. As the light turned green, he moved forward and a red Toyota pickup suddenly took a fast left turn in front of him.[4] Dom tried to swerve, but the truck hit him so hard that his body was launched into the air, hitting a wall near the sidewalk.

Two marines who happened to be trailing behind Dom witnessed the crash. They immediately sprinted out of their vehicle toward Dom, but one man noticed the driver of the pickup fleeing the scene, according to one of the marines. As one marine tended to Dom, talking to him and covering his lifeless body with his jacket, the other chased down the driver and detained him until police arrived.

One of the marines would tell Sabine that the driver, Juan Zacarias Lopez Tzun, not only tried to bolt from the scene, he also seemed entirely uninterested in the carnage his actions had caused. As Dom's body lay motionless, Tzun, according to the marine, gazed into the sky with a "Can we get this over with? I have places to go" attitude.

As time passed and there was no sign of Dom at the dispatch office, Dom's coworkers grew concerned. Dom was always a little late, bolting into the office with "boots untied and shirt untucked," according to

Sabine. He would cruise in just in time for the 6:00 a.m. briefing. Today, however, rather than receiving a reliably late Dom, the dispatch office received a concerning call: "Fatality on Pigeon Pass."

Dom's best friend was a motorcycle cop, who happened to arrive on the scene. He saw Dom's black and chrome bike lying on the sidewalk and thought, *No, no, no, that's not him.* The dispatcher ran the plate and a blocked identity signal popped up. She hit another button to uncover the owner of the bike: "Dominic Durden." Law enforcement had lost a brother in blue.

★   ★   ★   ★

Juan Zacarias Lopez Tzun, Dominic's killer, had a long and ominous rap sheet: grand theft, robbery, drunken driving, violation of probation. But Tzun was not just a criminal: he was a criminal who had no legal right to be in the United States. Tzun had illegally crossed the border before, and after a felony conviction for grand theft in 2009 he had been deported to Guatemala.[5] Undeterred, Tzun illegally crossed the border again. This time he earned a drunk-driving conviction and a penalty of three years' probation, a $1,660 fine, and a mere ten days in jail.[6] While on probation for his first DUI, Tzun was arrested for not having a license and a second suspicion of driving under the influence.[7] Tzun had no license, registration, or insurance, and he had a criminal record, but, remarkably, no deportation proceedings were initiated.[8] Instead, he was released on bail following his second DUI arrest, mere weeks before he crashed into Dominic.[9]

Sabine described it as a "drop-to-your-knees moment" when she found out about Juan's legal status. Although Sabine had already suffered the greatest of injustices, more injustice was yet to come.

Authorities arrested Juan after his collision with Dominic, and days later he was charged with misdemeanor vehicular manslaughter *without* gross negligence and driving without a license.[10] No gross negligence was charged despite the district attorney and judge acknowledging that Juan had made "an unsafe left turn," in their words.[11] As Juan awaited his trial, authorities eventually moved him from jail to U.S. Immigration and Customs Enforcement (ICE) detention.[12] In the face of multiple previous criminal convictions, the immigration judge nevertheless offered Juan the option of bail, which he readily posted.[13] At an early hearing, the judge also promised Juan a lenient nine-month jail sentence if he pleaded guilty, making this deal before Dominic's grieving mother had the chance to make her victim-impact statement to the court.[14]

During trial, Sabine watched as Juan gave his statement, taking "little responsibility for his actions," according to the *Riverside Press-Enterprise*'s Brian Rokos, who did extensive reporting on the case.[15] Although Juan sucked up to the judge during the trial, saying "You're the best" and "I so admire you," he never once apologized to Sabine for his fatal actions.

When the judge asked Juan about his reaction to the accident, Sabine remembers Juan snidely replying, "God gives life. God takes life. I was only on my way to work."[16] Audible gasps filled the courtroom in reaction to his unapologetic, callous statement.

When Sabine gave her victim-impact statement, she wearily stood with the judge to her left and the audience to her right as her two friends propped up her exhausted body.

"Lean back, lean back," her friends advised as Sabine tearfully faced her son's killer.

"Why do I have to lean back?" Sabine whispered.

"Just trust us."

Her friends tried to obstruct Sabine's view. "What is going on?" Sabine asked again.

"Don't look over there. They are mad-dogging you," her friends said.

As Sabine poured her heart out to the courtroom, sharing the life and the death of her only son, she looked out at a sea of weeping faces. All of the courtroom staff was bawling. But in the midst of all that empathy sat some members of the killer's family who seemed to smirk and sneer at Sabine in what she viewed as an effort to intimidate her. Undeterred, Sabine addressed Juan directly, "You had no license, no regard for anyone out there. You risked everyone's life who shared the road with you . . . You didn't just take Dominic's future, you took mine as well."[17]

While Juan was engaging in arrogant denial and evading justice, Sa-

Dominic and Sabine. *Courtesy of Sabine Durden*

bine coped with inconceivable loss. Upon arriving back in California in the direct aftermath of Dom's death, she asked to be taken to the scene. The blood was washed clean, but she stood at a marker, not realizing that she was standing on the very spot where Dom had died.

Sabine also had to make a heartbreaking phone call to her ninety-two-year-old mother in Germany to notify her that her favorite grandson had died. The family made sure a doctor was present, and when Sabine called, her sister could not even recognize her broken voice.

And then came the impossible task of laying her only child to eternal rest. "Thank God he had a helmet on," she said. That meant they could have an open casket. "He looked like he was asleep with a smirk on his face, but I knew his legs were mangled."

Sabine was forever changed, but Juan would walk away unscathed. Despite multiple convictions, a felony, two illegal border crossings, and an entitled, haughty attitude, Juan pled guilty, receiving only a nine-month jail sentence on a charge carrying up to a one-year sentence and five years' probation, just as the judge had promised.[18]

When Sabine heard the sentence, she recalls, "Everything in me went numb." Her two friends held her up and carried her out of the so-called River Hall of Justice, all three wearing "In Loving Memory of Dominic" T-shirts.[19] As her friends guided her to a bench outside the courtroom, Sabine cried, "Not one time [did he say] 'I'm sorry.' "[20] In addition to his sentence, Juan was also ordered to pay $18,800 in restitution to Sabine.[21] "That's my son's life," she lamented. Sabine hasn't received a dime from Juan, who had proved himself fully capable of paying his bail.

Even the judge seemed to acknowledge the injustice he had rendered. Rokos reported that the judge seemed "to question whether the charge against Tzun should have been a felony . . . [A]fter reading 16 victim-impact letters and hearing three tearful victim-impact statements, he appeared to regret promising that sentence."[22] The judge pointlessly told Tzun, "If I knew what I know now, I might have told the [prosecution] to find a way to charge you with a felony."[23] He even remarked to Brian Rokos, "This one [case] got to me."[24]

For Sabine, no amount of remorse from the judge would rectify the wrong. "This guy [Juan], he took more than just my only child," she told me. "He took his incredible future . . . He took away that I would never be a grandmother or a mother-in-law. So his friends are all getting married and having kids. And I'm happy for them, but inside it tears me up. I would have been them."

And his penalty? Because of a deal, Tzun spent only thirty-five days in jail.[25] Tzun's judge decided that the convicted felon could spend as much as two-thirds of his jail sentence in a work release program or in home monitoring.[26] Not only that, he gave Tzun credit for fifty-six days he had served in jail previously.[27] Local reporter Brian Rokos noted the implications of this decision just one day after Juan's conviction, writing a story headlined "Dispatcher's Killer Could Serve Only 34 Days in Jail."[28] And that is almost exactly what happened.

"He had all these crimes. He paid a little here, a little there. A little inconvenience. And the end game is thirty-five days for killing a U.S. citizen," said Sabine, who made it her mission to see Tzun leave the country.

Upon release, Juan was transferred to an immigration detention center, where he remained for just over ten months.[29] An ICE agent at the facility had warned Sabine that sometimes the guards let illegal immigrants out the back door when the place gets full: " 'We get a note from "the top," ' he said, 'and then we let some of the detainees go,' " according to Sabine. That same ICE agent promised to keep an eye on Tzun and inform Sabine each time he had a hearing.

Worried that Tzun might escape, Sabine and her fiancé, Anthony, visited the center weekly to fight for Tzun's deportation. Although they were not permitted to attend the deportation hearings, Sabine and Anthony would sit for a few hours to let everyone know that they were not going away and would be watching. "I didn't even have the right to sit in there while the murderer of my child talked to the judge," Sabine noted. Sitting before a steel door with a small window, Sabine would watch Tzun escorted into the courtroom in shackles. "I wanted him to see me when he came out of that little courtroom and had to walk the corridor . . . he would turn and see me and then look away. I wanted him to know I'm not going away. I'm going to see you out of here." She said he was shocked each time that he peered out the window and saw the face of the grieving mother whose life he had devastated.

In addition to fighting for Tzun's deportation, Sabine and forty friends wrote letters to the judge, highlighting the injustice of the outcome.[30] "Please Your Honor, don't let this happen to another victim's family," Sabine wrote. "Those wounds stay forever and when you get victimized again in court, by a judge, you will find it hard to believe in justice."[31]

The criminal justice system had failed Sabine, and now she worried that the federal government would too by failing to deport Juan. But in March of 2014, Sabine got the call: "He's on his way to the airport being taken to Guatemala." Juan was once again on board a U.S. Immigration and Customs Enforcement air operations flight back to where he belonged.[32]

But Sabine knows this is not the end of Juan's story: "He's [going to come] back. He's going to do it again because he didn't learn anything."

★   ★   ★   ★

After suffering unimaginable grief and witnessing severe injustice, Sabine became resolute: "I can't just go home. Be quiet. Not say anything." The pain was still unbearable. "I was going to kill myself. I was looking for ways," she said. Anthony knew it, which was why he would not even let her go to the bathroom alone.

Sabine felt hopeless until June 16, 2015, when a man came down an escalator and declared he was running for president. "I had planned my suicide to make it look like an accident," she recalled. "I couldn't take the pain. I'm going to end it. I'm going to join Dominic."

No one wanted to hear her story. No one would listen. She had the television on as then candidate Trump announced his bid for the presidency: "I will terminate President Obama's illegal executive order on immigration, immediately."

Sabine stopped in her tracks. It was a sign that someone cared, but not only that: it was an early predictor of what was to come.

For years, Sabine had sought to share her stories with her leaders. In 2015, Sabine testified at a Senate Judiciary Hearing, sharing her tragic loss as several lawmakers actually fell asleep![33] In the same year Sabine wrote a letter to President Obama. "Why do you continue to invite ILLEGAL ALIENS into the White House? WHEN do legal citizens that have been deeply affected by this Immigration issue, get a chance to share their side of the story with you?" she asked.[34]

Obama never responded, prompting Sabine to write to First Lady Michelle Obama. "My only child Dominic Durden was the best [thing] that ever happened to me. He was my only child and the love of my life. He was also of mixed race," Sabine wrote. "I told him that he could become any- and everything that he wanted to be. He corrected me and said: yes, anything but the President. That's only for Caucasian people. When your Husband became President (Dominic and I proudly voted for him) I reminded him of our conversation years back and we both smiled. The election showed that you CAN become anything you set your mind to." In the remainder of Sabine's four-page letter to the first lady, Sabine shared who Dominic was and her story of tragic loss.

"I am simply a grieving Mother writing to another Mother . . . I know as a Mom you are trying to imagine the pain all of us have and

I pray you will never have to feel this and know what it's like to wake up and go to sleep knowing you will never get to hug and kiss your child," Sabine wrote. This time Sabine received a response: a form letter. "Thank you for sharing your story with me," it read, with a few other added pleasantries and the First Lady's autopenned signature at the bottom. It was clearly a general letter sent to anyone who took the time to write to the First Lady's office.

Sabine felt insulted at the lack of empathy, and so Sabine picked up her pen again: "On August 29, 2014, I sent a letter to you . . . My heart was poured out to you from mother to mother," Sabine wrote. "On October 6, 2014, I received a reply letter from you. I do understand that you are very busy . . . May I suggest that one line may be added to letters that mentioned deceased loved ones. 'I am sorry for your loss.'" Shortly after, Sabine received a call from someone in Michelle Obama's office, apologizing for the mistake. Sabine then received a second letter written by Michelle Obama herself, recognizing her grief but not inviting her to share her story.

Sabine still felt betrayed by her leaders until July of 2015. That month Sabine received a call from a friend asking if she wanted to meet Donald Trump. "I thought it was one of Dom's friends playing a prank," she remembers. "I said, 'Yeah, right!' The friend instructed her to meet at the Beverly Wilshire Hotel in Beverly Hills, California. Sabine dressed up and arrived at the posh Italian Renaissance–style hotel to find a big room with a few families inside. Trump walked in and she remembers him having "such a presence." There was no media, no huge staff, just Trump and the fami-lies. For an hour and a half,

President Donald Trump and Sabine. *Courtesy of Sabine Durden*

Trump let each of the families share their stories of loss—all at the hands of an illegal immigrant.

Sabine said, "He listened. He cried with us. He laughed with us. And he said, 'So the common denominator is no one listens to you guys. Nobody wants to share your story . . . We're going to change that. Come with me.'"

The families exited the quiet room and entered another bustling one filled with media. Sabine remembered, "We were right by his side, and he told them 'These families suffered the biggest tragedy of losing their family to an illegal immigrant, and you guys are going to listen now.'" Someone had finally heard Sabine. Someone cared, and that was the soon-to-be president of the United States.

Sabine speaking at the 2016 Republican National Convention. *Courtesy of Sabine Durden*

Sabine attended several Trump rallies—in Costa Mesa, San Diego, and Anaheim—and a town hall meeting in Austin. And then she got a call in the summer of 2016: "This is the RNC, and we would be honored to have you as one of our speakers." *Another one of those prank calls,* she thought. But the request was indeed real, and on July 18, 2016, Sabine spoke to an audience of 35 million.

Sabine told me, "I was terrified of public speaking." Dom had a part-time job at the local television station in Moreno Valley, and when he laughingly stuck the microphone in her face, she would sweat, start shaking, and basically forget English. But on the night of the RNC,

On the CNN set at the 2016 Republican National Convention. *Courtesy of author's collection*

boldness overtook her. Before she went on the stage, she and the other two family members who had lost loved ones hugged and looked up, saying, "OK, boys, all three of you. You've got us, right?"

On the first night of the RNC, I watched from the illuminated red, white, and blue CNN set as Sabine stood boldly and confidently proclaimed, "We need to secure our borders so no other person has to ever go through this kind of grief, pain, and agony knowing this could have been prevented . . . Americans need to come first."

Sabine told me, "That was another moment with Dominic. He was right there with me. I felt him behind me. I couldn't have done it otherwise."

Trump continued to show Sabine that she was more than a prop to be used by a politician. When Moreno Valley, California, dedicated a portion of a rocky California hiking trail to Dominic's memory, Trump wrote her: "I was so glad to hear that they are dedicating a memorial for your son, Dominic. Though he has left this world, he lives on in you and all who knew him and loved him. I will honor his memory by fighting to deliver justice on behalf of your family and all American families who have suffered from such loss. We will never forget."

Sabine lost friends and family members because of her support for

Trump. She even got death threats. Social media users and bystanders at rallies and demonstrations called her a Nazi, a xenophobe, and a racist, among many other smears. All absurd accusations. Some people even told her, "It's good your son is dead."

At a question-and-answer session at UCLA, a questioner asked her, "What would you say to someone that accuses you of racism?" Sabine replied, "Meet my son," as she pulled out a picture of her mixed-race son.

And when she is accused of being anti-immigrant? She responds, "Meet me. I am a legal immigrant from Germany. I had to do it the legal way."

Sabine recognizes the media effort to drown out the story of victims of illegal immigrant crime. Most networks cut away from her speech at the RNC. She says "It's a scab on my heart" every time she sees a commentator who "has more

With Sabine at Naaman's Championship BBQ in Texarkana, Texas. *Courtesy of Sabine Durden*

compassion for illegals and their families than for us."

I told Sabine about a particularly fiery debate that I had had on the set of *Anderson Cooper 360*. When discussing Trump's executive order to curb illegal immigration, I pointed out to my Democratic colleague, Kirsten Powers, that there is a human face to the victims of illegal immigrant crime. Yes, most immigrants are good, hardworking people—as I said in the segment—and I appreciate their valued contributions, but what about the ones like Tzun, ending the life of an American citizen because our lawmakers didn't enforce the law? I specifically mentioned Dominic Durden. Powers curtly replied that these were "anomalies" and "a few tragic, tragic incidents."[35] What Kirsten had missed, I told Sabine, was that even if one American died—and Sabine instinctively said in unison with me—"that's one too many."

"And that's a few hundred too many," Sabine continued. "But it's that logic that is so twisted. Until it happens to them . . . On July 12, 2012, at 5:45 in the morning, if Juan Lopez [Tzun] would have been in Guatemala where he belonged, my son would be here today."

★　★　★　★

Today, Sabine recognizes two versions of herself. "BD," she says, was the person she was "Before Dominic." The other is the person she is now.

"If you would have met me BD," she said, "I was a completely different person. I didn't want to rattle the boat . . . my best thing was Dominic. I just wanted to be Dom's mom."

Today, however, Sabine boldly shares her story with others. She's used to the condemning, judgmental, unsympathetic eye of the media. During a segment on MSNBC where Sabine confronted an illegal immigrant, the host—who was comfortably seated in a New York studio and couldn't even get Sabine's first name correct—asked her, "Sabina [sic], Monica was talking about how she would feel if a wall was built. Monica, a woman who has been educated, pays taxes, [is] raising a family here in America. She's been here since she was three years old. Sabina, when you look at people like Monica and other immigrants who might not be documented but haven't committed any crimes, should they be deported?"[36]

Sabine reached into her purse and replied, "I believe so, and I wanted to ask Monica when she was talking about how she's worried about her family being separated, this is my son," Sabine said as she lifted out an urn. "This is what I have left of my family. His ashes. He was my only child. I would like to know what she would tell me. I'm a legal immigrant. I had to do it the right way, and yet this is all I have left of my family."

A producer told Sabine that there were audible gasps in the Manhattan control room. The producers were astounded when Sabine presented her son's ashes on television.

Sabine wishes she had the luxury of not being an advocate. "I would rather be home and just watching TV and saying 'Why don't they leave these poor illegals alone?' Then I wouldn't have to deal with this. But now that I do . . . [I'm glad] I have a voice."

In the aftermath of her son's death, Sabine has a newfound confidence. She explained, "I will never lose my composure . . . but I will hit you hard with facts and emotion . . . so you get a glimpse. Just a tiny glimpse of what my life is like every day when I drive in his truck, grasping the steering wheel and thinking, 'He used to touch [this].'"

Sabine clutched her necklace as she showed me the little locket containing some of Dom's ashes that she wears around her neck. And then she extended her wrist to display a tattoo that reads "Love Dominic" in her son's handwriting, copied from his last Christmas card to her. "I used to tease him: 'You write like a third grader.'" She smiled. "He's

Sabine holds hands with Anthony, displaying her "Love Dominic" tattoo. *Courtesy of Tara Probst / Moment in Time Photography*

everywhere I go. Pictures—here," she said as she lifted up her phone to display a picture of Dom prominently displayed on the back.

Sabine is not only more confident, she has a new lease on life. She says Dom always lived in a way that showed he knew life was so precious. "So now I have that chance. I enjoy life differently. [Before Dominic] I could never be by myself." Having been a victim of sexual and psychological abuse, Sabine "was frightened of the thought" of being alone. "But now I enjoy sitting anywhere by myself. Or I ride my motorcycle by myself and let my mind go to different places," she explained. "I can enjoy a beautiful sunset or the new pond we have in our front yard or the new flower sprout. Things that I took for granted [when] life was too hectic. I was more worried about 'O.K. I need the new Dooney & Bourke bag or new Gucci bag.' Now I would take a paper bag as a purse. It just doesn't matter anymore."

I asked Sabine about her faith in God, to which she quickly replied, "My faith got stronger. Big-time. One hundred times over." With excitement in her voice, she said, "I want to show you something." Sabine picked up her phone and began to search for a video while she told me the story. In November 2013 she was asked to testify before Congress. Although she was nervous, she reluctantly agreed. On the night before she was set to fly out to Washington, she sat at a sushi restaurant with two of Dom's friends. "I can't go. I'm not going to do it," she said. Dom's friends said she had to. They had even made her business cards. "I'm going to freeze up. I'm not going to know what to say." As she spoke about her fear, the teacup in front of her suddenly moved along the moistened tabletop. It moved again and again, and Sabine filmed what she knew was a reassuring sign from Dom.

Moved by her story, I said to Sabine, "There are so many stories like that from people who have lost children." I shared with her the story of a young girl I grew up with: Megan Carpenter. Megan was a family friend who was diagnosed with cancer at the age of eleven. She battled it for nearly six years even though her doctors told her she only had a few months. Megan's strength and Christian faith were an inspiration to all. Megan—a truly wise young angel—used to say to her family, "Don't be mad at God. He's watching after us." And when a six-year-old boy passed from the same rare cancer, Megan cried for her young friend and prayed for his family before observing, "He is well now, sitting with Jesus and feeling no pain." Our community used to collect feathers as a sign of hope for Megan. I would pick up a feather if I saw one throughout the course of my day and think of Megan.

On the last day of Megan's life, after battling cancer for nearly a decade,

Megan Carpenter. *Courtesy of Dana Carpenter*

Megan's mom cried in the hospital bathroom because she knew that Megan's short life was coming to an end. As she cried, a feather floated down from the roof. "Where does a feather come from in a hospital bathroom?" I asked Sabine. "That night Megan died, and that was God saying 'I've got her. She's going to be OK.'"

Sabine immediately replied, "Yep, yep. Right. That was her. Wow. You know, that doesn't even surprise me." After Dominic's death, Sabine took a flight to Germany to visit her family. It was the first time that she would make the trip without Dominic. She had a pillow with her that was made from Dom's sweatshirt. It read: FIRE DEPARTMENT. DOMINIC DURDEN. Sabine went to the bathroom, and when she returned, there was a white feather resting on Dom's pillow. "Inside a plane!" she exclaimed. "That was the first big sign. He sends many."

Sabine holds on to these moments and cherishes them in her heart as she deals with constant pain. "We put on a show. It's a 24[-hour-a-day], 360[-day-a-year] . . . pain all the time. There's never any relief. It's just [that] we learn how to work with it. How to deal with it." Sabine has dealt with it, in part, by moving from California to Arkansas. She no longer has to pass Dominic's elementary school or the scene of his accident. "The triggers are no longer there," she said. But she still cannot escape the horrors that now haunt her life. "The saddest part is every time a car turns in front of me, everything in me freezes up and [my] hair stands up because that's the last thing he saw," she said with a shaky voice.

In addition to driving Dom's truck, she cares for his dog, Cyrus, who wouldn't eat for weeks after Dom's passing. He would hear the garage door and run out to the driver's side of Dom's truck in the weeks after his death. One day Sabine found him sitting on a stair with his head through the slats. She sat next to him to find that he was "looking dead at Dominic's picture" hanging on the wall. "He did that until we moved," she said. Now she has a picture of Dom by his dog bed.

Sabine has her fiancée, Anthony, to help her through. "[Dominic] didn't like anyone I dated," remarked Sabine. "[But] he chose Anthony. We have been going on eight years. He never left my side . . . Through Dominic, I met this incredibly supportive man who God placed in my life, because God knew what was coming, and that man was with me. And he told me in Atlanta, 'I will never leave you.'"

Through her pain, though, Sabine said, "God showed me who I really am inside, that I am a fighter. Fierce. I am loyal to a fault.

"I'm still in control of my destiny, but this guy," she continued as she pointed up at the roof, "had all this planned out for me . . . Because of Dominic's strength and who he was, I became this woman."

★   ★   ★   ★

Four years after Dominic's passing, Sabine mustered the will to return to the place where she watched her son learn to fly. She had waited so long because, in her words, "it carried too much pain," and just the thought of it made her tear up.[37]

On her blog Dom Hugs, she described the experience this way: "The tears flowed freely as I walked into the airport and in Dominic's footsteps. I could hear his laughter and see his smile as I walked past the buildings and towards the planes. My knees almost buckled, but as I was holding on to his old headphones, I started feeling his arms around me and whispering: enjoy this mom, fly and feel me up there with you."[38]

Sabine seeks to hold government accountable for its failure to secure the border, a failure that cost her the life of her only son. She knows she will see Dom again, but in the meantime she keeps Dom's memory alive as best she can: "A bittersweet morning. A flight that lifted me up towards the clouds and seeing the world from Dominic's perspective one more time. Spread your angel wings, sweet son of mine. Soar and keep watch over us."[39]

Sabine and Dominic at the airport with their motorcycles. *Courtesy of Sabine Durden*

THE THIN BLUE LINE

Our Police Force

"Blessed are the peacemakers, for they will be called children of God."
—MATTHEW 5:9

Just off Officer Justin Winebrenner Memorial Highway—a stretch of U.S. Route 224 between Barberton and Akron, Ohio—is a tranquil sprawling green field with a strikingly tall cross, visible from every vantage point. The sounds of birds chirping and the quiet serenity seem to belie the field's purpose: it is a burial ground.

Through the winding, hilly paths and among the thousands of tombstones, one black granite memorial with blazing gold lettering stands out among the rest. While most of the grave sites display a flower or two, Justin Winebrenner's abounds with tokens of admiration.

Yellow flowers, a "Happy Easter" basket, and a glittery black and blue wreath. A Great Lakes Brewing Company beer bottle and an overturned shot glass. Coins scattered upon the base and soaring blue lights—

Justin's gravesite. *Courtesy of author's collection*

they all sit below those fateful but beautifully inscribed words from John 15:13: "Greater love hath no man than this, that a man lay down his life for his friends."

It is the resting place of a son who lies in eternal rest next to his mother and grandparents. If you stop by Justin's grave on any given day, you might find more than just inanimate tributes, though. You might very well encounter a group of young men having a beer with their fallen friend. A family sprawled out on a blanket having a picnic or flying a kite. Or you might even see an angelic little girl laying a donut on the grave of her father.

For there lies a hero whose light was extinguished far too soon.

★   ★   ★   ★

It was a dreary November day. A snowy, icy 20-degree chill pierced Akron, perhaps reflecting the mood of the town. Nearly three thousand people sat silently in the James A. Rhodes Arena, wiping tears from their eyes as they commemorated the life and legacy of thirty-two-year-old Justin Winebrenner. Although men and women of all races and backgrounds filled the audience, there was only one color they saw today: blue.

Justin's godfather and uncle, Charles Parson, stood just above the American flag–draped coffin and read several notes that he had written in Justin's voice—to Justin's father, Rob; his sister, Kelly; his fiancée, Tiffany; his little girl's mother, Alyse; and his four-year-old daughter, Charlee.[1]

To Charlee: "I'm sorry I had to leave you. I love you. You're my little Cherry Blossom princess and I am proud of all that you are becoming. My life shall miss sitting on the edge of your bed, wiping away the tears of your first broken heart, watching you graduate from high school and walking you down the aisle on your wedding day . . . I will not be far from you. I am now your guardian angel and I will listen to you anytime you look up in the air."[2]

At the end of the memorial service, Justin's family exited the arena as the sound of bagpipes filled the overcast skies. Justin's father, Rob,

Charlee and Rob salute Justin's casket. *Courtesy of WOIO*

held his sweet granddaughter, Charlee. Wrapped in her black puffy coat and with her brown hair drawn back by a blue bow headband, Charlee clutched her teddy bear—the teddy bear that she had not put down since her father's passing. She was the picture of innocence facing injustice far too soon.

As the patriotic coffin carrying Justin's body emerged from the arena, Rob, joined by two lines of police officers, stood in salute.

"What are you doing?" Charlee whispered to her grandfather.

"We're saluting your dad," Rob quietly told her.

The young girl raised her hand to her head in imitation of the saluting officers and saluted her fallen father for the first and last time.

Although the weather was snowy and uninviting, thousands of residents lined the streets with their hands on their hearts. Standing along Main Street, some held American flags; others held babies. New life clashing with life extinguished. Hand-painted signs displayed messages like "We will never forget!" and "Thank You." On Rosewood Avenue, blue duct tape formed the number 1301—Justin's Akron Police Department number—on the side of a black pickup truck.

The spontaneous show of support was visible from Rob's vehicle. As Rob looked out over the sea of people, he held on to the window.

"He was trying to touch all those people that were there . . . [P]eople couldn't see inside, but we could see out . . . [I]f he could've shook every hand that went by, he would have," Crystal, Rob's girlfriend, told me as she fought back tears.

Just one day earlier, Rob had done just that: shaken thousands of hands during Justin's six-hour wake. "My hand was swollen . . . I would shake [everyone's] hands . . . The first thousand wasn't so bad; the next thousand was much more difficult. But I thought . . . 'I've got to do this. These people are here.'"

As the Winebrenners rode down Waterloo Road, two fire de-

Officer Justin Winebrenner. *Courtesy of Akron Police Department*

partment cranes arched toward one another and joined to display an American flag above the entrance of Holy Cross cemetery. Officers on horseback guarded the cemetery's gates, which were swung wide-open in preparation for Justin's arrival. The once sprawling green landscape was now covered in powdery snow, but the towering brown cross stood tall nonetheless.

The narrow, circuitous roads to Section 22, Plot 1795, were dotted with leafless trees and lined with K-9 officers standing at salute as their dogs barked to greet the entrants. As the Winebrenners arrived at Justin's gravesite, they were unaware that they had entered the graveyard before the final car of the processional had even exited Rhodes Arena five miles back.[3]

For Rob and his daughter, Kelly, this second grim visit to Holy Cross Cemetery came far too soon. Five years earlier, the Winebrenners had sorrowfully laid their fifty-year-old wife and mother, Lori, to rest after a grueling battle with ovarian cancer. Now they said farewell to their only son and brother as well.

The police radioed that final announcement: "All cars, car 24. Number 1301 is out of service. We now have a moment of silence for our fallen officer Justin R. Winebrenner." It was the end of watch.

★   ★   ★   ★

For the Winebrenners, heroism ran in the family, and Justin was no exception. Rob was a police officer. His son, Justin, was a police officer. Several Winebrenners dedicated their lives to protecting their community. Rob's father, Robert Sr., was a decorated U.S. Army veteran. He had earned a Bronze Star in World War II for his heroism in Belgium during the Battle of the Bulge. Robert Sr.'s unit was under heavy machine gun and tank fire. Undeterred, Robert charged within one hundred yards of enemy guns and shot back for five hours, permitting the 289th Infantry to complete its mission.[4]

Robert Sr. worked until he was eighty-eight years old and never liked to talk about the war. "There's so many that didn't come home from the military. Why do they want to honor me?" he would say to his son. Robert Sr. instilled the values of hard work and humility into his family, values that his grandson, Justin, no doubt inherited.

During Justin's seven years in the Akron Police Department, he rescued a man from a burning car. "He never even thought twice. There wasn't hesitation," his fiancée, Tiffany, told me. "The police chief said one time that there are two kinds of men when a situation arises: the ones that run toward it, and the ones that run away from it. And he [Justin] was definitely the one that was always going straight in it. All the way. No second guesses."

When Justin heard about a four-year-old boy's stolen four-wheeler, he collected donations around town. Justin purchased a brand-new four-wheeler, picked it up in his truck, and surprised the little boy with a shiny new replacement. "Things you don't have to do and weren't expected to do . . . he would go out of his way to make sure they were done," Tiffany recalled.

Justin was not only kind, he was also immensely talented. After driving a golf ball four hundred yards and completing Firestone South, Hole

16—"the Monster"—in three shots, Rob laughingly told Justin, "There's something about you. I haven't figured it out yet."

"He was good at everything growing up," Kelly chimed in with a smile.

"There wasn't a sport he didn't like . . . He played football. He played basketball . . . but soccer was [his love]," Rob noted. He attended every Browns game as a proud season ticket holder, adorned in his number 33 custom-made "Crime Dawg" jersey. In addition to sports, he was an avid outdoorsman and

Justin's last buck. *Courtesy of author's collection*

meticulous about his hunting equipment. "I wasn't allowed to go with him because I used hair products," which would scare away the deer, chuckled Rob.

Taking a more somber tone, Rob continued: "He unfortunately got his deer that Saturday and shot it with an arrow . . . Got it home. Went out that night. And tragedy happened."

Motioning toward the back door of a log cabin, Rob and Kelly pointed at a six-point buck hanging above a framed folded flag and a plaque that read "In loving memory of Officer Justin Winebrenner. There is no greater love than this: That a man would lay down his life, for the sake of his friends."

"He was not supposed to be there," Tiffany said. "[But] he called early Saturday morning to say he shot a buck and would be back."[5]

When Justin returned to Akron, he and his fiancée attended a fundraiser for the Ellet Raiders Youth Football Team along with several other off duty police officers. After the fund-raiser, an announcement was made that attendees were welcome to continue the night at Papa Don's, a local restaurant and pub that Tiffany owned. Pulling in beneath the Papa Don's sign, displaying an affable looking gray-haired man in a light-blue shirt and the words "Rotisserie Ribs & Chicken—Steaks—Spirits," Justin and Tiffany made one final stop before ending their night.

Justin moseyed into the redbrick building he frequented and the bar lit up. Hugs. High fives. The life of the community had arrived.

As the couple chatted with friends, a woman came up to Tiffany and alerted her that an unruly man by the jukebox was harassing her. "I have a boyfriend," the girl had said, rebuffing his advances. "I don't care. I have a .40," he warned.

As Tiffany inquired about the situation, the man who claimed to have a gun, Kenan Ivery, approached her and the patron—yelling, angry, and loud. Tiffany asked him to please move to the end of the bar, and for five minutes she attempted to defuse the situation. Ivery refused to calm down and grew increasingly obstinate. Tiffany had no choice but to ask him to leave.

Recognizing Ivery from the fund-raiser, Tiffany said, "We have had a great evening to help raise money for a good cause in which your son was a part of, and I wish we could have ended this evening on a good note."

"I don't need cops or anyone else to pay for my kids," Kenan scoffed just before he exited Papa Don's.[6]

The problem had been successfully resolved, or so Tiffany thought.

That Kenan had a long history with law enforcement should come as no surprise. He had been booked at the county jail nearly a dozen times and gone to prison on three separate occasions.[7] In 2011, as the police approached his car in a McDonald's parking lot, Kenan put his gold Buick in reverse, slammed on the gas, and almost struck an officer, who had to dive out of the way to narrowly avoided being hit.[8] After finally yielding to law enforcement, officers searched Kenan's car and discovered a joint and nearly $40,000 in cash. At Kenan's home, they found a loaded Uzi submachine gun—an illegal automatic rifle—along with tools for making crack.[9]

Kenan's 2011 run-in with the law was the latest in a series. He spent three years in prison after a 2007 arrest for possessing 42.8 grams of crack.[10] He went to prison for another year in 2002 for a similar conviction, and he had a host of misdemeanors for resisting arrest and failure to obey police officers, among other things.[11] Despite an extensive history of criminal activity, Kenan was released early from the two-year prison sentence resulting from his 2011 conviction.[12]

With no sign of having reformed, Kenan's involvement in future criminal activity was a matter of when, not if, and on the night of November 15, 2015, at 1:52 a.m., Kenan's actions had fatal consequences.

Kenan left Papa Don's only to return eight minutes later, this time with a gun. "He was angry and wanted to shoot somebody," said Rob. "He kept saying 'I've got a .40.' No one knew what that meant until later when he came back with a .40 caliber."

When Kenan reentered the bar, Tiffany immediately approached him, and Kenan quipped "I'm not alone anymore" as he clutched his gun.[13] Tiffany asked Justin for help because "that's what he does. He protects and serves," she explained.[14]

Justin, unarmed and off duty, tried to get Kenan to leave. Others joined in the effort but, rather than leaving, Kenan began to shoot. According to one eyewitness, Winebrenner "went for the gun. It popped and everyone else moved and tried to go out the back exit."[15] Winebrenner succeeded in pushing Kenan out the front door, but he took two bullets through his torso in the process.

Amid the chaos, Tiffany ran to assist a wounded patron, but an employee urged her to come outside. "By the look on her face, I knew something had happened to Justin," Tiffany testified.[16] She saw Justin's motionless body on the ground in the parking lot and knelt beside him. "He wasn't really moving. I told him that I loved him and that he saved my life and that he had to stay strong for his daughter Charlee and that help was on the way."[17]

Having shot five people, Kenan fled the scene. Tiffany shared the bar's surveillance footage with the police to see which way Kenan had fled as emergency medical services transported Justin to Akron City Hospital.[18] Knowing time was of the essence, K-9 officer Jeff Edsall set out with his dog, Bronson, to find Kenan.[19] Meticulously wading through brush, Bronson eventually picked up a scent. Edsall and several others followed Bronson alongside the highway. A cruiser shed insufficient light on a pitch-black open field while Edsall and Bronson searched the area. Suddenly, Edsall heard on his radio: "Stop right where you're at. There's someone to the right of you."[20] He froze, slowly turned to the right, and illuminated the area with his flashlight. All he saw was the outline of a male figure.

"Show me your hands! Show me your hands!" he yelled. Other officers began to shout the order as well. The individual was lying face-down in a field of tall grass twenty yards away. When the suspect did not comply, Edsall ordered Bronson to subdue him. Bronson ran toward the subject and bit the back of the man's leg. Still not compliant, Bronson held on as the officers swarmed the suspect.

It was Kenan Ivery.

As the Akron Police Department swiftly apprehended Kenan, Rob got the dreaded 2:00 a.m. phone call instructing him to come to Akron City Hospital. He arrived to find twenty police officers with their heads down as he and his family were ushered to the family room. "When you've been a police officer, you know what's going to come next . . . It was like a ton of bricks hitting you in the face." And then came those words no father ever wants to hear: "Your son is dead."[21]

★   ★   ★   ★

Ten months later—just weeks before the one-year anniversary of Justin's passing—the Winebrenners faced the gut-wrenching task of facing their son's killer in court. Charged with eighteen counts ranging from felony murder to tampering with evidence and faced with damning video evidence and eyewitness accounts, Kenan still pled not guilty.[22]

The grueling trial, which spanned more than two weeks, "felt like forever," according to Tiffany. "Unfortunately, it was defined to us hundreds of times in a courtroom really what happened after [Kenan] got outside the door," Rob recalled. "The guy actually gripped two hands around his gun and looked at [Justin] and shot and killed him."

As Rob shared these horrifying details with me, I couldn't help but think of Justin's six-year-old daughter, Charlee. Running up to me with a huge smile on her face, Charlee presented me with a rainbow picture of a cat she had colored, next to the words "Thank You." This pure and wide-eyed young girl was left with mere memories of her father. Her future life—her senior prom, her wedding, her father-daughter dance, the birth of her children—would happen without Justin present. But she is nevertheless left knowing her father was a hero in every sense of the word.

Big Ball of Yarn

The picture Charlee drew for me.
Courtesy of author's collection

Justin lost his life to save many others. "He went toward that threat . . . and forced this man with the gun out the door . . . By forcing this man out of the door and the pub, he lost his life," explained Chief James Nice at Justin's funeral.

Kenan, during his testimony, falsely claimed that he began shooting that night at Papa Don's in self-defense—a baseless claim that the jury ultimately rejected when they found Kenan guilty of aggravated murder.[23] The Winebrenner family sought the death penalty to make Kenan realize the life-changing consequences of his actions. "He knew Justin was a policeman, and he never accepted that responsibility . . . [Y]ou [Kenan] never said 'This was my fault,'" Rob stated. But he could not evade responsibility entirely. During the sentencing hearing, Kenan finally offered a last-ditch show of remorse.[24] Nonetheless, the killer was sentenced to life in prison with no chance for parole, and the judge confidently told Kenan, "You will die in prison. You wreaked havoc and chaos when you marched back into that bar believing you were disrespected."[25]

In an emotional and moving victim impact statement, Rob addressed his son's killer directly: "To Kenan, I hope that someday you accept accountability and responsibility for what happened . . . [Y]ou are responsible for ruining a good family. We will get back up. We will survive. We will move on, but you did a lot of damage. While I may forgive you, that is basically so I can move on myself . . ."[26]

Kenan, outfitted in an orange jumpsuit, sat with his head down. He briefly looked at Rob when he heard the words, "Finally, I want you to know that as a parent." Kenan put his head back down as Rob concluded: "I am content standing here a proud father of a hero that is no longer with us. Knowing the last good deed that Justin did as a police officer was getting you off the streets forever."

★   ★   ★   ★

Two days after Justin died, Rob was asked how he could cope with such an unspeakable loss. "By believing in God, that makes it more accepting. I can believe his mother's in heaven and welcoming him," he said.[27]

Tucked away in a charming family-built log cabin in the heart of Wadsworth, Ohio, and seated at a long wooden table surrounded by Justin's closest family and friends, I asked Rob about his faith. "I lost faith when my wife died," he admitted candidly. "I told my wife nothing would ever happen to her as long as she was with me. As a policeman, I was her protector . . . we slept at night knowing that nothing was ever going to happen to her."

But Rob ultimately wasn't able to protect her. For two years Rob and his wife battled her ovarian cancer together. After six different combinations of chemotherapy over the two years, the doctor finally said it was time to prepare for hospice care.

"Am I going to die?" Lori asked Rob.

"I don't know. Not if I can help it," Rob responded.

Rob had a strong faith in God. He prayed every night and would think to himself, *Our faith says you're going to make it through this.* Rob told me, "Other people didn't see it, but I saw it. I said, 'Come on, we're going to beat this.'"

During her last seventy-two hours, the Winebrenners attended a concert, where Lori took to the stage amid roaring applause. Weak and fatigued, death was quickly approaching, but Lori held on just a few hours longer. She didn't want to pass on Justin's birthday. In the early hours of July 23, 2009, Lori left this world for the next.

"When she died, I became very angry with God," Rob admitted to

With the Winebrenners and friends at their cabin in Wadsworth, Ohio. *Courtesy of author's collection*

me. "Very angry. Even called him names . . . [saying], 'You know what, I don't need you in my life.'"

Nine months later, God brought Crystal—Rob's girlfriend of seven years now—into his life. Crystal prayed for Rob, and he soon realized that he was physically deteriorating without God in his life. "I thought if I don't forgive God . . . I'm going to self-destruct . . . I got back to where I was in a very strong relationship [with God]," he explained.

Fast-forward five years, and his only son was taken in a senseless act. "I got very angry again . . . How can you let this happen? This was the kid that I nurtured from a baby," Rob said. "I retired and he became a policeman. He was everything I wanted. I lived through him. And God took that from me."

This time, though, Rob realized right away that he was again physically declining without God in his life. His blood pressure was up. He stayed sick. Rob turned back to faith.

"His mother wanted him worse than I did," Rob said. Rob even did the unthinkable when he said he forgave Kenan. "Everyone looked at me like 'You're crazy. Why would you forgive?' But faith says forgive and you can live with yourself . . . I can't change it."

Crystal recalled, "He was sad . . . but never acted vengeful. It just showed how their family was raised and what they believe." She paused. "I watch Joyce Meyer."

"I love Joyce Meyer!" I interjected.

"I tape her every day," Crystal went on. "There was a pastor who lost his wife and he said, 'Lord, help me do this right . . . I'm representing you but yet my wife just died. I want to be angry . . . but help me do this right.'"

Upon hearing the sermon, Crystal and Rob started crying. "That reminds me of you," Crystal said to Rob. "Sitting through the trial and hearing these horrible things . . . you just stood tall."

And perhaps Rob stood tall because God never really left the Winebrenners. He shows himself in the subtlest of ways.

Kelly, Justin's sister, looked out the back window of her Wadsworth, Ohio, log cabin one day to find a striking blue and black butterfly perched on her deck. Hurriedly grabbing her phone, Kelly quickly snapped a picture. A few months later she attended a retreat for the families of fallen officers hundreds of miles away in Missouri. Just before Kelly participated in her first event, she noticed something sitting on the bench: a blue and black butterfly. "Like, the same butterfly!" she exclaimed.

The following day at the retreat offered a new experience for Kelly: skeet shooting. She had never shot or even touched a gun. In fact, Justin was supposed to take her to the shooting range, but they never got that opportunity.

"It was a big day," she said.

As Kelly drew the rifle in front of her, poised and ready to shoot for the very first time, her friends yelled, "Stop and look down!" A blue and black butterfly had landed on her foot. "Don't move! Don't move!" her friends said, marveling at the sight. After a few minutes of admiring the friendly creature, Kelly finally shot her gun.

The blue butterfly on Kelly's shoe.
Courtesy of Kelly Winebrenner

As the loud bang of the rifle reverberated around her woody surroundings, she gazed down in bewilderment to find that the glistening butterfly had never left her foot. In fact, it remained with her the entire time she shot.

"I walked all the way back real carefully, and it stayed on my foot the entire time," Kelly remembered. "And then it let me pick it up and stood on my hand. And then I moved it all over and it wouldn't leave. This beautiful blue and black butterfly."

It was as if Justin had found a way to take his little sister shooting after all. "I needed him there, and there he was," Kelly said, smiling.

The blue and black butterfly even made its way to Rob at a separate retreat in Arkansas. "I'm just sitting there and this blue butterfly just comes down and lands on the railing right next to me." He quickly snapped a picture and sent it to his daughter. Rob says, after the passing of his wife, "You tend to notice more things. You see bluebirds now. I would see cardinals everywhere, but now I see blue jays in the tree

The blue butterfly on Kelly's finger. *Courtesy of Kelly Winebrenner*

where the cardinals were at. I thought, 'That's weird. I've never seen blue jays before.'

"Whether that's a sign or not"—Rob pauses for a brief moment before confidently announcing—"faith."

★   ★   ★   ★

Justin was murdered ten days before the Ferguson, Missouri, grand jury announced its decision not to charge Officer Darren Wilson in the shooting death of Michael Brown. The decision was met with very memorable violent reactions. Buildings were set ablaze and the sound of gunfire blazed across America's television screens, even though President Obama's own Justice Department later concluded in a quietly released memo, "It was not unreasonable for Wilson to fire on Brown . . ."[28] Justin's death, meanwhile, garnered no national headlines or cable news coverage.

Regarding this disparity, Rob said, "Nobody got crazy . . . nobody stood up for my family and started screaming and breaking things . . . Not that that's what I want, but all this is happening elsewhere; it would be immediate if it was reversed."

Rob was pointing out a hard, cold truth.

There was a 10 percent increase in officer deaths in 2016.[29] Sixty-four officers were shot and killed last year, twenty-one of them callously ambushed. Ask yourself: How many can you name?

For many reading this, the answer is probably none. That is because when an officer is killed, his or her story rarely makes national headlines. The broader public does not pause to take notice. Their sacrifice is not appropriately honored. You rarely see the valiant portrayals of officers like Justin Winebrenner; instead, officers as a whole are demonized.

A May 2017 FBI report acknowledges this. The study analyzed fifty police killings and attempted to understand the motives of the killers. In a section titled "Assailant Study—Mindsets and Behavior," the study exposed this mischaracterization of officers: "It appears that immediately following the incidents, assailants were exposed to a singular narrative by news organizations and social media of police misconduct and wrongdoing."[30]

It was in reaction to this unfair media narrative that I mentioned Justin Winebrenner during a December 2014 appearance I made on *The O'Reilly Factor*. That is how I came to know this family: through an attempt to elevate a hero amid a slew of negative police coverage.

A pointed Facebook post on Rob's page (from an unattributed source) states, "'When did we become the enemy?' For centuries the sheepdog has protected the flock. Standing guard, on the lookout, and ready at a split second notice for the evil to arrive and prey upon those that have the luxury of forgetting that the evil does exist."[31]

In support of this, one of his friends replied with the telling revelation that she once displayed the so-called thin blue line flag: a black and white American flag with a blue stripe through the middle, representing the thin blue line of police officers that guard between civilized society and anarchy. When people told her they were "offended," Rob's friend removed the commemorative flag and gave it to someone in law enforcement.

Whether due to media bias or our forty-fourth president "leading the chorus in slandering and maligning the character and the integrity and the service and the sacrifice of our nation's law enforcement officers," in the words of Sheriff David Clarke, one thing is for sure: our courageous officers have been forgotten.[32]

In Rob's victim impact statement, he isolated two reasons for the seemingly ever-present violence we see almost daily: a godless society and a lack of respect.

"Our laws are based on God's laws," he said. "God was in our courtroom. In fact, his name was mentioned several times. Unfortunately, we are becoming a godless society."

Rob remembers giving a lesson to a classroom full of students years ago. On the way out he merely said, "Have a good weekend. God bless!" Shortly after, he was called down to the principal's office and warned that he could not say "God." He hadn't even realized he said it in his quick and casual good-bye to the students. "We have so many influences in our school, and I don't think God is a negative one personally," he told me.

The second problem is respect. "Kids are not taught respect in the family. We show little respect for teachers and authority in the schools.

Therefore, we will have little or no respect for police or authority on the streets. This is what led us to where we are today. We need respect," Rob proclaimed in his statement.

As for politics, Rob said, "I wish everybody would just not be so political, fix things, and not have to worry about Republicans and Democrats . . . [There's] so much fighting."

Justin's story, like the stories of so many other police officers, was overlooked by our national leaders. Perhaps that is why so many of our men and women in blue voted for Donald Trump in the 2016 election. Just one day after the election, Michele McPhee wrote in the *Boston Globe*, "The vote that didn't show up in the polls, the secret groundswell of support that stunned the media establishment and the pundits and those who proudly stood with her [Hillary Clinton], was not about race or gender or ethnicity. It was about blue."[33]

But for Rob, the answer was never government but a societal shift toward mutual respect and understanding. The solution can only be found in the American people opening up their hearts, coming together, and seeing past the obstacles that divide us.

★　★　★　★

Two years have passed since Justin's murder, and for Rob the pain is still real. Describing his daily reality, Rob said, "I don't know when I'm going to fall over. I really don't . . . [T]he fact that sometimes I still reach for my phone and try to call him. His number's still in my phone. Maybe I haven't 100 percent accepted everything."

For Charlee, the passing of her father is a daily reality. "Now [Charlee] will have to learn to do things without her dad," Rob told the courtroom during his victim impact statement.

"She couldn't invite him to her preschool class this year the day they had donuts with Dad. All the other kids were there with their dads. I went in his place. I felt her pain. After we went to the cemetery and visited her dad where he lays next to his mother. Together we talked. We prayed. She left him with a donut. That made her feel a little better."[34]

And then there was Charlee's first day of kindergarten. "She had to start her first day of kindergarten without her dad. I went in his place. Along with her mother and other family members and a host of fifty law enforcement officers across the county."[35]

But even though Justin has passed, he is still very much alive.

He's alive in the toasts his friends routinely make in his honor, raising Justin's favorite drink into the air. He's alive in the "You should be here" poster with his picture that's affixed to his friend's camper during Country Fest. He's alive in the three hundred feet of blue rope light that covers Papa Don's. He's alive in the "Crime Dawg" jerseys his family wears to the Brown games and the blue "1301" bracelets that several friends vow never to take off. And he's alive in the seven thousand blazing blue lights his father has worked tirelessly to place on porches throughout the community. In fact, Justin is alive right here as I write this passage under the glow of a blue light bulb that Rob gave me in Justin's memory.

"The blue lights make you smile," said Justin's best friend, Joel. "They make you smile because you think of Justin." Charlee's mother, Alyse, said her daughter "counts them all the time. There's one. That's two. That's three!"

This past November, the community hosted an event titled "A Night to Remember" at the Fraternal Order of Police, Akron Lodge 7, to commemorate the two-year anniversary of Justin's passing. Far from being a tearful reminder of loss, the anniversary was a joyful celebration of life. Beer. Music. Guitars. Smiles. There was hope, not despair. Joy, not sadness.

Crowded around a campfire, the community lit white Chinese lanterns and released them into the night sky. Several years earlier Rob had performed the very same tribute for his wife.

Now it was Justin's turn.

Hundreds of glistening lanterns pierced the darkness as the sound of bagpipes playing "Amazing Grace" ascended to the heavens. Rob's shirt displayed that perfectly suited second Bible verse inscribed on Justin's tombstone: "Blessed are the peacemakers, for they will be called sons of God."

Liberty

THE SILENCING

Freedom of Speech

---

*"Have the courage to have your wisdom regarded as
stupidity. Be fools for Christ. And have the courage to
suffer the contempt of the sophisticated world."*
—JUSTICE ANTONIN SCALIA

I nervously climbed the winding staircase of the twelfth-century church
in the heart of Oxford University. The church turned library was appropriately set in the middle of a graveyard, for as I ascended the narrow, circuitous stairwell, I felt that I was walking to a grave of my own.
I clutched my ten-page paper on U.S. foreign policy, knowing that I
would have to read it aloud to my international relations tutor. In Oxford's tutorial system, professors—called "tutors"—systematically dis-
mantle your arguments and writing in an effort to build strength. As
a Western-minded, Israel-loving Republican, I was afraid that my esteemed tutor—a former representative of the Palestinian Liberation
Organization—would attack my views. My fear was justified, because
she did just that.

I left my first tutorial with tears running down my face, not because
my tutor had critiqued me unfairly or not listened to my arguments
with an open mind. In fact, she had, but she presented me with a set of
arguments I had never earnestly considered. After dozens of these one-
on-one sessions, I grew to have a deep respect for my tutor. She had not
changed my views per se—I am still a Western-minded, Israel-loving
Republican—but she instilled in me a level of compassion for and open-
ness to hearing the other side. She wrote me a moving letter of recom-

mendation, and to this day she remains one of my favorite in a long line of educators. Through this academic experience, an Israel-loving Westerner and a more Eastern-minded Palestinian met and developed a mutual respect.

The relationship I built with my Palestinian tutor was the academic ideal, but it was far from the academic reality. For far too many conservatives, the academic reality is hostility, marginalization, and sometimes even penalization. But it was during my time in graduate school that an even harsher reality took hold of America's campuses: the outright criminalization of conservatism.

★   ★   ★   ★

I gazed out the window of my Harvard Law apartment and onto the famously serene streets of Cambridge, Massachusetts. Night had fallen on my cozy, quiet community, and its residents were sheltered from the cool November night. I took a seat at my glass table, littered with neon sticky notes and stacked with books, ready to study my dense criminal casebook by candlelight. As I enjoyed the tranquility of the sleepy four-hundred-year-old town, the scene that transpired on my television screen could not have been more distinct.

There were buildings ablaze, their flames reaching far into the sky. Hundreds of bullets and rocks crisscrossed the smoky backdrop. Tactical assault vehicles rolled down the streets while heavily clad armed officers patrolled in gas masks. Looters ravaged local stores. It looked like a combat zone but it was not. The jarring images were not set in the war-torn streets of a far-off land but beneath a "Seasons Greetings" sign adjacent to a McDonald's in our very own backyard: Ferguson, Missouri.

The Ferguson grand jury had rendered its decision: Officer Darren Wilson would not be charged in the shooting death of Michael Brown. Wilson had acted in lawful self-defense against an aggressor in a situation wrongly characterized as "hands up, don't shoot," in which Brown was erroneously portrayed as nonthreatening and compliant. Though the American legal process had delivered justice, Ferguson rioters insisted upon injustice, pillaging and razing their neighbors' businesses in the dead of night.

While Ferguson was a critical flashpoint for the nation, it was a decision point for law students. The evening's events were sure to dominate the discussion in my criminal law class. I had a choice: speak my mind in support of the grand jury and suffer the condemnation of my predominantly liberal peers, or stay quiet in the hopes that some brave soul would speak for me. I decided on the latter—at least for now.

★　　★　　★　　★

The next day the mood on campus was predictably grim. Students wore black shirts in protest and opined about the injustices of the courts, but the true firestorm of anger wasn't unleashed until after Thanksgiving break, just as our onerous fall exam period approached. Upon arriving back on campus, the signs of impending upheaval at Harvard Law were not just felt: they were seen.

Every morning before class I walked through Harvard's esteemed Wasserstein Hall past a sea of faces. On the wall were portraits of the world's greatest legal minds—hundreds of black-and-white pictures of professors at Harvard both past and present who have made valuable contributions to our legal system. I always looked at these faces with a hint of both nervousness and disbelief. Nervous that I might be the victim of one of these instructors' infamous cold calls, where I would be ruthlessly grilled on a case in front of my peers. Disbelief at the opportunity I had to engage with these great minds. Both emotions were embedded in a deep respect for my elders, with whom I might disagree but would never disrespect.

This December morning I saw that the gallery of faces that typically greeted me had been covered with signs. Written across them were striking words:

"You shot me."

"I can't breathe."

"Please don't let me die."

As I moved closer to get a better look at the signs, I saw the hashtag

"#LastWords" and the names of individuals who had died during an interaction with a police officer.

Student activists had covered our faculty's faces with "last words," and yet some of these very faculty members had devoted their entire lives to defending individuals who uttered last words just like these. I found the defacement to be both profoundly confusing and deeply disrespectful. These professors had done more for social justice and civil rights than all of these insolent students combined, and yet here their portraits were marred with words of protest. Why tarnish the images of the very people who have tirelessly worked to counter injustice? It made no sense!

The visible signs of protest were accompanied by a flurry of campus activity. Protesters blocked traffic, chanting "No justice, no peace, no racist police" and "Hands up, don't shoot."[1] Harvard medical students held a "die-in," where they lay on the ground in their white lab coats.[2] And, in an amusing clash, a group of student protesters intentionally held a silent demonstration during a biannual Harvard tradition called "Primal Scream," where inebriated undergraduates run naked across Harvard Yard in a last act of liberation before exams.[3] The protesters' "White silence is white violence" sign came face-to-face with noisy buck-naked college students. To silence the raucous undergrads, the protesters repeated "Silence, silence" to which the streakers replied, "U.S.A.! U.S.A.!" One protest organizer told the *Harvard Crimson* that she was "disgusted" because when the crowd shouted "U.S.A.!" they were "upholding a system that is oppressing black people."[4] Meanwhile, most of the drunken undergrads were blissfully unaware of the silent demonstration intentionally designed to interrupt their event.

Harvard was not alone in its protest activity. Ferguson was a flashpoint, setting off waves of activity on our nation's campuses. In some cases the school administrators acknowledged it, and in other cases they coddled it. At Columbia Law School, students asked for exam extensions, complaining that "in being asked to prepare for and take our exams in this moment, we are being asked to perform incredible acts of disassociation that have led us to question our place in this school community . . ." Taking exams are an extreme act of disassociation? I was bemused. Our singular requirement as law students over an entire four-month-long semester was to show up for that four-hour block of time to complete an exam. And now, as *National Review*'s Charles C. W. Cooke so eloquently put it, these students were claiming "Social justice ate my homework."[5]

Attempting to mimic our Ivy League peers, my classmates implored Harvard Law dean Martha Minow for exam extensions and safe spaces. "Your silence denies humanity to the lives lost and minimizes the gravity of the palpable anguish looming over campus . . . we are traumatized," they admonished the dean.[6] Being forced to take exams denied humanity? How were my peers going to survive in the real world, where a troubling news cycle is no excuse for absence?

Columbia Law caved and permitted exam extensions for "trauma related to recent non-indictments," in the words of the student senate.[7] Harvard did not acquiesce, although they did provide an extraordinary level of support: a space for reflection, one-on-one support, and a session on concentrating amid strong emotions—all deemed unacceptable by the protesting students.

In the month after Ferguson, I remained silent. But that was about to change. Tired of what I saw as the vilification of cops on campus, I approached *The O'Reilly Factor* about the happenings at Harvard and received an invitation to appear on the show. I traveled from Boston to New York City for the program and, after taking an eight-hour online exam in my hotel room (for which I could have used the grand jury exemption my peers sought!), I joined Bill O'Reilly on *The Factor*.

I used the platform not just to express disagreement with the exam extension request but also as an opportunity to advocate for law enforcement. Sitting across from Bill, I said, "You know what really disturbs me, Bill? A cop dies every fifty-eight hours. Thirty-nine have died by hostile gunfire [in 2014 alone]. And, in fact, one week before Ferguson, off-duty police officer Justin Winebrenner confronted a gunman and was killed. There were no protests. There was not a peep." After I mentioned Justin on television, members of his Akron, Ohio, community reached out on Facebook to thank me for bringing attention to his heroism. Officer Justin Winebrenner's story was, of course, the previous chapter of this book.

What my classmates were missing was this: while there are indeed instances of police brutality that should be addressed and condemned, these incidents are not the norm. The majority of officers are good people working a hard and thankless job, and some are even as heroic as Justin, bravely running into danger and receiving little thanks or appreciation for it.

During my two years at Harvard, I was astounded by the lack of respect for authority—for police and professors alike—on the part of my fellow students. In a profession founded on the principle that everyone receives a defense, the police received none on my law school campus. In a field committed to finding truth, the truth had been buried. The "hands up, don't shoot" scenario had been proven false—at this point by the Ferguson grand jury—but my fellow students nevertheless continued to chant it on the streets.[8] Months later, President Barack Obama's own Justice Department would corroborate the Ferguson grand jury's decision.

I chose to speak up, and I incurred the wrath of my peers because of it. Dirty looks in the halls. Private, behind-the-back shaming. In Harvard Law School's highly publicized annual parody, students planned to include a reference to me despite the long-standing policy of not attacking students. It was removed at the last moment after the Federalist Society president threatened to go to the administration if the joke was not removed.

There was even an anonymous blog post titled "A New Low" in which a faceless colleague labeled my pro-police views "vitriolic" and wrote this concerning my appearance on *The O'Reilly Factor*: "Going on national television to mock your fellow students for their activism and the pain they've endured is a new low . . . and defending state-sanctioned terrorism."[9] State-sanctioned terrorism? The irony is that the very author of this post would most certainly be calling on the so-called state-sanctioned terrorists if suddenly in harm's way.

My very public career first at CNN and now as national RNC spokesperson puts me in the middle of a storm of criticism—go check my Twitter feed or Facebook page!—but it doesn't bother me much. What does bother me—intensely—is the vilification of opposing views. Academia is meant to be a bastion of free thought, where your ideas are questioned, countered, and engaged. As a conservative student, liberal academia proved particularly rewarding, since it gave me a meaningful opportunity to challenge and sometimes concede to opinions that are different from my own.

Like the time when my professor of criminal law, Ronald S. Sullivan, presented two cases in an attempt to illustrate racial disparity in the criminal justice system. The cases were from the same place and had similar though not identical fact patterns but the verdicts could not have been more different. In one famous case, a white man shot at four young black men on the subway. The penalty? A conviction for carrying an unlicensed firearm and acquittal on all other charges. In the other, lesser-known case, a black man defended his home by shooting a white teenager who charged at him and allegedly slapped his gun—an action that would ordinarily be protected by the so-called castle doctrine, or the right to defend your home. His penalty? A conviction for manslaughter.

My professor asked the class how these similar cases could have turned out so differently. My answer echoed that of the black defendant's attorney, who said: "Race has so much to do with this case . . . that it's painful."[10] As a conservative student, I was fortunate to have a professor like Sullivan who engaged me in the friendly manner of a wise educator shepherding his green student. He opened my eyes to disparities in the law. I was enriched by the fair-minded alternative views academia offered, but my effort to add a conservative viewpoint was disparaged by some of my peers. Sure, they had every right to falsely caricature me, but the coming months would show their intent was not just to bully but to silence.

The criticism I encountered on campus, while far-reaching, was mild compared to what Bill Barlow, the emerging conservative hero on campus, had to face. His exposure of our snowflake counterparts earned him baseless and unfair labels like "white supremacist" and "serial killer." In my eyes, and in the view of many others, though, he was a rock star, and his ability to out-argue our radical peers was nothing short of epic.

★   ★   ★   ★

Before I tell you Bill's story, a little background. Following Ferguson, Harvard experienced a deluge of snowflakes—literally. Yes, 2015 was indeed a year of record snowfall. But that is not the snow to which I refer. Rather, I am referring to liberal snowflakes: the individuals who dare not hear dissenting thought lest they melt.

A group called the Students for Inclusion began an anonymous blog called Socratic Shortcomings with the apparent aim of giving slighted Harvard Law School students a place to whine about instances in which they felt victimized.[11] Purporting to be open to all points of view, the site claims to give voice to "students of all identities and backgrounds, named or anonymously."[12] However, we would later find that the group allegedly censored a variety of posts that they did not agree with.[13]

On Socratic Shortcomings, the topics vary: most center on race or gender, but there is the occasional slighted conservative. For instance, one student said she felt "disheartened" to see some of her liberal friends "celebrate the death of Justice Antonin Scalia."[14] How can they claim to support human rights by opposing the death penalty but rejoice at the passing of a man who left a wife and nine children? A fair point to which I think any rational human being would agree.

Most of the posts, however, are far less logical and give you a window into the mind of a snowflake. Here is a preview:

- "Chalk Offensive"—"On my morning walk to campus, I saw a TRUMP 2016 chalk message . . . This is an unacceptable affront to all POC [people of color] at HLS."[15]

- "Holy Cow"—"I very much dislike the way that op-eds . . . repeatedly make use of the 'holy cow' idiom to refer to free speech . . . If the goal is to resist white supremacist, please don't use idioms that were invented by white people to disparage a certain kind of brown person."[16]

- "The Jail Bird"—"I cringe every time I have to order a chicken sandwich at the grill at the HLS dining hall. The reason for this is that the grill menu apparently has an incarceration 'theme': the french fries are called 'Felony Fries,' the onion rings are called 'Crime Rings' and the chicken sandwich is called 'The Jail Bird.' Incarceration is not a joke . . ." [17]

- "The Framers"—"I don't want to interpret the documents that house my most basic rights as . . . American by reflecting on what 'The Founders,' in all their infinite racism, sexism, and elitism, thought hundreds of years ago. The continuous validation of this historical perspective in our classrooms and the opinions we read is offensive and oppressive." [18]

- "Legal Profession"—"The number of times the old white guys teaching our Legal Profession class (which, I underline, is an ethics class) have used racist terms like 'off the reservation' . . . is just unacceptable. ETHICS CLASS. You can't write this irony." [19]

The snowflake complaints were also coupled with attacks on certain groups of students. I'll never forget receiving an e-mail sent from the official student government account "on behalf of the Affinity Group Coalition." The e-mail was addressed to "white allies" of the minority student affinity groups, and its aim was to teach "white allies" how to be a "good ally." One recommendation in particular stood out: "continue acknowledging your privilege."

The demand seemed stereotypical and tone-deaf. There are many white people who grew up as victims of poverty, crime, or sickness. Summing up a group as homogeneously "privileged" was off base. This was the same broad categorization of a group that we oppose in the fight against prejudice!

Indeed, the snowflakes were out in full force, but they met their match in a fierce conservative fighter who would be silent no longer. I first heard about Bill Barlow from my roommate. "You have to get a copy of the *Harvard Law Record*, Kayleigh. There is a bombshell op-ed you will love," she said. I grabbed a copy of the *Record* and found an op-ed titled "Fascism at Yale." It had gone viral, and a quick perusal of the article revealed why. [20]

The article concerned an incident at Yale, our school's Ivy League rival. Yale's Intercultural Affairs Committee sent an e-mail cautioning students against wearing offensive Halloween costumes. A professor questioned the email, arguing that "American universities were once a safe space not only for maturation but also for a certain regressive, or even transgressive, experience; increasingly, it seems, they have become places of censure and prohibition."[21] When the professor's argument was met with protest, she personally went to engage with the protesters.

Here is how the students responded to her willingness to have a dialogue. In a manic, screaming voice, a student shouted at the professor, "Why the f*** did you accept the position?! Who the f*** hired you?! You should step down! . . . You should not sleep at night. You are disgusting."[22]

Barlow's op-ed pairs this disturbing Yale incident with another that occurred just days later. At an event held by the William F. Buckley, Jr., Program—a conservative group at Yale—dissenting opinions escalated to physical assault when activists literally spit on attendees. Speaking of the protesters, Barlow lamented, "The problem is that no one is willing to stand up to them. If we are going to begin anywhere, we are going to begin by calling them by their rightful name. They are fascists. They are fascists. They are fascists."[23]

With this article, Barlow began the process of doing just that: standing up to them. His article gained so much traction that he was asked to appear on Lou Dobbs's show on Fox Business Network. Just as my *O'Reilly Factor* appearance had been met with mockery and belittlement a year earlier, so too was Barlow's. Soon after Barlow appeared on Fox, a Facebook thread developed with Harvard students maligning him and falsely labeling him a "white supremacist."

Students further criticized Barlow not for his words but for his appearance, saying he looked like a serial killer. Barlow said he laughed it off, wisely noting that "as long as they're expressing their opinion in the shadows, it doesn't do anything," but at this point he realized that he was enemy number one on campus when it came to politics—a status that he readily embraced.

★   ★   ★   ★

The liberal forces on campus—ignited and emboldened by Ferguson—organized, and as their movement gained momentum, their protest tactics grew increasingly more childish. Activist students formed a group called "Reclaim" that aimed at ridding Harvard of a variety of alleged racial and gender disparities. In one member's words, "I #ReclaimHarvardLaw because HLS perpetuates the white supremacist patriarchy . . ."[24]

Harvard Law—a "white supremacist patriarchy"? Give me a break! Harvard, the alma mater of W. E. B. Du Bois and more recently Attorney General Loretta Lynch is a bastion of diversity and inclusion, not a place where white supremacists lurk around every corner. The accusation was ludicrous!

Reclaim had a list of demands to remedy this perceived white supremacy overtaking Harvard Law School—among them, mandatory implicit bias training for incoming students and the addition of a section on student evaluations to report professor bias. As Barlow wisely countered, implicit bias training "would be taught in a highly partisan fashion" as it was at University of California, where students are cautioned not to say offensive statements like "Everyone can succeed in society if they work hard enough."[25] Seriously? And as far as professor biases go, there was only one bias I encountered among faculty: liberal.

In pursuit of their demands, Reclaim showed a deep aversion to alternative thought, a militant demeanor, and an uncalled-for irreverence toward authority. For instance, when Dean Martha Minow received the Gittler Prize for "mak[ing] a lasting contribution to racial, ethnic or religious relations," Reclaim students traveled to Brandeis University to shout her down during her acceptance speech.[26] Minow, a candidate on President Obama's shortlist for the Supreme Court, had worked tirelessly on behalf of refugees and desegregation, but here were her own students rudely heckling their elder and ally at a ceremony in her honor.

In defense of Dean Minow, Professor Randall Kennedy—a professor at Harvard Law for more than thirty years and a renowned advocate for racial justice—said, "It seems to me that it is altogether fitting that she [Dean Minow] should get this prize at this moment."[27] Ironically, Kennedy—who has dedicated his entire life to promoting racial equality—became the target of Reclaim's ire when he wrote in the *New York Times* that two tendencies worried him on campus: "exaggerating the scope of the racism that the activists oppose and fear" and "minimizing their own strength and victories that they and their forebears have already achieved."[28] After acknowledging several of the activists' concerns that racism does still exist, he concluded in saying, "Reformers harm themselves by nurturing an inflated sense of victimization."

It was nothing short of remarkable: here was a professor who was an activist himself pointing out the "inflated sense of victimization" among activists on campus. These were the wise observations of a civil rights icon to a younger generation of activists who would have none of it. Incensed by his gentle guidance, dissenters—some of whom belonged to Reclaim—scoffed at Kennedy and accused him of being out of touch, confronting him angrily as he tried to communicate his point of view during a class discussion. As a southerner who grew up in a home where "Yes, ma'am" and "No, sir" were mandatory, I was taught that disagreement was acceptable but never disrespect. My Reclaim counterparts had crossed that line in a big way.

Irreverent toward authority and dissatisfied that Harvard was not yielding to their every demand, Reclaim resolved to occupy Caspersen Student Center, a warm and inviting student common area with fireplaces and grand light fixtures.[29] Covering the wall in signs promoting their cause and the floor with sleeping bags and air mattresses, Reclaim dictatorially declared ownership of half the room, creating their own sort of safe space right in the heart of campus, directly in the path most students take to class. It couldn't be missed.

Barlow grew increasingly frustrated as he walked to class. Every day he dealt with liberal professors and liberal classmates, but now on the way to class he had to "see a literal wall of propaganda," in his words. He got an idea: Why not show Reclaim just how annoying it was to walk through a common area plastered in signs you disagree with? Let them see what it was like to have "a daily barrage of disagreement," in his words. If Reclaim could put up signs, why couldn't he?

Besides, he believed that Reclaim was "authoritarian at heart," intolerant of contrary opinions. Many students mildly agreed with Reclaim.

Who cares if they're occupying a space and proffering a list of demands? They aren't acting authoritarian, many students thought. So Barlow devised a plan: fill the other half of Caspersen Student Center with signs of his own and put Reclaim in a position where they would be forced to choose between tolerance and intolerance.

For his first sign, Barlow wanted to make a strong point that was sure to get noticed. It was the heat of the 2016 primaries, and while Donald Trump was exceedingly popular among Republican primary voters, he wasn't exactly the top choice on a liberal law school campus in the heart of the so-called People's Republic of Cambridge. With this in mind, Barlow made a provocative statement on his first batch of signs, alleging that Trump and Reclaim were alike in censoring dissent. It wasn't that Barlow believed Trump was anything like Reclaim; rather, he knew a Donald Trump analogy would have the biggest impact in challenging the liberal activists. Moreover, he said, "The only way that you could get a Trump sign into Harvard's halls without getting murdered was to have it in a negative light."

As Barlow put up the signs in empty wall space, members of Reclaim approached him and a "tense but civil" thirty-minute conversation ensued during which Barlow explained his right to dissenting speech. But it seemed to him that "people were angry at the fact that I was even talking." One student pointedly said, "The fact that we are having this conversation is a reinforcement of white supremacy."

About an hour after the conversation, Barlow received word that the Trump portion of his signs had been taken down. He had posted several sheets of paper on the wall, and the one that specifically mentioned the presidential candidate was detached but the others remained. Barlow also received an e-mail from the dean of students' office asking to meet. In their meeting, an administrator pressed Barlow about whether his signs were placed on the wall as a deliberate attack on Muslim students, apparently because of its reference to Trump. The assertion was as outrageous as it was nonsensical, and a very distant stretch from Barlow's motive of promoting free speech. According to Barlow, the administrator's line of inquiry was prompted by Reclaim students, who had approached the dean of students to complain about the signs and ascribe to them

Bill affixes signs to Caspersen Student Center. *Courtesy of Jim An, The Harvard Law School Record Corporation*

an anti-Muslim bias. The administrator then explained that the Trump sign might offend some students and run afoul of Harvard's 501(c)(3) status, a claim Barlow argued was inaccurate. The dean of students confirmed to him that non-campaign signs were permitted, and she also verified that students, not the administration, had removed the signs.

Despite the fact that the administration approved the signs that did not mention Trump, Barlow received a text from a friend informing him that all of his signs had been taken down. Intent on getting his message across, Barlow returned to post a second round of signs. This time the message read, "Censored by Reclaim Harvard Law." As he attached the signs, a Reclaim member curtly warned in what Barlow describes as a faux nice voice: "All signs must be approved by the plenary committee. You can place an application, but you're not permitted to just put up signs."

What was this so-called plenary committee, you ask? It wasn't composed of faculty or recognized by the administration. In fact, the administration had already explicitly given Barlow permission to hang his signs. The plenary committee was a group of hard-core Reclaim students who had appointed themselves the authority for deciding what type of speech was permissible in Harvard's student center.

Barlow told the student that their group had no right to do that and he continued to put up his signs. The student replied, "This is our territory, our property. You can put those up, but we will tear them down." Their property? This was a *common* space for *all* students, funded by every student's tuition, that Reclaim was unilaterally claiming as its own. As Barlow put up his signs, Reclaim began to take them down right in front of him. Barlow's friend asked the students why they were doing that, and they replied, "Because it's offensive." My activist classmates could not tolerate Barlow's harmless but accurate assertion that "Reclaim is against free speech," and so they removed it. In doing so, they were proving Barlow's very point: they were censoring speech!

Barlow's friend explained to Reclaim that several of their signs were an affront to him but he nonetheless let them remain. Reclaim's response? "Oh, the eggshell-white male! You are overly sensitive and can't take criticism," Barlow remembered them stating as they removed all of his fliers. Here was a group whose purported purpose was racial equality blatantly insulting a student because of his race. The off-the-cuff comment wasn't Reclaim's only race invocation. They also tweeted: "White man desecrates #BelindaHall!"[30]

At this point, thirty-six of Barlow's signs had been removed, and he said it was the angriest he had ever been, because it was a blatant infringement on his rights. Barlow was nevertheless undeterred. He returned—for a third time—with a new batch of signs whose message read "Reclaim Harvard Law = Suppression of Free Speech." What came next was to be expected, but this time the irony could not be more blatant. After Barlow posted the sign on the wall, Reclaim removed it—and his friend got it all on tape.

After three attempts to post his signs, Barlow approached the administration, who said they would speak to Reclaim. Barlow returned to the Caspersen Student Center with a fourth batch of posters: "56," they stated, with the explanation that Reclaim had removed fifty-six of

Barlow's signs up to this point. Once more Reclaim removed the signs, bringing the total to sixty-eight.

At this point, students around campus began to take notice of Reclaim's totalitarian tactics. The *Harvard Law Record* published an article detailing Barlow's efforts, and other students also began to place signs around campus that were critical of Reclaim.[31] These signs were of course removed. Dean Martha Minow, to her credit, sent an e-mail to all students noting that "when a shared space is made open . . . for protest and discussion . . . the values of free exchange that define an academic community require that every member of the community has the right to use that shared space to express views, to express differences, to engage in debate. That freedom to disagree makes us stronger and better." It is simply bewildering that Harvard Law School's administration had to remind the nation's top law students about the importance of free speech and the First Amendment, but they did.

With the power of the administration behind him and the support of many classmates, Barlow entered the lounge in Wasserstein Hall to make a fifth effort at posting his messages. Reclaim, evidently angered by Barlow's efforts, had sectioned off the lounge into two areas: the "silenced" area and the "privileged" area. A stark red line ran down the center of the wall. On the left it read "Silenced" in black. On the right, "Privileged" in red. Oddly, Reclaim posted its own signs in the "silenced" space—even though they themselves were the ones doing the silencing! They insisted that alternate thought be posted on the "privileged" side. Any signs that Barlow placed on the "silenced" side were moved over to the "privileged" portion of the wall. Never mind that Barlow was in fact the one being silenced!

The paradoxes were twofold. As Barlow noted, by having two separate silenced and privileged areas, Reclaim—the group that seeks racial equality—was engaging in its own form of segregation. Students recognized this, as signs reading "Tear Down This Separate-but-Equal 'Free Speech Zone'" dotted the so-called privileged zone.

Reclaim even went so far as to move a Harvard Law School veteran's sign to the "privileged" zone. The sign read, "I fought for your freedom. Don't take away mine. HLS Vets for Free Speech." Imagine that: privileged Harvard Law millennials with the audacity to label themselves "silenced" while labeling our veterans—military men and women who put their lives on the line to defend our freedom—"privileged"!

Reclaim continually proved Barlow's contention: the far-left students were engaging in authoritarian behavior. Barlow noticed, "Reclaim's Twitter feed taking an odd, Orwellian turn." The group retweeted, "Free Speech is nothing but a shield used to protect ideas that contribute to the harming of the oppressed."[32] *What?* Unrelenting, they continued: "What is it [free

Silenced/Privileged Zone enforced by Reclaim. *Courtesy of author's collection*

speech] doing to eliminate prejudice except protecting the rights of the bigoted to spread hate speech."[33] *Excuse me? Free speech is the bedrock of a democratic society!* Barlow notes that the group even retweeted an article that argued for abridging the freedom of speech.[34] My fellow students in Reclaim clearly had not been paying attention in class. Speech—even speech that is repugnant to America's core values—is nevertheless protected. To make matters worse, these Reclaim students were not even objecting to repugnant speech but completely innocent, harmless speech that challenged their methods and censorship.

Through it all, and despite Reclaim's vicious attacks on him, Barlow remained intellectually honest and even-handed. Upon learning that someone had defaced Reclaim's signs with the message "Stop censorship," Barlow wrote: "We don't know who did this, but acts of defacement are never acceptable, even if the victims don't abide by the same standards." He had been maligned as a serial killer, a white supremacist, a racist, and a bully, among other things, but here he was defending the very people who had tried to intimidate him.

Bill fought valiantly against the militant far left on Harvard Law's campus, and in doing so he showed them to be enemies of freedom of expression. He exposed the culture of victimization, which was evident in the grievance-filled blog Socratic Shortcomings and the Reclaim movement. Barlow saw the Reclaim movement as a reflection of what liberals at large do. He noted, "If you want to understand [the] left, it's not an ideology, it's a social hierarchy. Victimization gives you status and identity. It gives you currency within their social system." Barlow had exposed the so-called victims and, in doing so, showed himself to be the real victim—the victim of an intolerant ideology that wishes to deprive him of speech. He, of course, would never describe himself that way, for victimhood isn't in the conservative DNA.

Barlow became a conservative icon on campus, one whom many—including myself—silently applauded. When I asked if he got quiet confessions of support along the way, he replied, "All the time." Much like the silent Trump voter, college students dare not profess conservatism. For if they do, they risk belittlement by a professor, lower grades, or condemnation from peers. One student put it this way on Socratic Shortcomings, in one of the rare conservative posts the site did not censor: "I think HLS is one of the only places in the world where I am judged more for being a member of FedSoc [the conservative student society] than I am for being gay."[35] It was a sobering reminder of the status of conservatives on college campuses.

Barlow said that throughout his undergraduate experience at Duke University, he pretended to be liberal to get good grades. I too felt pressure to stay neutral or echo left-wing points during my time at Georgetown University and Oxford University, and during my two years at Harvard Law School. Some liberal professors were open-minded and encouraged—sometimes even rewarded—thoughtful dissent. But as a conservative student, one proceeds at one's own peril, never quite sure how to distinguish between the tolerant and the intolerant. Barlow strategically chose to speak out in his second year at Harvard Law after he had gotten his job offer. He wanted to make a real, tangible difference, and there's no doubt that he left his mark on the campus of Harvard Law School. He will remain a legend, whispered about from one generation of conservative students to the next.

The fear of speaking out on campus seemed to closely mirror the position of many Trump voters, who were afraid to express support for Trump lest they be accused of being racist, xenophobic, or misogynistic, among other horrible things. I asked Bill Barlow whether he thought the militant suppression of conservative thought on the Harvard Law School campus paralleled what happened nationwide in the 2016 election. Bill replied, "I absolutely think [so]." He noted that when he goes on Reddit and looks at Donald Trump–related posts, nothing gets people more fired up than when a conservative speaker gets canceled from campus. "For younger voters, rebellion against [the] political correctness environment was one of the top issues, if not the one," he observed.

Academic silencing of conservative voices is indeed pervasive. Using data from the Foundation for Individual Rights in Education (FIRE), I discovered that 83 percent of canceled speakers were disinvited in 2016 because of a challenge from the left, while a minute 4.2 percent were silenced because of a push from the right.[36] As I wrote previously in *The Hill*, "There is just one recorded incident in 2016 of a university canceling a left-wing speaker."[37] My piece went on to note several distinguished and mainstream voices that incurred the wrath of the left. Liberal students took aim at distinguished *Wall Street Journal* columnist Jason L. Riley, a black conservative, because of his book *Please Stop Helping Us: How Liberals Make It Harder for Blacks to Succeed*. In 2013, students shouted down former New York City police commissioner Ray Kelly for a full thirty minutes, forcing a cancellation of his speech. And in 2017 student protests led to the cancellation of Republican senator John Cornyn's commencement speech at a historically black college.[38] In each of these cases, usually left-leaning administrators seemed to recognize the absurdity of their liberal students. Virginia Tech issued an apology to Jason Riley and re-invited him to speak; a Brown University administrator noted to the crowd screaming down Ray Kelly, "I have never seen in my 15 years at Brown the inability to have a dialogue"; and Texas Southern University invited Senator Cornyn to speak at a later date.[39]

Indeed, an atmosphere of politically correct suppression has led many to embrace the unadulterated realspeak of Donald Trump. Voters were exasperated by the eloquent poll-tested prose robotically read off a teleprompter by a scripted politician. Instead, they preferred Trump's off-the-cuff realism. When Trump declared his candidacy, I was drawn to his bold, anti–politically correct style. I wondered whether America was ready for unfiltered straight talk.[40] But witnessing suppression on my campus made me realize this was exactly what America needed and pushed me forcefully into Trump's corner very early in the primaries, where I later became a daily advocate for the president on CNN.

In explaining my early conversion to Team Trump, I wrote: "During my time in academia, it became increasingly clear that prisons of political correctness with peer-engendered public shaming are now the academic reality . . . It was this kind of mindset—the hostile advocacy of platitudes over polite dissent, dictatorial silencing over thoughtful engagement and censorship over free interchange—that took me from reticent acceptance of Trump's approach to passionate advocacy . . . Trump has set the politically correct walls aflame."[41] A flame he rode all the way to the presidency.

Thanks to Barlow, the politically correct walls at Harvard were aflame as well. Barlow remembers attending one of the two campus-wide meetings that Dean Minow held to give students a platform to speak during a time of activism and protest on campus. The room was filled with mostly Reclaim students, taking to the mic and listing their grievances before their mostly applauding peers. Barlow felt afraid, but he knew he had to say something in a room full of people who seemed to despise him. Grabbing the microphone, he briefly said, "I think we are being far too angry. This administration is handling this well." He feared making such a simple statement, knowing other students would disparage him for it, but once he did it, he felt liberated. Asking him how he overcame the fear, he told me quite confidently: "Once you've done it, you're free of all of it. You don't have the oppressive feeling anymore. You are liberated."

The silence was broken.

THE FORSAKING

Freedom of Religion

---

*"I consider it an indispensable duty to close this last solemn
act of my Official life, by commending the Interests of dearest
Country to the protection of Almighty God, and those who
have the superintendence of them, to his holy keeping."*
—GEORGE WASHINGTON

*"America will never be destroyed from the outside. If we falter and
lose our freedoms, it will be because we destroyed ourselves."*
— ABRAHAM LINCOLN

Our Military

Silence filled the nondescript auditorium at Travis Air Force Base as
two men dressed in military uniforms stood facing one another. The
men waited for the distinct music to commence, each holding the edges
of an unfurled American flag. As the trumpet-laden chorus broke the
silence, the servicemen folded the flag before an audience gathered to
celebrate the retirement of Master Sergeant Chuck Roberson from the
749th Aircraft Maintenance Squadron.

Hearing his cue, Master Sergeant Oscar Rodriguez took three resolute steps toward the front of the room to deliver his speech.[1] Oscar had
written his now-famous rendition of the standard flag-folding speech
during his thirty-three-year tenure in the United States Air Force. His
oration had received wide praise from elected officials like Democratic

congressman John Garamendi, who
complimented the speech in a hand-
written note, and fellow servicemen
like Chuck Roberson, who asked
Oscar to perform it at his ceremony.
"God bless our flag. God bless our
troops. God bless America." Oscar
had declared those closing words more
than one hundred times before. He intended to do the same today.

Just before beginning his speech—
this time at the request of the retiring
Roberson—a uniformed airman approached Oscar. Three other servicemen in the front row leaned forward

SMSgt. Oscar Rodriguez, USAF.
Courtesy of Oscar Rodriguez

to observe the encounter, seemingly in anticipation. "You're not going to
do this are you?" the airman asked Oscar.[2] In a split second, two other
airmen from different corners of the room hastily rose, bolted to the
stage, and surrounded Oscar.

A bit puzzled by the interruption, Oscar nevertheless started speaking. His booming voice rang out, "Our flag is known as the Stars and
Stripes." In an effort to silence Oscar, the surrounding men firmly
pressed their hands against his chest and pushed him toward the exit.[3]
Struggling to remain at the front, Oscar continued speaking—his voice
now taking a more urgent tone—but he could not resist the shoving of
the airmen, who succeeded in evicting Oscar from the stage. As they cor-
ralled and expelled Oscar, he could be heard shouting the second line of
his celebrated speech: "The union consists of white stars on a blue field,
symbolic of a new constellation. Each star represents one individual state
and together they stand united indivisible."[4]

Why was Rodriguez removed from a retirement ceremony whose
honoree requested that he give a speech he had given dozens of times
before? The answer provided by Oscar and Chuck is sure to disturb any
believer in the First Amendment: he was removed because he planned
to mention the name of God.

★   ★   ★   ★

Master Sergeant Oscar Rodriguez loves this country and served it valiantly. From a young age, he shone with patriotism. "When I was a child,
during baseball games, one of the most emotional parts of that was the
national anthem," he told the First Liberty Institute.[5] "I would always
try to hide my tears from my brothers because I knew that many men
died for that freedom to be able to have a hotdog and watch a baseball
game."[6]

Oscar dreamed of serving his country, and for more than three decades he did just that, but not without cost. In exchange for his service,
"his reward was bankruptcy," Democratic senator Mary Landrieu announced from the Senate floor.[7] In 2002, after more than twenty years as
an Air Force reservist, the Air Force gave Oscar just eight hours' notice
that he would be activated abroad for an entire year.[8] With no time to
prepare for the abrupt change, Oscar left his construction business in the
hands of his wife and daughter. Although his family tried tirelessly to
save the company, they could not. The Rodriguez family's income fell

Master Sergeant Oscar Rodriguez. *Courtesy of First Liberty Institute*

by 80 percent, and their house went into foreclosure.[9] Oscar told CBS News, "I lost the bids for my construction projects. I lost my savings. I lost my credit. My credit history—it's in shambles."[10] His daughter remembered, "It was hard seeing my mom. I mean seeing her stressed and seeing her cry—it hurts a lot."[11]

The hardship Oscar had endured as a result of his service made the betrayal at Travis Air Force Base all the more troublesome. "I have given more than three decades of service to the military and made many sacrifices for my country." Oscar told First Liberty.[12] "To have the Air Force assault me and drag me out of a retirement ceremony simply because my speech included the word 'God' is something I never expected from our military."[13]

As a Christian and a fierce defender of our civil liberties, I too was surprised. In fact, I gasped out loud when senior counsel for the First Liberty Institute, Jeremy Dys, told me about Oscar's assault. I told Oscar's First Liberty attorney, Mike Berry, that what made his case most surprising is that it occurred in a military setting, where there is a strong, Christian, conservative strain. "Not anymore," Berry immediately interjected. "I can only say that eight years has done a lot of damage." He told me that if you graphed religious suppression in the military in the past three to four years, it would be shaped like a hockey stick with the number of incidents taking an almost vertical trajectory upward.

Oscar's forcible removal from Chuck's retirement ceremony came after an overt effort to impede Oscar from attending the ceremony altogether. After hearing about Oscar's invitation to attend the ceremony, Lieutenant Colonel Michael Sovitsky told Chuck to disinvite Oscar, citing the fact that Oscar, who had previously served on the Travis Honor Guard Team, had been released for "misconduct" many years ago—a fact that First Liberty attorneys rightly point out is irrelevant.[14] Oscar is now a private citizen, as deserving of First Amendment rights as any other U.S. citizen, and Sovitsky's request was an unfounded pretext for silencing Oscar, who had a sterling thirty-three-year record in the Air Force. Not wanting to defy his commanding officer, Chuck informed Oscar about the situation.

"The commanding officer wants me to tell you not to come," Chuck said.

"Well, what do *you* want?" Oscar asked. "This is your retirement. You only get to retire one time. Let's make this about you."

"If it were up to me, I would have you there," Chuck replied.

Chuck had previously told Oscar that it would be the highlight of his retirement ceremony to have Oscar deliver the speech, so both men resolved to make it happen. Chuck and Oscar knew that Sovitsky did not have the authority to bar Oscar from the ceremony. He was not an installation commander, and only someone with that title could keep someone off the base. Even so, Chuck and Oscar did not want to cause trouble, so they made several efforts to assuage the problem.

They suspected that the disinvitation request had something to do with the religious references in Oscar's speech. Oscar had served in Sovitsky's unit before and was well aware of Sovitsky's disdain for Oscar's speech. In fact, Oscar had performed a flag-folding speech one month earlier, and when Sovitsky heard the speech, he was very upset, allegedly remarking, "Oscar is never to do that in my unit." Unlike the official Air Force flag-folding script, Oscar's speech made reference to God.

Chuck made several efforts to contact higher authorities and approve Oscar's speech. He offered to put a warning on the door of the auditorium, telling attendees that the word "God" might be mentioned at the ceremony. He likewise offered to allow offended individuals to leave during those parts of the ceremony. Having received no response, Chuck told Oscar to come to the ceremony, and if he heard his unique flag-folding music begin to play, that would be his cue to give the speech. Chuck put Oscar's name on the seating chart, placing him in the very front row as a distinguished speaker, and when that familiar music rang out, Oscar knew it was his time to speak.

While Sovitsky did not have the authority to bar Oscar from the base, he did have the authority to remove someone if they were being disruptive. This was the rationale Sovitsky used in the aftermath of the assault. He claimed that Chuck had never actually invited Oscar to attend, according to Oscar's attorney. Chuck immediately contested that, saying that he had not only invited Oscar, his name was on the official guest list. "That the Air Force would do this to me, as it's my retirement, I was very embarrassed and humiliated in front of all my family and friends," Chuck said.[15]

Oscar echoed Chuck in a First Liberty video, calling it "one of the most humiliating experiences . . . To even imagine that I would be removed while the American flag is being unfurled and opened—the flag which represents freedom of speech, freedom of religion, freedom of the press . . . it's horrifying."[16] And to compound the situation, Mike Berry, Oscar's attorney, added, "They took glee in doing this to him. They were waiting for this opportunity."

Following Oscar's removal, he filed a complaint with his congressman, and Senator John McCain demanded that the Air Force conduct a full and thorough investigation into the matter. When First Liberty approached Oscar about taking legal action, he was very frustrated about what had happened but was uncertain about whether to pursue litigation. After taking the weekend to think about it, Berry said, "[Oscar] realized what happened was really wrong. This shouldn't happen to anybody, and [he realized] 'if I don't do something, I'm letting this perpetuate.'" Berry sent a letter to the Air Force on Oscar's behalf, seeking an apology. "All we've ever wanted out of this is to make things right. No one is interested in going to court," Berry explained.

The Air Force did not apologize, but it did release a statement reaffirming its commitment to the First Amendment: "Air Force personnel may use a flag folding ceremony script that is religious for retirement ceremonies . . . The Air Force places the highest value on the rights of its personnel in matters of religion and facilitates the free exercise on religion by its members,"[17] Its release was carefully timed and conflicted with the Air Force's 2005 mandate requiring use of an official, nonreligious speech.[18] Acknowledging the conflict, an Air Force release stated, "The Air Force acknowledges the AFI [Air Force Instruction] does not reflect the current policy . . . We acknowledge that the Air Force Instruction should have incorporated the supplemental guidance."[19] Convenient.

The Air Force conducted an internal review of Oscar's case and maintains that Oscar was not removed because of his religious script but for "not being a planned participant of the ceremony/not on the retirement script, and previous misconduct."[20] The IG report makes vague references to previous "misconduct" while Oscar was in the honor guard without citing specific examples. Moreover, the report even acknowledges Sovitsky's concern that Oscar would not use the approved Air Force script for retirement speeches, which makes no religious reference, and would instead use his personal script, which closely mirrors the approved script but makes reference to God.[21] Vague "misconduct" appears not to have been Sovitsky's only motivating factor.

Aside from Rodriguez's personal story, two excerpts from the IG report stand out to me as troubling:

> On a military installation, to maintain good order and discipline, the commander also has the authority to preserve dedicated military facilities for activities consistent with their intended function.[22]

How is Oscar's widely hailed retirement speech—celebrated by a sitting congressman and praised by the military community—inconsistent with the "intended function" of a retirement ceremony? The report goes on:

> Although Mr. Rodriguez is a civilian, not subject to a military commander's direct command authority, he is not free to exercise his right of freedom of speech whenever, wherever, or however, he chooses, *in contravention of substantial military interests.*

How is a harmless speech making reference to God at the personal request of a retiring serviceman "in contravention of substantial military interests"?[23] The report does not provide an answer. First Liberty continues to fight for Rodriguez's First Amendment rights and is now suing the Air Force for unlawfully withholding the results of one of its two investigations into Rodriguez's removal.

It is perplexing to see hostility toward faith take hold in our military of all places when you consider that so many of the rank and file are people of faith. Berry said it's because the military is increasingly becoming "politically correct and risk averse." Those ascending the ranks in a given branch hide their faith. "They're afraid," Berry told me. "These loud outsized voices on the outside [are] threatening to sue them just for having a Bible on their desk."

Indeed, a court-martial convicted United States Marine Corps lance corporal Monifa Sterling for posting a Bible verse on her computer after a supervisor removed it and put it in a trash bin.[24] A trial court and appeals court ruled against Sterling, and the Supreme Court chose not to review the case.[25] "The climate of political correctness did not arise 'suddenly,'" Berry pointed out to me. "It's been a steady onslaught. It mirrors what we observe in our culture. The military rewards those who don't take risks—and thus don't make mistakes—and go along with the political current. The problem with this is when government officials begin to sacrifice our constitutional rights at the altar of political correctness."

Religious suppression in the military has potentially far-reaching consequences, and not just for those who seek to practice their faith freely. A full 66 percent of active duty servicemen identify as Christian.[26] With this in mind, Berry said, "If we are worried about national security, national defense, our ability to keep and maintain a strong, resilient, ready military, then we have to worry about recruiting." This means creating a hospitable environment where servicemen and -women are free to practice their faith. Berry continued: "If you create a culture in the military that is hostile to people of faith, that chills their religious expression, then those people are eventually going to get the message 'We are not welcome here.'" And this is the disturbing trend that Berry has witnessed firsthand in his efforts to defend religious freedom. He said, "I can't tell you how many mothers and fathers across the country who have said, 'I served . . . I loved serving in the military and I love my country, but I could never let my son or daughter join the military having seen what it's become. Why am I going to send my kids to do something that no longer represents my values?'"

But military-related restriction on religious liberty is just one example in a long and growing list of infringements. Religious liberty is under attack in all aspects of American society: the workplace, the school, the courts, and even in the home. A survey of First Liberty Institute's cases described in the pages to come—many of which had successful outcomes for the plaintiffs—reveal attacks on religious liberty in all these settings and a disturbing and ever-increasing hostility toward people of all religious faiths.

Christians, in particular, face a rather disturbing picture both at home and abroad. As CNN reported, an Open Doors USA survey found that 2015 "was the most violent for Christians in modern history, rising to 'a level akin to ethnic cleansing,'" with 7,100 Christian faith-based killings worldwide, a 3,000-victim increase from the year prior.[27]

A 2016 LifeWay Research survey noted a reflective hostility toward Christians in the United States, with 63 percent of Americans noting that "Christians increasingly are confronted with intolerance in America today"—up a full 13 percent from just three years ago.[28] Although the survey noted a dramatic increase in Americans' recognition of Christian persecution, the survey also revealed a smaller but substantial increase of religious persecution generally, with 60 percent noting that "religious liberty is on the decline in America," up 6 percent in three years.[29] The shocking stories that follow help make an anecdotal case that faith is under attack.

Our Places of Worship

Rabbi Yaakov Rich leads a small congregation in the bottom floor of his son's North Dallas home in a neighborhood called Highlands of McKamy. Because Orthodox Judaism prohibits travel on the Sabbath, members of Congregation Toras Chaim have to walk. The rabbi's home in North Dallas is the only place close enough for congregants to reach by foot. Every Saturday, Rabbi Rich's congregation would walk down Meandering Way in their reverent holy day attire, past the mezuzah (a piece of parchment with the Shema, one of the essential Jewish prayers, in a small case mounted on the doorframe) at the entrance to the redbrick home, and into their place of worship, where about two dozen white folding chairs sit behind a matching table that prominently displays a large Torah.[30]

Bothered by Rabbi Rich's congregation, an angry neighbor spearheaded a lawsuit, claiming that the meeting infringed on the residential-only restrictive covenant in the neighborhood. At a prior residence, the lead plaintiff had sued a neighbor for putting up a fence that obstructed his view of the country club.[31] Rabbi Rich's religious practices would be his next target.

Although Congregation Toras Chaim was aware of no complaints during its three years of worship in a neighboring community, a small group of neighbors in Highlands of McKamy listed several frivolous-sounding complaints, including needing to stop for a blind person and a woman pushing a stroller crossing the street and the claim that it looked "odd" and "unusual" when congregants left the religious meetings.[32] The lead plaintiff also initiated a separate lawsuit against a neighbor and member of Congregation Toras Chaim "for erecting a ceremonial structure called a sukkah in his driveway, for the weeklong harvest festival of Sukkot," calling the symbol "unusual" and an "eyesore, according to the *Dallas Observer*.[33]

The lead plaintiff claimed to have no problem with Orthodox Judaism; rather, as the *Dallas Observer* noted, the homeowners' complaints were "ostensibly grounded in secular complaints."[34] But therein lies the problem of so many of these religious liberty cases. As in Oscar Rodriguez's case, the suppressor can disguise his objections to certain language or actions by citing unrelated concerns—Oscar Rodriguez's "misconduct" or Congregation Toras Chaim's bothersome traffic pattern—when in fact those are a mere pretext for the real motive: religious suppression. In Rabbi Rich's case, subsequent events would suggest that anti-Semitism was at play, if not on the part of the lead plaintiff, then certainly from others in the community.

As Rabbi Rich fought for his right to freedom of worship, he became the target of anti-Semitic hate crimes. The mezuzah was ripped from his door. Cars drove by with passengers shouting obscenities. And then there was the horrific moment when Rabbi Rich's son interrupted his religious gathering to alert him that a large swastika had been smeared across the trunk of his Honda.[35] But Rabbi Rich did not give in to the threats, and he won the case against his neighbors in Collin County District Court. Although the neighbors and homeowners association claimed that the members of Toras Chaim had violated the community's bylaws, the court ruled that religious liberty laws protected the congregation.[36] Congregation Toras Chaim prevailed, only to be sued by the city of Dallas on the grounds that the congregation had violated onerous regulations regarding sprinkler systems and parking requirements.[37]

First Liberty attorney Justin Butterfield told the *Dallas Observer* that if plaintiffs succeeded in shutting down Rabbi Rich, it would "effectively end Orthodox Jewish practice in the community."[38] Butterfield warned, "If they can shut this small Orthodox Jewish congregation down, they can shut down the prayer meeting, the Bible study, even the person who just has some friends over for dinner."[39] While Rabbi Rich and Congregation Toras Chaim are the target today, it could be your congregation tomorrow.

The Workplace

Alexia Palma, a thirty-two-year-old Guatemalan immigrant, loved working at her local health clinic in inner-city Houston. In keeping with her Catholic faith, her job—which she described as "my American dream come true"—allowed her to help the vulnerable.[40] Part of her job entailed teaching several courses, including a lesson about contraception, a practice that violates her Catholic faith.[41]

Alexia was committed to always putting her faith first, even when it wasn't easy. God had been there for Alexia when she endured a difficult childhood. "I never had a stable home, but there was always one place I called my stable home, and that was the Church . . . it's the only true home I've ever had," Alexia told First Liberty, growing teary-eyed as she expressed her love for the Church.[42] Her faith saw her through abuse and likewise saw her through thoughts of suicide.[43]

To avoid violating her Catholic faith, Palma asked her employer if she could show a video instead of her personally teaching about contraception. The company agreed, and for a year and a half there were no problems. Alexia would play the video for the class and a nurse would answer any questions students might have.[44]

But when a new supervisor joined the company, she demanded Alexia not only teach the course herself but also attend mandatory training at Planned Parenthood. "I immediately informed them that I was being accommodated for my religious beliefs and the only reason I had ever been close to Planned Parenthood was outside praying," Alexia told LifeSite News.com.[45] Alexia offered her new supervisor several compromises, like having the course taught by another employee who had eagerly volunteered to fill in, but the supervisor refused. The supervisor's refusal was in line with the company's alleged pattern of isolating Christians: forbidding talking about God during breaks, barring religious items from desks, and now actively forcing an employee to violate her conscience.[46]

Alexia told First Liberty, "I began to cry. I told them, 'I'm sorry, I can't do that. My faith comes first.'" Despite having an excellent work performance, the company fired Alexia over her religious objections even though her previous accommodation affected less than 2 percent of her job.[47] Thanks to First Liberty's efforts, Alexia won a settlement payout from the company.[48] But she was nonetheless faced with a grueling choice that no American should face: "choosing between their faith and her job," according to First Liberty senior counsel Jeremy Dys.[49] "She chose her faith and was fired because of it."[50]

The School

On any given fall Friday night at Bremerton High School, in Bremerton, Washington, assistant football coach Joe Kennedy could be found taking a knee at the 50-yard line. Alone on the field, he would quietly kneel and pray to God, thanking him for this opportunity to win or lose. Coach Kennedy carried on this tradition for seven years with no complaints.[51] Some of the players took notice over time and asked if they

Coach Kennedy kneeling at the fifty-yard line. *Courtesy of First Liberty Institute*

could join their coach at the midfield marker. The former Marine Corps gunnery sergeant turned coach would say, "This is a free country. You can do what you want."[52]

After each game at Bremerton High, students from both teams would gather around Coach Kennedy, who started delivering what one player described as a "postgame speech."[53] "He didn't say 'under God' or anything involving religion," the player pointed out to the Daily Signal, the news platform of the Heritage Foundation.[54] Coach Kennedy neither forced nor encouraged students to participate. Rather, it was an organic movement of students supporting a coach they loved. It became somewhat of a postgame tradition. "During the game we're enemies, but then he would bring us together like we're one big family," one student said.[55] Another player described it as "just magical."[56]

But Bremerton High School demanded Kennedy end the seven-year tradition, ordering him not to even bow in silence privately after the players left the field. The demand was confounding, especially considering that another assistant coach was permitted to recite a Buddhist chant at the very same fifty-yard line.[57] In an effort to stand up for religious liberty after the homecoming game—and surrounded by players from both teams and members of the community, who huddled around him in support—Kennedy knelt at midfield in defiance of the order.[58] After encircling their coach, the team enveloped him in a bear hug before cheering and pointing up in unison.

Because of Kennedy's refusal to sacrifice his First Amendment rights, the school suspended him despite his many years of service and glowing reviews from fellow coaches and players. Sitting by Coach Kennedy, one player shed tears over the decision, saying, "I was going through some troubles at home with my dad and [Coach Kennedy] helped me. Sat me down. Talked to me about how it was going to get better no matter what. I wanted him there because he was there for me."[59]

But in August of 2017, the Ninth Circuit dealt an appalling blow to Kennedy's First Amendment rights when they held that "when Kennedy kneeled and prayed on the fifty-yard line immediately after games while in view of students and parents, he spoke as a public employee, not as a private citizen, and his speech therefore was constitutionally unprotected."[60] First Liberty did not seek monetary damages or extraordinary accommodation. Berry said, "All we're asking is for Coach Kennedy to be reinstated and for the school to allow him to continue to pray alone at the 50 yard line after the game."[61]

As First Liberty considers their options, the faith community maintains hope that the Ninth Circuit will be rebuked by the Supreme Court, as they so often are, with an 88 percent reversal rate in 2016.[62] In the meantime, Fox News' Todd Starnes sums up the status quo in America quite well: "Welcome to the America that was fundamentally transformed by President Obama and his activist judges. It's a nation where football players can take a knee to disrespect the flag, but a coach can't take a knee to pray to the Almighty."[63]

The Church

It seemed like an ordinary Sunday for Vintage Church lead pastor Rob Wilton. Standing before his Metairie, Louisiana–based evangelical congregation, Wilton began to preach the word of God to the bustling tent of believers until he was interrupted by Jefferson Parish officials. The police issued Wilton a criminal summons, taking his fingerprints right there in front of his entire congregation while the rest of his staff was threatened with "physical arrest."[64] Wilton's crime? Using microphones and amplification equipment that exceeded 60 decibels, equivalent to the sound of a typical conversation or a dishwasher.[65]

Doing his best to comply with the city's demands, which had been prompted by the complaints of a neighbor, Wilton hired sound technicians and resisted using any amplifier equipment. But his best efforts proved insufficient. Wilton's Sunday service was again interrupted when six police vehicles pulled up, and seven law enforcement officials, including the sheriff, entered the church.[66] Wilton quickly told the men that he had avoided any use of amplifier equipment, but the officers demanded to inspect the premises, finding only unplugged and idle equipment.[67] Wilton was nevertheless issued a second summons for noise above 60 decibels.

Pointing to a glaring double standard, First Liberty attorney Justin Butterfield told Charisma News, "The parish allows lawn mowers and jackhammers starting at 8 a.m. on Sunday while placing the burdensome restrictions on the church."[68] Litigation is ongoing as the church that provided hope to so many in the aftermath of Hurricane Katrina fights to keep its doors open.[69]

The Home

It was a peaceful November evening at Mary Anne Sause's apartment in Louisburg, Kansas, but it soon turned into "one of the worst nights of my life," in her words.[70] Sause, a retired Catholic nurse, lived by herself and grew nervous when she heard loud banging on her door. Unable to see through her broken peephole, Sause—a rape survivor—feared letting in the two men, who did not identify themselves.[71] They left, only to return and demand entry again. Realizing finally that the two men were police officers, she obliged and let them inside. When they asked why she had not let them in initially, Mary Anne handed the men a pocket Constitution.[72] "That's just a piece of paper . . . doesn't work here," the men replied.

Mary Anne would provide a disturbing account of what happened next in the lawsuit she would file: The officers offered no explanation for being there and said that Mary Anne should prepare to go to jail. Mary Anne asked for the reason, and one officer answered, "I don't know yet."[73] Mary Anne asked if she could pray, and with the consent of one officer she got down on her knees and prayed to God. The second officer took notice and demanded she "get up" and "stop praying." She complied, but the officers charged her with "interference with law enforcement for refusing to open her door" and "disorderly conduct."[74]

In June of 2017, the Tenth Circuit dismissed Sause's case, finding that even if the officers violated Sause's First Amendment rights, the police officers are barred from liability due to a special protection called qualified immunity.[75] First Liberty's Jeremy Dys stated, "No one should face the prospect of being arrested for praying in their own home."[76] A simple response to a complaint that Sause's radio was too loud devolved into a grave issue of religious infringement in the most intimate of places: the home.[77]

★　★　★　★

The cases that First Liberty takes on are numerous and increasing, and should be worrisome to people of faith. Stories of religious infringement from First Liberty alone could fill the entirety of this book. In October of 2016, amid the waning days of the presidential election, I heard about one of First Liberty's cases during a sermon at my own church. In a sermon titled "America's Hope" by Dr. Stephen Rummage of Bell Shoals Baptist Church. Rummage advised the congregation to "vote based on policies not personalities," placing the sanctity of human life and religious liberty as the two paramount issues for Christian voting. At the time, the likelihood of the only pro-life candidate in the presidential race, Donald J. Trump, winning the presidency seemed dim, if you listened to the pundits. Without mentioning any specific candidates,

Dr. Rummage reminded us, "Don't lose sight of God's sovereignty." My family and I left the sermon revitalized, knowing that God would guide the hearts and minds of our citizens in the right direction. I kept my sermon notes in my laptop case for the remainder of the 2016 election. Before walking on set at CNN to argue for the values I hold dear, I would inevitably stumble upon those notes as I took out my computer. Every time I would remember what I was fighting for: the right of religious people everywhere to practice their faith.

With religious suppression on the rise, America's faith community felt voiceless in the fall of 2016. But on November 8, 2016, they made sure they were heard. President Trump earned 58 percent of the Protestant vote and 52 percent of the Catholic vote.[78] He outperformed John McCain, Mitt Romney, and President George W. Bush in 2000, earning a greater percentage of both Catholics and Protestants. Only President Bush in 2004 tied Trump among Catholics and beat him by 1 percentage point among Protestants.

"The community of faith voters that had been demonized by the left showed up," Trump's son-in-law and senior adviser, Jared Kushner, told me. They showed up because for too long they had been left behind by their elected officials and actively disparaged or caricatured in the mainstream media. Trump offered to fight for America's faith community by appointing a conservative Supreme Court Justice to replace the valiant warrior we had in Justice Antonin Scalia. In the early days of his presidency, Trump made good on his promise in the nomination and confirmation of Justice Neil Gorsuch.

Despite the president's best efforts, however, the ultimate solution to religious suppression lies beyond government. First Liberty's Mike Berry said, "I don't think we can legislate our way out of this . . . what it's going to take is for Americans to wake up and realize that our constitutional freedoms are only as strong as our willingness to stand [up] for them." The silencing of Americans like Sergeant Rodriguez and Coach Kennedy and Rabbi Rich can be ameliorated in the appointment of freedom-loving judges, but it cannot solve the problem entirely. The answer lies not in government but in the American people. The problem will not ultimately be fixed until our culture is fixed.

"I think there's really a fundamentally very simple solution," said First Liberty senior counsel Jeremy Dys. "The solution to this issue is that Mom and Dad will sit down at the dinner table each night and regularly look their kids in the eyes and say, 'Kids, this is what religious liberty is' . . . [and] tell them the stories of our Founding Fathers." Dys concluded, "Religious liberty, being our first liberty, is the one in which all the rest of our freedoms are built. You remove that and all the other freedoms topple along with it."

When the faithful are forsaken, the freedom of all is forfeited.

Pursuit
of
Happiness

THE CLEANSING WATER

The Flint Water Crisis

---

*"Blessed are those whose transgressions are forgiven, whose sins are covered.
Blessed is the one whose sin the Lord will never count against them."*
—ROMANS 4:7–8

As brown, lead-laden water gushed from the faucets of Flint, Michigan, twenty-eight-year-old Noah Patton, the single father of three, faced yet another affliction in a long line of tragedies. But this time Noah's plight drew the eyes of a watching nation:

"'Our Mouths Were Ajar': Doctor's Fight to Expose Flint's Water Crisis"[1]

"Flint Mother: I'm Worried My Son Will Wake Up Different"[2]

"The Poisoning of an American City"[3]

The headlines appropriately reflected the anguish of a city already ravaged by problems and once labeled one of "America's most dangerous cities."[4]

Noah's youngest daughter, Mercedes, was exposed to lead at the young age of two. "I don't know if she's a crybaby because of the lead. I don't know if she whines because of the lead . . . as of right now, I really don't know the effects yet," Noah told me. "I don't know about lead, but I'm sure they call it poison for a reason."

The level of lead poisoning in the children of Flint was so high that some experts said it was equivalent to children's lead exposure in war-torn countries like Iraq. Dr. Mozhgan Savabieasfahani claims, "The high level of extremely toxic lead in children of Fallujah resembles very much the same amount of lead poisoning in the children of Flint."[5] The consequences of such exposure can be life changing. Lead is linked to "lower IQs, less verbal competence, worse speech processing, and worse attention."[6] In addition to developmental effects and brain damage, lead exposure has been linked to miscarriages, hair loss, and other physical ailments.[7]

In January of 2016, a federal state of emergency was declared in the blighted Michigan city. Two years earlier, the city of Flint had changed its source of water from neighboring Detroit to the Flint River.[8] For decades, the Flint River had received all sorts of toxins from the automotive plants that dotted its shores.[9] Now the lead- and toxin-filled water streamed right through the faucets and showerheads of Flint's homes. Flint residents complained about the putrid, discolored water for eighteen months, but Flint officials assured everyone that the water was perfectly fine.[10] "There are a lot of bigwigs in Flint," Noah told me. "Some people who worked in the city were drinking bottled water before they told us." Although these Michigan Department of Environmental Quality officials claimed the bottled water was provided in response to a city health notice and not because of lead poisoning, residents like Noah are understandably frustrated that they were encouraged to drink from their taps.[11]

But Flint wasn't always a town plagued by problems and forgotten by government. For much of the 1900s, Flint was a booming auto hub, with General Motors employing nearly half of the residents. For many in the African-American community, Flint represented hope.

"My granddad comes from Clarksdale, Mississippi," Noah informed me. "He used to tell me all the time that his granddad was a slave. He showed me a piece of cotton and everything." Noah explained that when his grandparents and great-grandparents lived in the Mississippi Delta, they would pray to God for opportunity. "Places like Flint were made for an African-American gentleman to actually thrive and slam his Cadillac door and pay his bills and, you know, buy land," Noah detailed. "It wasn't nothing like down South. You know, Flint was up North. And it was free, so Flint was the American dream for a black person for a long time."

Flint was the American Dream in large part because companies like

GM were willing to invest. Not only did GM invest in their factory, they invested in the community as a whole. In fact, Noah's childhood home— once vibrant, now vacant—was built by General Motors in 1919. His neighborhood, Civic Park, was the first planned subdivision in Flint. "Our city is beautiful—*was* beautiful," Noah caught himself. "And we got, like, big old homes and everything. Everything is big, but then the shops left out of nowhere." Now foreclosed homes dot the streets. Drifters and drug addicts languish where enterprising families once lived. Schools once buzzing with students stand vacant and decaying. "Once the money left . . . our city just diminished," Noah recalled—right before his very eyes.

At its height, some 80,000 Flint residents worked for GM. Today, just 5,000 Flint inhabitants work for the automotive company.[12] After GM closed, there was a mass exodus out of Flint. More than 100,000 people fled the area, leaving Flint with a population of just over 97,000.[13] In addition to being one of the most crime-ridden cities in America, Flint is also one of the poorest, with more than 40 percent of residents living in poverty.[14]

"The feeling of depression is still around Flint," Noah said. "If I didn't know God, I would be like everyone else running around here, feeling like we living in the end of time. That's what it feels like when you walk through Flint. You don't have any clean drinking water. Every house but two houses on the street is abandoned. At least five people get killed every other day." In fact, a young man and fellow church member portrayed in a short film about Noah's life was killed at age twenty-seven, shortly after filming was completed.[15] The devastation in Flint closely mirrored the personal affliction that racked Noah's early years of life. But for Noah an encounter with the poisoned water of Flint would change his life forever.

★   ★   ★   ★

On Wednesday, November 13, 2003, fifteen-year-old Noah Patton lazily opened his big brown eyes as light poured into his white-walled, window-filled childhood home. It seemed like just another ordinary day: school and breakfast with his three siblings and mother crowded around the kitchen table. But today was not ordinary. Far from it. It was a day he would never forget, a day that would send his life into a downward spiral.

But, you see, Noah was aptly named after a biblical character like his three siblings and dozens of his cousins. Noah was well suited for the youngest Patton son. In the infamous Genesis account, Noah's ark saves him from the deadly waters that flooded the earth and rid it of violence and corruption. A similar torrential storm was heading the teenage Noah's way, one filled with death, suicide, guns, violence, and drugs. Even though literal floodwaters were not approaching Noah's Flint home, poisonous water of another kind was. And unfortunately, at least at first, Noah would not have an ark to save him.

As Noah got ready that Wednesday morning, his sister abruptly entered his room. "We can't go to school today," she told her brother. "Mom is feeling depressed." Noah's mom, Lynn, suffered from manic depression. But after several stints in the hospital, she seemed to have overcome the illness. With big black-rimmed glasses dominating her petite face, Noah and his siblings jokingly called their mother, a former Navy sailor turned stay-at-home mom, "Dexter" from Dexter's Laboratory.[16]

Noah's dad worked at General Motors, the lifeblood of Noah's hometown of Flint. Noah's parents constantly fought. "By the time that I was born . . . my dad was pretty much done with the whole situation . . . when GM left, he left with GM," Noah said.

Noah's dad still works at GM to this day. "I never had a relationship with him, none whatsoever," Noah told me. "I think I met him one time for thirty minutes when I was, like, seven."

With Noah's dad absent, his grandfather, Roy, stepped in to fill the role of father. Noah, his brother, and his two sisters would live with their grandparents during his mom's trips to the hospital. "That was how we got most of our learning about the Bible," Noah said. As a Bible scholar and man of deep faith, Roy instilled in his grandchildren a love for Jesus Christ and a trove of biblical teachings.

Every Sunday, Noah and his siblings would load up their grandfather's minivan with Bible tracts. The kids would then pile into the vehicle and fill the mailboxes of Flint with little booklets that explained the Christian faith. As Noah and his siblings walked the streets each week, handing out biblical literature, his grandfather would trail closely behind. "We were in the middle of the hood," Noah told me. "But he followed us, so nobody messed with us." After the family finished their missionary work, Noah's grandfather would treat the kids to a meal at Burger King before returning home for evening Bible study.

"That's when Flint was full of houses," Noah reminisced. Today, Flint is full of abandoned buildings and broken dreams. Forty percent of its residents live in poverty as they face the infamous lead poisoning water crisis that dominated the headlines in 2016. But when Noah was a kid, Flint had promise. Now, just pain.

Noah's personal pain started on that memorable Wednesday when he stayed home from school to care for his mom, who began pacing their family home back and forth and talking to herself. She spent Wednesday night in the hospital but left the very next morning. On that tragic Thursday, Noah remembers being in the kitchen and watching his mom cook tacos. She was mumbling to herself and singing gospel songs before pausing to give Noah instructions. "Don't look up, but look for the cameras," she told him. Realizing that she was still in a delusional state, Noah kissed his mom on the head and replied, "OK, Mom. You're losing it, but I love you. I'm going upstairs."

"It scared the crap out of me, because I thought she was saying maybe there was cameras in the house or something like that. You know what's funny?" Noah said to me. "After she passed, somebody told me maybe she was talking about the movie cameras." It was long before Noah would become the subject of a short *National Geographic* film, but his mom seemed to have some kind of intuition.[17] After having that last conversation with his mom, Noah joined his brother and sister in his room. The three siblings sat around the bedroom turned makeshift music studio when their stepdad suddenly appeared at the bottom of the stairs. "Call an ambulance!" he yelled.

Noah bolted from his room. As he descended the staircase, the young teenage boy had a haunting suspicion that his mom had committed suicide. "As I got down to the kitchen, I began to smell the gunpowder . . .

it smelled like a firecracker. God was just preparing me for what I was about to see," Noah believes. "As I hit the corner, I see my mom laid back on the bed with a gunshot wound to her head."

A cascade of tears poured out of Noah's eyes as he took in the sight of his fallen mother. Noah's sister followed just behind him and let out a piercing scream. Her cry reverberated around the house as she shook her mom's body. Although Noah's mom was still alive and evidently clinging to life, she was brain-dead and unable to speak. Petrified, Noah fled the scene, hiding around the corner at his best friend's house. Noah's world had been turned upside down. His grandfather had passed. His dad was out of the picture. And now his mother was gone.

"It hurt so bad. Mom, why would you leave us? Why would you leave us here?" Noah asked in his *National Geographic* film.[18] From that day forward, discord enveloped the parentless family. Noah's siblings fought constantly. "I was forced to kind of, like, fend on my own in the house," Noah related. Eventually his siblings moved out, and Noah found himself in a silent home without running water, heat, or electricity.[19] He was sixteen and entirely alone.

"I waited," Noah told the film crew of his documentary. "I thought my brothers and sisters were going to come back home, and the lights were going to be back on one day, and it was going to be just like the day before Mama passed. It never happened."[20] When Noah turned seventeen, he briefly moved in with his grandmother, the only parent figure he had left. Six months later Noah turned eighteen, became an adult, and returned to live alone in the crumbling, abandoned family home in the heart of Flint. He fell into a seven-year pit of hopelessness and crime until a stint in jail and a step in faith changed his life.

★　★　★　★

"I was always a soldier, but I was a soldier in the wrong army," Noah told *National Geographic*.[21] That's how Noah describes the period of his life when he descended into crime and self-destruction. "I was riding down the road, smoking weed," he explained. "I had to keep a gun because I was always either getting over on somebody or somebody wanted to shoot my house up." Noah's home got shot up so often that he kept an AK-47 and a MAK-90 submachine gun with a seventy-five-round magazine wind-up drum on it for protection. Noah recalls watching his toddler children step over his AK-47, prominently displayed in his kitchen, as they scurried toward the breakfast table each morning.[22] "I had a fascination for guns," he said. Noah was so proud the day he got his first .40-caliber. "I picked up that gun every day and checked it and talked about my .40s," he recalled. He vividly remembers his four-year-old son picking up the gun and pointing it at his dad. "Here, Dad, here goes your .40," the young child said, mimicking his father's actions. "That was one of the first wake-up calls for me. Although it would take a lot more before I got the message," Noah told me. "I can never forget that morning."

To make money, Noah started "scrapping"—removing copper and aluminum pipes from the slew of vacant houses in Flint. He also bought and sold firearms illegally. "I was like a walking pawnshop," he said. At the age of eighteen he got arrested for the first time when he was caught stealing aluminum siding. He had several other run-ins with the law after that: operating a chop shop, where stolen vehicles were quickly disassembled for their parts; possession of marijuana; fleeing a police officer; two high-speed chases; and two standoffs with the police. "Literally, the police [were] outside. I'm in the house. I've got my gun. They've got their gun. I did that twice," Noah said.

Noah quickly became known as the rich guy in Flint. He ran the chop shop in his backyard. It was a lucrative endeavor, but when the police noticed all the stripped-down cars behind Noah's house, it eventually earned him one hundred days in jail. "I've got pictures of me in a 1980-something Mercedes-Benz, and I had over seventy-something cars," Noah said. "I was determined to be successful. I still had all the aggression in me from what my mom did." Being well-off in Flint made Noah a target in town. He knew his days were numbered, and he said he was "ready to die in the streets."[23]

But even though Noah briefly lost his way, that faithful young boy was still buried inside him, urging him to come back home to God. "I had a lot of teaching in me," Noah said. "I knew what I was doing wrong, but I was doing it to get to the next level. I just didn't know what next level I was getting to." Noah's Bible-based roots crept up even during the rough period in his life. Although he smoked weed, he refused to try any other drugs. "I wouldn't allow anybody to sell drugs out of the house because the house was where I learned all my Bible scriptures," Noah emphasized. His grandpa's library of Christian books still sat adjacent to where Noah slept. Everyone had to respect his family home.

"I prayed to God before I would go do something stupid . . . And I actually made it home safe," Noah said. One time a bullet broke through Noah's window and hit his couch. When he went to retaliate, he only managed to shoot once before the gun jammed.[24] "God's always seen a way out of it. I've never been shot. I've never been stabbed. It just seemed like God had a purpose for me." And he did.

★ ★ ★ ★

"I was working for Satan and didn't know it," Noah remarked to me. "In my mind I thought that I'm surviving. You know, it's not my fault that I got left with no parents, so I'm just going to do what I've gotta do. Anybody get in my way, oh, well, they're going to catch my wrath." Young men in Noah's neighborhood recognized his financial success and haughty attitude, and they looked up to him as a role model. "All of them would run up to my car because they know I was the guy who used to have nothing at fifteen and sixteen, and now I got rims and the biggest clip and I got a bunch of money. I was promoting bad," Noah lamented.

When Noah went to jail for his chop shop operation, he befriended another inmate. Both men were barreling toward destruction but agreed in jail that they would leave as new men, putting their criminal pasts behind them. "I need to use you," Noah heard God telling him in jail. "If I let you out, you have to work for me." Noah started to realize that God had a purpose for him, but how could God possibly use him? He still had an open case for selling illegal guns, which carried a possible two-year prison sentence.

When Noah finished his hundred-day jail sentence, instead of leaving reformed, he returned to his old ways and reneged on his decision to change. Months later, Noah encountered his former jail mate. Something was different about him.

"Man, how you staying out trouble?" Noah asked.

"I just be at the church," his friend told him.

Intrigued by his friend's conversion, Noah began volunteering at Joy Tabernacle, a tiny yellow-brick church with a dozen or so brown pews. "That right there started the process of changing me," Noah said. Within weeks of volunteering and after seven years of a life filled with crime, Noah Patton gave his life to God. He soon realized his purpose: to show the young men who looked up to him there was a better way to live.

"I took my calling as a preacher out of nowhere, with pending charges," Noah pointed out as he let out a slight disbelieving laugh. "I'm serious: with pending charges, on my way to prison!" We both laughed at the contrast between prison and preaching, but the juxtaposition wasn't foreign at all to our shared Christian faith. After all, God used the imperfect to bring about revolutionary change: Moses killed a man before leading the Israelites out of Egypt; Peter denied Jesus three times before becoming the rock of the church; and Paul persecuted Christians before authoring much of the New Testament. The idea that Noah could go from prison to preacher was the very meaning of Christian redemption.

"I hold a lot of guilt," Noah admitted. "I sold a lot of people guns and stuff, and they got killed or, you know, they ended up in jail. And my image was so messed up that I kind of was scared to move on and be a preacher." One day Noah had a breakdown: "I was feeling kind of bad. Scared to move forward with the kids and kind of feeling all of the weight of not having nobody and scared to go to jail and everything." But his preacher offered wise words. "You've got to let go and let God," the preacher advised, before physically washing Noah's hands with Flint water.

The irony could not be starker. Here was dirty, lead-tainted Flint water—ruined by man and rejected by all—cleansing the hands of Noah Patton of all of his wrongdoing. What man had destroyed, God used for good. "It symbolically washed away all my pain. It washed away all the

things I did in my hands, all the things I stole, all the things I took—
everything." Noah marveled. "It just became a symbol of restoration in
my life because I don't have a father. I hadn't had anybody to care about
what I did with my hands."

It was so simple and yet so meaningful. Just as the waters in Genesis
had wiped away a corrupt and violent earth, the water of Flint purified
Noah's hands, removing his past transgressions and renewing him in
the eyes of the Lord. The biblical name Noah's parents had bestowed on
him now seemed all the more fitting: God had given the biblical Noah a
vessel for rescue and the modern-day one a savior for redemption.

"That was so instrumental to my changing . . . [My preacher] just
had to do something as simple as say, 'You free. You know I'm washing
your hands for free. You don't have to worry about the past. Just let go
and let God change.' And I did it, and God is doing it."

When Noah turned back to God, all of the bad in his life seemed to
fall away, though not initially. The mother of his three children left town
with the kids, and Noah became depressed, alone in his house and without his children. But even through his struggle, he stayed in the church
and leaned into God. "The next thing you know, I end up getting my
kids because she ended up abandoning [them]," Noah said. "Keep in
mind, I still have pending charges." Because Noah had outstanding light
bills that he couldn't pay, he and his three children resorted to using
candles. "I had illegal lights. Kids. The water crisis . . . And I was worried about going to jail," Noah recalled. "But I still went to church every
Sunday. I still read my Bible. I still taught Sunday school. I preached my
first service. I was still basically walking with God."

Then, seemingly out of nowhere, a once-in-a-lifetime opportunity
came Noah Patton's way. The Community Foundation visited Noah's
church, seeking to film the life of someone struggling through Flint.
They selected Noah. His mother's final words to him, "Don't look up,
but look for the cameras," suddenly made sense. "The day before the
film crew came, a warrant popped up for my arrest for the two-year
prison charge," Noah said. Conflicted over whether to turn himself in
immediately or shoot the movie first, Noah decided to share his story.
"I don't know if you notice in the movie, but I had a hood on," he re-

marked. "I was wanted for a warrant that happened two years before that. I had already changed everything good in my mind, my heart, in everything. But that warrant popped up out of nowhere."

In addition to the warrant, Noah's probation officer finally gave him a court date for one of his high-speed chases. Noah pleaded for a delay in the court appearance. "I understand you're doing good now and the case is old, so I'll give you some time. I'll give you until the twentieth of June to turn yourself in," the man graciously offered. With an outstanding warrant, Noah took a risk by being filmed. "Even if I did have to go to prison, I was going to be able to touch somebody's life and let them know that they don't have to go through this. I was trusting in God," he acknowledged. Noah's riveting documentary, filmed by Dana Romanoff and published by *National Geographic*, was featured on YouTube, where it has touched the lives of more than thirty thousand people and counting. God was working through Noah even when he couldn't see it.

On Father's Day, Noah's son got baptized, and on the very next day Noah turned himself in to the police. "In my mind, I'm about to go ahead and do these two years. When I get out, I'm going to be a better person, and so I went to jail," Noah explained. Noah spent the whole summer in jail, mentally preparing himself for the prison sentence that likely awaited him. "I was really just walking by faith," he said. He faced a daunting five felony charges and significant prison time. But God had others plans.

Noah's church and many reputable members of the community wrote letters to the prosecutor, attesting to Noah's changed life. It made a difference. "To God be the glory, I didn't have to go to prison!" Noah exclaimed. When Noah arrived at court, instead of two years in prison, he was given two years' probation. "That never happens," Noah pointed out. "If you're a felon in Michigan and you get caught with a firearm, it's two years minimum—no ifs, ands, or buts about it. But the prosecutor had favor on me." Supporters of Noah's movie bonded him out, and Noah was now free to continue walking down the path God had laid before him. "When I got out of jail, the movie finally came out, and I didn't have to go to prison. I got full custody of my kids," Noah gleefully stated. "I'm just a living testimony from that part on." Like his biblical namesake, "Noah found favor in the eyes of the Lord."[25]

★   ★   ★   ★

Noah found strength within himself to overcome an abandoned home, poverty, and a life of crime. While he took responsibility for his actions, the same cannot be said for the government in the wake of the Flint water crisis. It was a twenty-first-century betrayal of epic proportions, and accountability was notably absent. Democrats blamed the Republican governor, while Republicans blamed the Democratic Environmental Protection Agency.

The blame game between parties bothered me, leading me to say this on CNN's set after the Democratic primary presidential debate in Flint: "This shouldn't be a political issue . . . When you have poisonous water in Flint, Michigan, this happens in third world countries. This doesn't happen in the United States of America. We need to get to the bottom of it. Whatever party official, you're out . . . and you should resign if you knew about it."[26] Instead of putting party aside and people first, politicians pointed fingers. In the end, the regional EPA chief and the state director of Michigan Department on Environmental Quality resigned amid criticism.[27] "All those bigwigs run together, I'm pretty sure," said Noah, placing blame on both the government and the automotive industry that contributed to polluting the Flint River.

Both 2016 presidential candidates acknowledged the crisis in Flint. "The people of Flint deserve to know the truth about how this happened," Hillary Clinton said.

Standing in a Flint church, Donald Trump remarked, "It used to be that cars were made in Flint and you couldn't drink the water in Mexico. Now cars are made in Mexico, and you can't drink the water in Flint. That's terrible."[28] But neither pitch got Noah's vote. He chose to sit out the 2016 election.

"I didn't trust neither one of the candidates, to tell you the truth. I didn't," Noah told me. "Because I mean we're talking about the government"—the same government that instructed Noah and his family to drink the water. "It was safe," they claimed. "So in my mind the government is corrupt altogether, so I trust in God," he explained. "I pray for government, and I trust in God."

Betrayed by government and left behind by big business, the residents of Flint, Michigan, are left to pick up the pieces of their broken city. How does a broken inner city without hope move forward? "I think the answer is the residents," Noah suggested. "The people that live in Flint should start basically venturing out in a positive manner and rebuild the city ourselves . . . Let's buy our own grocery stores . . . We need to own our own banks . . . We need to start our own businesses."

"Exactly," said Ben Carson, secretary of Housing and Urban Development (HUD), when I shared Noah's outlook with him. "When you start thinking the way you just described . . . you're going to find a way out. You're going to find a way to develop your talents. You're going to find out how to help people around you develop theirs, and you're going to be thinking more in terms of what you can do rather than what you can't do. It makes all the difference in the world in terms of how you approach something."

In this vein, Reverend Reginald Flynn, pastor of Foss Avenue Baptist Church and North Flint Reinvestment Corp, is trying to open a locally owned grocery store.[29] Noah himself is in small-business boot camp and just accepted a loan from the city to start his own lawn care service. His new venture cuts the yards of vacant lots, transforming the visible decay in Flint.[30] Lawn by lawn, Noah is reviving his Flint community. Noah suspects that government looks at his community and thinks, *They're killing each other already. There's nothing we can do.* "The people need to stick together," he said. "I think when people in Flint start to wake up and say, 'Hey, they're treating us like slaves. Let's buy ourselves our freedom,' I think that would help."

This, of course, does not mean that there is no role for government in urban renewal. Secretary Carson explained, "The government should be focused on how to develop human capital . . . They can do things like encourage public-private partnerships by creating win-win situations." This means incentivizing big business to invest in blighted areas, looking from a thirty-thousand-foot view and connecting willing investors with populations of people in need of opportunity. Under Carson's leadership, HUD is utilizing an underused government program called Section 3. Section 3 mandates that beneficiaries of certain HUD funding hire local, low-income individuals, train them, and offer contracts to their businesses.[31] "It has largely not been used over the fifty years that it's been on the books," Carson said. "We are now putting a major push on using that." For decades, contractors claimed that they were unable to participate in Section 3 because local residents did not have enough training. Carson maintains that there is a very simple answer to that: advance notice to contractors and training programs for residents. "It simply means that you have to think ahead," Carson said. "You know a year or two or three ahead of time that you're going to do that, so you train them then, and they're ready to go at that time and they have marketable skills that allow them to escape dependency. It's not a matter of how many people you can get in public housing, it's how many you can get out of it."

I asked Noah what he would say to the federal government if he had the chance. Here's what he wants his leaders to know: "Nobody wants to be a failure, but when you're raised around a fallen environment, it becomes natural to fall. And Flint has some residents that just haven't given up, that just have enough fight in them to say, 'I might have messed up in the past—like you see this tattoo on my face and now I'm a preacher—but, hey, I want to live. I want to be successful. I was young. I didn't know better.' I think the government needs to know that."

Rather than dismissing an entire segment of society as lazy or unmotivated, Americans in general ought to recognize the fighting spirit that still resides in the heart of many Flint residents. Even though people may lose their way, they are not hopeless. "It takes time for people to grow up. It takes time for people to grow out of depression. It takes time for people to grow out of being abused and neglected," Noah said. "And now that we're growing out of it, we deserve a push to help us get where we need to go because all the odds was against us for so long . . . and now that we see better and we want different, we need help with changing our past for the future."

I shared Noah's message with Secretary Carson, who understood it all too well. He grew up just over an hour away from Noah, in Detroit. His dad left when he was young, abandoning Carson, his brother, and his mom. Stuck in an impoverished community and a seven-

hundred-square-foot single-parent home, Carson refused to let his surroundings determine his future. Thanks in large part to his mother,
Carson overcame the odds, earning his undergraduate degree from Yale
University and an MD from the University of Michigan Medical School
before doing his internship and residency at the nation's most selective
medical school, Johns Hopkins. At the age of twenty-three, he became
the nation's youngest chief of pediatric neurosurgery. Describing his
mom, Sonya, Carson fondly stated, "She refused to be a victim. She refused to allow us to be victims. That was probably the greatest thing that
she gave to us."

★　★　★　★

Even though Noah's future was uncertain at times, his unwavering faith
in his Father in Heaven was not. When Noah grew up, he recited the
Twenty-Third Psalm every night with his brother and sisters. It reads,
in part:

> *The Lord is my shepherd, I lack nothing.*
> *He makes me lie down in green pastures,*
> *he leads me beside quiet waters,*
> *he refreshes my soul.*
> *He guides me along the right paths for his name's sake.*
> *Even though I walk through the darkest valley,*
> *I will fear no evil, for you are with me;*
> *your rod and your staff, they comfort me.*

Noah grew up lacking much in the eyes of the world—little money,
a broken community, crime-ridden streets—but he was taught by his
grandfather to say he lacked nothing. And Noah did walk through the
"darkest valley": a fatherless home, a mother who took her own life,
and a once-bustling home full of siblings now empty. But Noah's faith
in something bigger than this earthly life helped him overcome his past
and defy the odds in building a prosperous future.

Now, instead of praying the Twenty-Third Psalm every night, Noah
prays the "Our Father" with his children. When Noah faced the daunt-

ing prospect of a life in prison, his faith gave him the strength to keep fighting, for himself and for his children. Taking a knee in between his kids' twin beds, Noah worried he would have to leave them behind for a life behind bars. With only a candle for light, he nevertheless began to pray.

"Our Father . . ."

"Our Father . . ." his three little babies echoed behind him.[32]

". . . who art in heaven . . ." he continued.

". . . who art in heaven . . ." the three little ones repeated.

". . . hallowed be thy name . . ." Noah said.

Noah, of course, never did have to go to prison, and he continues to pray that prayer with his children every night. "That's just to keep them in the mind-set," he said. "You know, they watched me go to sleep every day listening to gangsta rap and smoking weed, so now I have to reset their minds and reset the vision of where we're going in our life. I didn't have a vision, I didn't have goals, so by praying and taking them to church and everything like that, I'm giving them hope for a future. I'm letting them know this is what [we're] riding with now."

Noah aims to shepherd in the right direction not only his children but his neighbors as well. He has shared his story far and wide, but never for money or fame. "It's not for my recognition," Noah said. "I really want the young man that's standing outside the corner store trying to sell a bag of weed . . . to know that it's not the end of time. You can stop right then and there, and God will pick you up and bring you into the next day."

There is one thing that Noah wants people to know about Flint: "We've been survivors since day one."[33] While Flint might be down, they're not out. It is a city full of fighters and, despite its troubles, a wellspring of faith. Though lead-filled, poison liquid flowed from the faucets of Flint, the cleansing eternal waters of change transformed the heart of one man, Noah Patton, who is in turn changing the hearts and minds of those around him. Just as in the story of Noah's ark, there is always a rainbow just beyond the unforeseen waters that flood our lives.

THE BETRAYAL

Jobs

"Labor is prior to and independent of capital. Capital is only the fruit of labor, and could never have existed if labor had not first existed. Labor is the superior of capital, and deserves much higher consideration."
—ABRAHAM LINCOLN

On February 10, 2016, Brian Easton pulled into work an hour early, just as he had done every day for the past twenty-five years. The big, burly, blue-eyed man entered the large beige warehouse beneath a soaring American flag. It was the same factory that his wife worked at and his two kids too. He got his coffee, inventoried his parts, and prepared for a hard day's work. But something was different today. *That's weird,* he thought as he observed a platform that had been erected near the front of the room. Not thinking too much of it, Brian continued with his normal routine.

T. J. Bray also arrived at Carrier's furnace plant in Indianapolis that chilly Wednesday morning, the same company that five of his aunts and uncles had dedicated 125 years of their working lives to. Carrying on the family tradition, T.J. joined his two cousins in working at the plant. "It was kind of meant for me to work there . . . I've almost been there half my life," the friendly thirty-three-year-old midwesterner told me as he reflected on his fifteen years of work. "It's the only adult job I've ever had," he said. "I graduated high school on May 22, and my first night of work was May 21, so I had to miss my second night of work to get my diploma." Missing work was rare for T. J. Bray. Rain or snow, bronchitis or flu, it didn't matter: T.J. always showed up for work. It was in his DNA.

T.J. remembers when his mom briskly woke him up one morning as a freshman in high school. "There's something wrong with your dad," she told him. Rushing into the other room, T.J. arrived to find his dad lying on the floor in a pool of blood. "It looked like a murder scene," he recalled.

"Get me up," his dad implored, fighting against the crimson liquid that his body exuded. "I'll get in the shower and head to work."

"You probably lost 20 percent of your blood. You're not going to work!" T.J. replied.

"No. no. I'm good."

"Let's help him up," T.J.'s mom insisted.

The fourteen-year-old T.J. helped his husky, six-foot-one-inch father to his feet and they waited for an ambulance. At the hospital Terry Bray found out that he had a ruptured ulcer, a potentially life-threatening condition if left untreated.

Unconcerned with the news, Terry asked the doctor, "Can I get a phone? I've gotta tell my boss I'm going to be late."

"Buddy, you're probably not going to be at work for a while," the doctor replied.

"When am I going to get out of here so I can go back to work?" T.J.'s father repeatedly asked.

T.J. vividly remembers his dad's disappointment at his inability to return to work. Mr. Bray worked for Federal Express his whole life, and T.J.'s mom started out as a waitress at Steak 'n Shake in the 1970s. Spending decades with the fast-food joint, Rhonda became a manager and then a district manager before finally earning a spot on the corporate side of the company. "She never called in sick," T.J. said. "There were no off days for her and my dad." It's memories like these that instilled in T.J. a relentless work ethic.

Brian Easton, T.J. 's coworker and friend, was cut from the same cloth. On June 7, 2014, Brian had an ACL replacement, a surgery that keeps most people inactive for six months.[1] On July 7 of that same year, he had spinal fusion surgery on his L4 and L5 vertebrae, another major surgery that can cause pain for up to six months.[2] Despite two serious operations, Brian was back on his feet at the Indiana plant on August 7, exactly one month later. "It was hell for six months," Brian said.

T.J. and Brian were tough, high-caliber workers and they were loyal. But on that February morning, they found out that loyalty only ran one way. Just before 10:00 a.m., T.J. received a text from the union president. "Hey, I need everyone up front right now. I've got bad news." T.J. dropped what he was doing and barreled toward the front of the room. As he made his way to the gathering of union stewards, he could hear a voice over the PA system calling every department up front, one factory line at a time. *Something ain't right here,* he thought.

T.J. approached the small group of union leaders and noticed the same stage that Brian had curiously observed earlier that morning. Big event-style speakers sat on either side of the stage, where roughly two dozen suited men stood waiting. A rope separated the indifferent corporate suits from the growing crowd of workers. Security guys stood watch with guns firmly planted on their hips.

As T.J. joined the group, blissfully unprepared for the news he was about to hear, Brian's radio blared: "Tell all the forklift drivers to pull up, get off their fork trucks, and head up front." Brian and his fellow group leaders then got additional instructions. "Tell all the press operators to shut down their presses," the voice demanded. "They shut down all the lines," Brian recalled. A bustling factory now stood motionless.

Brian encountered a high-level boss during his walk to the stage. "As soon as I saw his face, I knew what was going on," Brian said. "He looks like he saw a ghost." Not wanting to ask a question that would prompt an unwanted answer, Brian nevertheless probed his supervisor: "What's up?" "Just go up there," the man replied. Brian knew in his heart what was about to happen. As he made his way up front, Brian's sister called him on his cell phone. "Are they hiring yet?" she asked, inquiring on behalf of her niece. Carrier started hiring in the spring, and they always prioritized family first.

"I don't think that's a good idea. I think we're getting ready to lose our jobs," Brian answered.

"No way."

"Yeah, I think we're getting ready to lose our jobs," Brian repeated.

Across the room, the union president told the blue-collar union stewards huddled alongside a few dozen disaffected suits: "They're getting ready to tell these people their jobs are going to Mexico." T.J.'s heart sank.

"What?!" they all said in disbelief.

"OK, that's not funny," one union steward countered.

"We thought it was a joke," T.J. recounted.

"No, I am dead serious," the union president sadly replied.

T.J.'s thoughts immediately turned from himself—a husband and dad of two—to his coworkers. He had just taken the position as their union steward two short weeks earlier, and now he was burdened with delivering the terrible news. *I have to text as many of my coworkers as I can,* T.J. thought.

"I was trying to get it to everybody before they heard it from that guy," T.J. said. "I've got a lot of family there." He texted his cousins and friends, receiving replies like *No they're not* and *BS.* Brian was among those who received a text from T.J. *We're closing down,* the message read. *Oh my God,* Brian thought as he tried to process his confirmed suspicion. His entire family would be losing their jobs.

With a crowd full of men and women in sweatpants, ball caps, and T-shirts standing before him, the man in the crisp suit and tie took to the stage. He calmly began to deliver his prepared remarks. Wanting to capture the moment, T.J. kept his phone down by his waist and began filming. Even though filming wasn't allowed, one young woman held her phone high in the air in defiance, capturing the corporate official's every move and every word.

As he built up to those unwelcome words, the room grew eerily silent. In a monotone voice, the man stated, "The best way to stay competitive and protect the business for the long term is to move production from our facility in Indianapolis to Monterrey, Mexico." The crowd instantly erupted into impassioned boos and jeers. "You f***ing sellout!" Brian cried out repeatedly in a booming voice. One man put his hand over his mouth in visible shock, while another man in a Pittsburgh Steelers beanie and safety glasses left the scene in apparent frustration.

While the audience reacted in audible confusion, grief, and outrage, the man on the stage impatiently stated, "Listen, I've got information that's important to share. If you don't want to hear it, other people do, so let's quiet down." Shouts and boos continued across the room as 1,400 Americans learned that they would be losing their jobs in what was "strictly a business decision." After giving the loyal employees a mere two minutes to take in their new reality, the man reminded the crowd, "Throughout the transition, we must remain committed to manufacturing the same high-quality products" before admonishing, "Once again, please quiet down."

A subsequent speaker told the crowd that they would have the remainder of the day off, but most of the workers just stood around in shock, hugging and crying. T.J. stayed for a while before rushing out of the factory in the hopes of telling his wife he had lost his job before she saw it on the news. After hearing the news, T.J.'s wife left work and suggested the couple meet at Chili's for a beer. When T.J. got to the well-known bar and grill, the first thing he did was post the audio he captured on Facebook with the caption "Wow. 14 years down the drain."

"I was hurt," Brian said. "And I'm not going to lie. You know, I made it until I got home that day." When Brian returned to his house that Wednesday afternoon, the big, burly hunter with bulky tattooed arms cried his eyes out. "I went in the house. I went up there to the spare bedroom and shut the door and cried like a little baby." After fifteen minutes he regained his composure and went back out to his family.

"Just calm down. It's going to be OK. We're going to figure something out," his wife reassured him.

Brian was proud to work at Carrier. He had attended college for one year and quickly realized that it just wasn't for him. When he got hired on at Carrier in 1997, he thought to himself, *I can move up around here. This doesn't just have to be a job. This can be a career.* Within five years he became a press operator. Within seven, a fab tech. And within eleven he became a group leader in the fabrication department.

During his time at Carrier, Brian eagerly did anything his supervisor asked him to do. He volunteered to test every new product, a sometimes arduous task. He took classes on lean manufacturing and learned how to set up lines. "I did it because I wanted the place that I work at to be successful. Not only did *I* want to be successful, but I wanted *them* to be successful," he explained. "But then, to find out in the end they want to be successful but they don't give two shits about us . . . you know that's tough." Brian's hurt eventually turned to apprehension. "I was nervous. I was scared," he said.

It wasn't just individuals who were scared but entire families. "Everybody there just about has got a family member working there," Brian explained. "I mean, heck, the Thermans—"

T.J. interjected: "The Thermans, the Brookens. I mean. they've got four or five brothers and sisters that all work there."

While some families learned their fates that morning in a face-to-face interaction, the night-shift workers learned from Facebook, text messages, or their local news before officially finding out that night during a meeting of their own. T.J.'s phone lit up with text messages all day and night. *Is this true?* they asked.

For years the workers at Carrier had heard rumors: maybe one day Carrier would go to Mexico. But there were no indications that February 10, 2016, was the day. On the contrary, all the writing on the wall suggested Carrier was staying right there in Indianapolis. Over the last five years the company had spent millions of dollars investing in the facility: refurbished lines, new equipment, renovated office areas, modern furniture, and flat-screen TVs. "They spent millions of dollars just on epoxy floor," Brian remembers. On top of the investment, the Carrier factory was winning awards for its parent company, UTC—quality awards, industrial awards, environmental awards. Every year management told the workers, "You're UTC's gold standard, making record profits." Thinking back, T.J. reflected, "Why would we think anything was wrong when we're making record profits?"

In the intervening months, T.J. and Brian both grappled with hurt, anger, and even self-blame. "You look at the decisions you've made in life," Brian said. "You've alienated yourself just to this one path. Factory workers are a dying breed. Why have I done this to myself?" By Brian's estimate, there have been at least thirty major manufacturing facilities that have left Indianapolis since the late 1980s, maybe more. Including the smaller factories, that number is probably closer to one hundred, he thinks.

Two weeks before the announcement, T.J. began to question his path. "What have I done in my life?" he asked. "I worked at a factory. Like, if I die right now, what would people say? What did I do in my life?" As T.J. wondered about his career choice, the union asked him to become a union steward. After some hesitation, TJ agreed to a role that would set him on an unforgettable journey.

When Carrier made the unwelcome announcement on that brisk winter morning, they told the workers that there would be no impact on jobs until 2017, providing them more than a year's notice. "It was a curse and a blessing that they did that," T.J. said. "It was a blessing because we had a year and a half to figure out what to do next, but a curse because you're just standing around, waiting for your funeral." Unbeknownst to T.J., it was a funeral that would never come. T.J. was about to become a national figure, and the intervention of a presidential candidate would change everything.

"Something put me on this path. I was questioning," T.J. said. "If I die tomorrow, my kids will have all these newspaper clippings and photos of stuff I've done. And they can say, 'Man, look: Dad stood up for something he believed in.'"

★   ★   ★   ★

When the callous corporate official announced to a room full of Carrier workers that they were losing their jobs, he was likely unaware of the young woman filming just beyond the stage. And the young woman filming was admittedly unaware of the momentous reaction her video would provoke. In just one night three million people viewed that video, taken from the phone of a Carrier employee and posted on YouTube. Brian can be heard screaming his terse "F***ing sellouts!"

"I still can't watch the video," T.J. told me during our first conversation. "I have to turn away." The video brings back the stomach-dropping memory of betrayal. The curt announcement contrasted starkly with the audible reaction of distraught workers. America took notice.

"It seemed like every channel you turned on, that video was on there," Brian remembered. It was one of the few news stories that broke through the near-constant coverage of the presidential primaries.

Shortly after the video went viral, then-candidate Donald Trump tweeted out a still shot of the video and wrote, "I am the only one who can fix this. Very sad. Will not happen under my watch!"[3] During the CBS Republican presidential debate that evening, Trump mentioned the Carrier workers. Describing the video, he vividly recounted the scene to a watching nation, "They're laid off. They were crying . . . it was a very sad situation . . . I'm going to tell them right now, I am going to get consensus from Congress and we're going to tax you when those air conditioners come."[4] Trump was the only Republican candidate in that debate to mention the Carrier workers, who would become a constant line of reference for him on the campaign trail. On the Democratic side, Bernie Sanders highlighted the plight of the Carrier workers, joining them at a rally at the Indiana statehouse.[5]

I asked T.J. and Brian how union members felt about Trump, Sanders, and Clinton during the primaries. "Nobody was for Clinton," T.J. instantly replied.

"It was NAFTA, Benghazi," explained Brian. "The whole white-washing of her servers."

"It was trust," added T.J.

"And not to mention the list of people that seem to die around the Clintons," Brian replied with a sarcastic chuckle.

"[S]he was for TPP [the Trans-Pacific Partnership] and then she was running for president—oh, now she's against TPP!" T.J. quipped, then returning to a serious demeanor, "So I think a lot of people had no trust in her . . . I don't know one big Clinton person last year at all."

"I really didn't," Brian confirmed.

T.J.'s and Brian's political leanings in 2016 are emblematic of the political divisions within Carrier and among unions nationwide. T.J. supported Bernie Sanders because he wasn't a "corporate candidate" like Hillary, propped up by the DNC, while Brian supported Trump because of an article he read years ago. In the article Trump mentioned that one of the things that made him successful was not being afraid to let someone go who was incapable of doing the job. "I see that around me every day. I see people that are incapable at doing their job, and we just hold on," Brian explained, a rationale he would later expound upon in surprising detail.

"Trump was the first Republican I voted for," Brian said.

"There was a lot of Trump," T.J. told me.

"But it wasn't visible," Brian pointed out. "There was this persona that if you were a Trump supporter, you were—you know—you're racist."

"You're racist, you're this—" TJ said.

"It got so bad," Brian recalled. "There were people that would come up and approach my wife and say something: 'If your husband feels this way, then why are you with him? He's obviously racist.'"

"And he's married to a black woman," T.J. added, to emphasize the ridiculousness of the accusation.

"It just got to a point where I just wouldn't post anything [on Facebook anymore]," Brian said.

In the primary, T.J.'s local union endorsed Bernie Sanders, but in the general election they endorsed neither Trump nor Clinton. The United Steelworkers, by contrast, endorsed Clinton during the general. In fact, more than forty unions and trade associations endorsed Clinton during the 2016 general election, while just three officially declared their support for Trump. But endorsements didn't seem to matter: there was a mutiny among the rank and file, who rebelled against their leadership and voted for Trump in droves. It was those crucial votes of rank-and-file union members in places like Michigan, Pennsylvania, and Ohio that ultimately made the difference in electing Trump.

It was a very real phenomenon that the *New York Times* pointed to in a January 2016 article headlined "Union Leans Democratic, but Donald Trump Gets Members' Attention."[6] This prescient passage from the article grabbed my attention when I read it just days before the Iowa caucuses: "[Union leaders] fear that Mr. Trump, if not effectively countered, may draw an unusually large number of union voters in a possible general election matchup. This could, in turn, bolster Republicans in swing states like Ohio, Pennsylvania, Michigan and Wisconsin, all of which President Obama won twice."[7]

With nearly a year to go before the general election, the reporter at the *Times* had managed to isolate the very states that would be essential to Trump's victory. Trump indeed went on to carry all four of those states in November, and the Democrats never saw it coming. Throughout the election, as Clinton counted blue-collar support as a foregone conclusion, Trump remained sharply focused on the plight of the American worker and recognized the struggle of workers like Brian and T.J.

"I know my parents, their generation, they could say, you know, if you were willing to work and work hard, you could make a decent living," Brian said.

"Yeah, and it's going to pay off," T.J. emphasized.

"And have nice things and, you know, live this so-called American dream. It's getting to the point now where you can't."

"It's not happening anymore," T.J. observed. "Now you have to have both parents working . . . Everything's going up. Food prices are going up. Gas price is going up. You know education is so outrageously, ridiculously expensive. My wife's going to pay for school loans for the next thirty-three years."

But it's not just in the manufacturing hubs of Indiana that the apprehension of the American citizen was found during Election 2016. Economic angst was felt nationwide. It was felt among the 57 percent of Americans who told Gallup in September of 2016 that they believed the economy was getting worse.[8] It was felt by the 60 percent of battleground voters who said the economy was rigged against them.[9] And it's felt by the middle-class families who will see their health care premiums rise by 22 percent.[10]

And in the face of this economic malaise, President Barack Obama boasted that "America's economy is not just better than it was eight years ago—it is the strongest, most durable economy in the world."[11] Obama's remark reminded me of an out-of-touch encounter I had on a television set during the presidential race. A Democratic pundit held up a copy of the *Wall Street Journal* and said, "Oh, look, wages are going up. If only we could get the news out there, people may vote for Clinton." I thought to myself, *You shouldn't have to tell voters how to feel about their paycheck. They should feel it. They should see it in their paycheck. It should be tangible.*

Nevertheless, my peer was making a mistake that politicians throughout the 2016 primary were making: they were telling voters how to feel rather than listening to them. Listening is something that

Donald Trump did and excelled at. Rather than using focus groups to test his words or adhering to the party line during the primary, he opted for unscripted straight talk and used common sense when discussing the issues. It earned him the ire of his peers, but it also earned him the presidency of the United States and, for the moment, leadership of the people's movement to take back government.

Just five minutes into the first presidential debate against Hillary Clinton, Trump turned the focus to workers, and Carrier in particular. "All you have to do is take a look at Carrier air-conditioning in Indianapolis: they fired 1,400 people, they're going to Mexico. So many, hundreds and hundreds of companies, are doing this. We cannot let it happen," Trump admonished.[12]

Some union members, like Brian, heard this and showed up for Trump. Others, like T.J., didn't. But distrusting workers like T.J., despite not supporting Trump, were still integral to Clinton's defeat. "I left it blank. I didn't vote for Hillary and didn't vote for Donald," T.J. said.

"I mean, your average person that was a Democrat, they would say they were going to vote for Clinton. They didn't want to," Brian added.

"They didn't want to," T.J. echoed.

Silent support for Trump propelled the president to victory on November 8, and neither T.J. nor Brian was prepared for what would come next. T.J. noted, "If you would have told me that day when I lost my job, 'Oh, yeah, President Donald Trump is going to be here announcing he's going to save my job,' I'd be, like, 'OK, you're full of shit.'"

★　★　★　★

T. J. Bray was in New York City for the Macy's Thanksgiving Day Parade when he got the surprising call. Trump had just been elected president weeks earlier, and T.J. had done an interview with *NBC Nightly News*. In the segment, the reporter stated, "Workers say they have high expectations for the president-elect," after which, T.J. can be heard saying, "If he [Trump] can come here and save these fourteen hundred jobs tomorrow, I'll gladly vote for him again."[13] Later in the nationally tele-vised piece, T.J. sent a message to the incoming president: "We want you to do what you said you're going to do. We're going to hold you accountable."

Just over a week later, while T.J. was vacationing in New York, he received a phone call from a coworker, delivering some surprising news. "Hey, did you see Trump's tweet?" the coworker urgently inquired. T.J. pulled up Twitter and found an unexpected announcement from the president-elect: "I am working hard, even on Thanksgiving, trying to get Carrier A.C. Company to stay in the U.S. (Indiana). MAKING PROGRESS—Will know soon!"[14] About an hour later, Carrier also tweeted, "Carrier has had discussions with the incoming administration and we look forward to working together. Nothing to announce at this time."[15]

What prompted this? T.J. wondered. No one seemed to know.

Back home at Carrier, things were quiet. The union knew noth-ing, and for five days the workers pondered the prospects of a deal. The local union's president, Chuck Jones, expressed skepticism. "I think it's a long shot. I hope they aren't playing with people's emotions," Jones told CNN.[16] Others, like Brian, were confident. "I had a pretty good idea there was a chance that our jobs were being saved, but I didn't want to get my hopes up," he said. "I figured the announcement would come at Christmastime." But the deal came much sooner than expected.

Just after Thanksgiving, Carrier night-shift workers noticed men in suits entering and leaving the plant. "We never see corporate people. Never. So everyone was, like, 'Who are these people?'" T.J. said.

"Facebook was blowing up," Brian remembered. "People were in-boxing, 'What's going on? We've got secret service up here. A bunch of guys in suits. People with guns.'"

Windows in one of the big meeting rooms were covered so people couldn't see in. Something big was brewing. "I was up until 3:00 a.m. in the morning," Brian said. "I had to be up at 4:30 a.m., but I just couldn't go to bed, you know?"

On the night of Tuesday, November 29, Carrier made the announce-ment: "We are pleased to have reached a deal with President-elect Trump & VP-elect Pence to keep close to 1,000 jobs in Indy. More details soon."[17] Three hours later came the almost simultaneous news that Trump would be visiting Carrier. "I will be going to Indiana on Thursday to make a major announcement concerning Carrier A.C. staying in Indianapolis. Great deal for workers!" he tweeted.[18]

"I didn't expect it to come as soon as it did, and I was, like, 'Wow!'" Brian said. The media predictably tried to find a negative spin on an undeniably pro-Trump story. Rather than headlines giving the president-elect hard-earned credit, they read:

"Trump Saved Jobs at Carrier by Making a Bad Deal for America"[19]
"Is Trump's Deal with Carrier a Form of Crony Capitalism?"[20]
"Trump's Carrier Shakedown"[21]

The headlines insinuated that Trump had promised some sort of nefarious payoff to keep the Carrier jobs here. The revelation that Carrier would be receiving $7 million in incentives over a decade to stay in the U.S. was immediately derided. This was corporate cronyism, they cried! In reality, the $500,000 a year in state incentives was mere "window dressing" that "rarely change a firm's behavior," according to experts.[22] The money paled in comparison to the $65 million Carrier would save in moving to Mexico. Carrier's rationale for staying in the U.S. was more likely the very one the company cited: an improved economy under the incoming Trump administration.[23]

The next few days were eventful ones for the 1,400 Carrier workers as the soon-to-be leader of the free world prepared to head to the Indiana factory. A hand-selected group of workers were chosen to attend Trump's speech based on seniority, criminal background check, and other criteria. T.J. was among them.

The next day T.J. arrived to find Secret Service agents everywhere and metal detectors at Carrier's point of entry. Shortly after he got in the room, an HR boss tapped T.J. on the shoulder. "Hey, T.J., can you come here?" the boss asked. "I want you to meet this woman, the vice president of communications for UTC [United Technologies, Carrier's parent company]." The boss escorted T.J. into a hallway and to the waiting executive. "Hi, Mr. Bray," the woman said, introducing herself. "I just got a phone call from the Trump administration. They have specifically asked that you sit in the front."[24]

What's going on? T.J. wondered.

"Is that a good thing or a bad thing?" T.J. jokingly asked.

"I think it's a good thing." [25]

T.J. took his seat, right in the front. As he sat among his Carrier co-workers, a voice broke the silence. "Ladies and gentleman," the voice said as the workers simultaneously raised their phones to take video. "Please welcome the chairman, the chief executive officer of United Technologies, Greg Hayes." Hayes walked up to the podium as three security men crossed in front of him. Standing behind a podium with the blue and white Carrier logo emblazoned and in front of a backdrop littered with dozens more Carrier logos, Hayes told the crowd that the incoming Trump-Pence administration's planned to improve the U.S. business environment "through tax reform and through a more thoughtful approach to regulation." [26] The new presidency gave UTC renewed confidence in the future and the ability to keep 1,100 jobs in Indiana.

Vice President elect Mike Pence followed Mr. Hayes and proclaimed, "Thanks to the initiative and the leadership of President-elect Donald Trump, Carrier has decided to stay and grow right here in America." [27] After describing the inaction of the Obama administration, the vice president elect said, "President-elect Donald Trump did just what he said he would do . . . He picked up the phone and talked from one American to another . . . He made the case for America." That made the difference. "It is my high honor and distinct privilege," Pence continued, "to introduce to you a man of action, a man of his word, and the president-elect of the United States of America, Donald Trump."

As President-elect Trump emerged from behind the curtain with victorious music reverberating around the room, the Carrier workers stood in applause, raising their phones higher into the air. After some brief introductory remarks and thank-yous, that surprising revelation came out, the one T.J. didn't expect.

"I'll never forget. About a week ago, I was watching the nightly news. I won't say which one because I don't want to give them credit because I don't like them much. I'll be honest. I don't like them, not even a little," Trump said as the room broke out in laughter. "But they were doing a story on Carrier . . . They had a gentleman. Worker. Great guy. Handsome guy. He was on, and it was like he didn't even know they were leaving." T.J. began to gather that the incoming president might be referring to him. "He said something to the effect, 'No, we're not leaving because Donald Trump promised us that we're not leaving,' and I never thought I made that promise," Trump continued, describing how the nightly news then played a clip of Trump saying "Carrier will never leave." Trump clarified that that was a euphemism, but he understood how it could be interpreted the way the worker heard it.

Then came that unforgettable moment for T.J. "So now, because of him, whoever that guy was, is he in the room by any chance?" Trump asked, looking around for the young worker. T.J. prepared to stand and be acknowledged, but before he could, one of his coworkers in the far back of the room shouted, "That's my son!" Trump responded, "That's your son? Stand up. You did a good job. You did a great job, right? That's fantastic. And I love your shirt." The woman stood up, proudly displaying her Trump shirt to the cameras. Several of the Carrier men and women were perplexed, knowing that was not T.J.'s mom. She was the mother of another Carrier factory worker, but T.J. was the one who had gone on *NBC Nightly News*.

After Trump saw T.J.'s segment in early November, he immediately recognized that he had to do something. The very next morning, he called Mr. Hayes to try and save those jobs. He told Hayes, "We have to do something . . . we can't allow this to happen anymore with our country. So many jobs are leaving and going to other countries." Days of active negotiation resulted in the saving of American jobs.

When the speech ended, T.J. went to shake the president-elect's hand and thank him, taking pictures as he moved along the rope line. "I wanted to make sure I shook his hand," T.J. said. When he returned home to join his wife and her family, T.J.'s mother-in-law and brother-in-law, big Trump supporters, prodded him, saying, "I want to shake your hand because you shook his!"

After Trump's Carrier speech, news networks scrambled to find the mysterious Carrier man whose nightly news interview prompted Trump to save jobs. "Well, I'll tell you who that guy was," one CNN anchor said. "We just grabbed him and put him in front of a camera." The anchor asked the worker, "Do you remember the day that you were interviewed by a news network about jobs leaving your company?" The young man looked from side to side and took a very long, awkward pause. "No, I don't. No, I don't, actually." [28] The employee was indeed the child of the mom who had stood up during Trump's speech and took credit, but he was not the man whom Trump had seen on the nightly news.

Later that afternoon, T.J. received a call from a CNBC producer. "I think Trump was talking about you," the producer said. "Let me make some phone calls and get back to you." The producer called back. "We just talked to someone from the administration, and they said that's why they called you up. They wanted to acknowledge you," the woman said. The next day *NBC Nightly News* ran a piece highlighting T.J.'s role in saving the Carrier jobs. Like dominos, other outlets ran with the story: the local news, CNN, Fox News. T.J.'s words had prompted action, and the media took notice.

I asked Brian whether the president-elect saving jobs swayed any Carrier Democrats his way. "No," he said. "There were some people that wanted us still to lose our jobs."

"*Really?*" I exclaimed.

"Yeah," they both replied simultaneously.

"They just wanted to be able to say that Trump couldn't do it . . . Now, that's spiteful," Brian said.

The thought seemed shocking, and yet, the days that followed the president-elect's announcement would showcase some of the ungrateful attitudes Brian had referenced. About a week after Trump came to Indiana, Chuck Jones, the president of United Steelworkers Local 1999, told the *Washington Post* that the president-elect "lied his ass off" when he claimed to save 1,100 jobs. [29] In reality, according to the union leader, he had only saved 730 production jobs, meaning 550 workers would still lose their jobs.

But Trump was not lying. As the Carrier workers explained to me, when Trump echoed UTC in saying 1,100 jobs were staying, he was including four hundred white-collar and research-and-development jobs already slated to stay. Even so, the workers were understandably dismayed. When Carrier tweeted out that a deal had been reached, naturally, all the Carrier employees just assumed they were staying. The confusion prompted Chuck Jones to call the president-elect a liar.

"Did most people like Chuck Jones saying Trump lied his ass off?" I asked the workers, half expecting them to say yes.

"No!" T.J. said.

"No, no," Brian echoed. "See, that's what pissed me off. Because I feel like Chuck Jones slit the throats of the employees at Rexnord."

Rexnord was another company a mile down the road from Carrier that announced it too was leaving the United States. T. J. Bray had been fighting, not just for Carrier, but also for Rexnord—the plant that his grandpa had spent forty years at. After jobs were saved at Carrier, the Rexnord employees' hopes were raised. "Trump tweeted twice about Rexnord," T.J. said. "And so they had a lot of hope."

"The world's eyes were on us," Brian said. "There was an opportunity for Rexnord to seize the same thing we were getting . . . to steal a little bit of that thunder too and possibly save their jobs. And then here comes Chuck Jones running his mouth. It's, like, 'How dare you?'"

It wasn't just that Jones stopped the momentum for some unrelated neighboring company: he actively represented Rexnord too as president of Local 1999. Incensed by Chuck Jones's actions, Brian asked, "Why would you let your personal pride get in the way of helping people that have not only worked there but have mouths to feed, have families, have kids, [all] to have a pissing contest with Donald Trump?"

"Carrier people were saying, 'Man, I can't believe Chuck did that. He f***ed with people," T.J. remembered. T.J. texted some Rexnord employees in the aftermath and asked their thoughts on Chuck's comments.

"We're mad as hell," they responded.

★   ★   ★   ★

The story of the workers at the Carrier manufacturing plant is the story of many in twenty-first-century America. America's trade deficit with China, repeatedly decried by candidate Donald Trump, has cost approximately 3.2 million jobs over the course of a decade.[30] A host of factors—not least among them bad trade deals—has prompted the closing of sixty thousand U.S. factories.[31]

Experts have written an array of textbooks and academic papers explaining the loss of U.S. manufacturing jobs. Some say it's NAFTA offering cheap overseas labor; others say its automation displacing the American workers. While these theories all have some merits, there's a perspective that the experts inevitably miss because they've never looked through the eyes of factory workers.

"They say robotics and technology are going to take over," Brian sneered. " I don't buy that. I've seen or heard percentages as high as 85 percent of factory jobs are going to be eliminated because of robotics. Impossible! Especially in a sheet-metal shop." It's as if the so-called experts and pontificating pundits had no grasp of the complexity of Brian's job.

Brian went on to explain a manufacturing procedure called "stack up." "There's plus or minus 3,000 allowances on this part, 3,000 allowances on that part. If each one of them is just a slight bit out, but still within spec by the time you get to the end of it, you're talking 10 or 12 thousandths out [of spec]," he said. "Will a robot be able to perform the tasks you need to do now? Chances are, no. Not on a consistent basis."

To put it simply, I was lost. Burner assembly? Tolerance? Variance? I felt like I was in a foreign physics class. It was like Brian was speaking a different language—and he was: the language of manufacturing. As Brian explained his job in vivid detail, I gathered that he was not only highly skilled in a niche area but he was also extremely intelligent. He spoke a language that not a single one of my co-panelists on CNN could speak. Pundits throw around fancy words like "automation," but did they have any appreciation for the complexity of Brian's job?

Not only do many in the talking class fail to understand the work of a manufacturer, some actively put down the non–college-educated lifestyle. T.J. told me that he had just seen Mike Rowe from *Dirty Jobs* make this very point. "Plumbers. Handymen. They're portrayed as dumb [on TV], like Tim Allen, and Dan Conner [John Goodman's character] on *Roseanne*," T.J. said. Rowe posited that the disparaging media portrayal of blue-collar workers produces a culture that doesn't respect these jobs and pushes kids away from them at a young age. "It's really a vicious cycle," T.J. explained. "High schools aren't pushing those vocational classes no more, like welding, woodshop, fabrication classes. You don't see that no more."

And that's not always for the better. When T.J. grew up, there were shop classes in school. "We learned how to build stuff," T.J. said. "You look at the kids nowadays, all they know how to operate is their tablet or phone. They don't know how to build anything."

"Zero problem-solving skills," Brian added.

T.J. and Brian are workers at heart, and hard workers at that. Even so, Brian admits that you have to get on board with technology. "The unions are so hard against it; they don't realize they're slitting their own throats," Brian said. Automation may cost some jobs on the front end, he explained, but when you learn the process, you open yourself up to new skill sets. The day after Trump came to Carrier, the head of UTC announced a $16 million investment in automation—a worrisome development for T.J. and Brian.[32] "If we're going to have robots in here, who are we going to have run them?" T.J. asked. Why not train Carrier workers to move into these new roles?

Beyond technological change, T.J. and Brian also cite corporate greed as a reason for disappearing jobs. To many corporations, employees are faceless numbers, on the backs of whom big-time CEOs amass empires. An erosion of appreciation now plagues companies in even the smallest of ways. "When my dad worked at FedEx when I was a kid, man, they used to have so many things for you," T.J. reminisced. "Events. Christmas dinners. Bonuses. At Carrier now, you don't get nothing. You don't get nothing."

"Yeah, I remember we used to get a turkey at Thanksgiving, and then that stopped," Brian added.

"We used to have cookouts for the Indy 500 in May," T.J. said. "They'd have a big tent out there, and the [Carrier] race car out there, and all the supervisors would give people hot dogs. They don't do that no more."

Brian's daughter works at an apartment complex. It's not a billion-dollar corporation, just a tiny company with a tight budget. "She got a $500 Christmas bonus. A nice little gift bag with stuff in it," Brian marveled. "And I'm thinking, 'Damn, we don't even get a damn turkey.'"

Now, please don't misunderstand. It's not that Brian and T.J. demand a whole bunch of gratuitous handouts. That's not in the DNA of workers like them. The slow elimination of acts of appreciation is a symptom of a bigger problem: nothing seems to matter to twenty-first-century corporations except their bottom lines.

"It started in the eighties when you let Wall Street get in all these government officials' pockets," T.J. said. "That's where stuff started. The greed started, where it was just all about money."

"So you're like a cog in the wheel, not a human being?" I asked him.

"Yeah, you're just a number to them," T.J. said.

"There's a problem. It's not the United States anymore. It's corporate America," Brian offered. "These special interest groups aren't negotiating anything in my interest, his interest, or your interest. It's about whose back they can scratch." Brian said to just look at UTC's board of directors and you'll see the kinds of political affiliations they have. One member of the board is a retired general. What does he know about running a company or air-conditioning manufacturing? Not much. He's there for one reason and one reason alone: to lobby for U.S. military contracts.

"Nothing's about the people," Brian said. "Everything's about shareholders, about the CEO. The CEO is making twenty-five times the average worker, and yet they want to blame us? We make too much money?" Brian explained that UTC just bought out a board member for a whopping $195 million.[33]

"It was a lot for him to walk away," T.J. said.

"Just for him to go away."

"But yet they *need* $65 million to stay in Indianapolis?" T.J. asked.

Trump succeeded in capturing more union workers than any Republican presidential candidate in the last three decades because he elevated the sentiments expressed by T.J. and Brian. Just before the 2016 crop of Republican primary candidates entered the race, Vice President Joe Biden warned a group of union leaders that Republicans are "willing to sacrifice your needs on the altar of ideology . . . They act as if you are the problem, as if you caused the recession."[34] Biden alleged that Republicans had "dismissive contempt" for unions.[35] However, the Vice President had no idea that Trump was waiting in the wings.

Three months later, Trump declared his candidacy and offered an anti-trade, pro-worker message, foreign to the Republican establishment but primed for the union rank and file. Unlike many of his predecessors, Trump acknowledged that hardworking union workers were getting a raw deal, and he vowed to rectify that.

Brian and T.J. don't place all of the blame on the company for jobs disappearing. They recognize the blameworthiness in some of their coworkers. Brian noted that on any given day Carrier operates with 20 percent to 30 percent absenteeism because of FMLA—a Clinton-era program that allows an individual to take up to twelve weeks off every year.[36] Although the program was designed to assist new parents or gravely ill individuals, workers now take off for "stress" or "migraines," and the company cannot refuse you.

"So if I come into work and see I have a hard job today, and I don't want to be here, I can go to medical and say, 'Hey, I'm stressed today,' and leave," Brian pointed out.

"And they have to let you leave. They can't say no," T.J. added. "So many people just take advantage of it and abuse it." Brian and T.J. told me that coworkers will take FMLA and then gloat about it on Facebook.

"They'll leave early on FMLA and you'll see 'Oh, I'm at the mall' or 'Check in. I'm getting my nails done,'" T.J. remarked.

"Or 'I'm at the park' or 'It's such a nice day, I'm chilling at the pool,' Brian said. And he would think, *Didn't you leave on FMLA?*"

"So many people abuse it. This past week has been rough," T.J. recalled. "And really that's what's frustrating."

"We have a second chance," Brian said. "But it's like they don't care about anyone else. It's just selfish. 'I don't care whether I cost everybody else their job. I don't feel like being here today' . . . During football season, Tuesdays are hell. For some reason everybody's had their issues on Tuesday after *Monday Night Football*."

T.J. explained that HR uses a point system for absenteeism. Mondays are three points against the worker, whereas every other day is just two points, and yet Mondays are the worst days for absenteeism. "Of course everyone's there on payday on Thursday," T.J. remarked. Absenteeism and abuse of FMLA has gotten so intense that HR now claims that FMLA must stand for the "Friday and Monday Leave Act." "What's sad is we've all lost our jobs and still there's people that just don't give a shit," T.J. said.

Brian noted that the unions enable this kind of behavior. "If you feel the necessity to cuss out a supervisor, you don't deserve a job," Brian asserted. "If you tell people you don't care, well, then [they should] fire you. If you're sitting at 30 something points on an 18 point system, you don't deserve your job, but the union will fight to get your job back."

It's this kind of attitude of self-responsibility that motivated Brian to vote for Trump. Brian seeks accountability in the workplace, not excuses and willful blindness. Brian described one guy at Carrier named Harold Gillespie. Harold has had forty-plus years at Carrier, and he's getting ready to retire. He's had a kidney transplant and he's half-blind. He's also a diabetic who has had to have two to three toes cut off on each one of his feet. "He will outrun any employee I've got in my area or any employee in my plant. He runs his numbers day in and day out, and it's unreal," Brian said. "He's one hell of a worker."

By contrast, Harold's nighttime counterpart is a young guy half Harold's age. The buff, able-bodied worker is constantly complaining. He gets just half the numbers that Harold gets. "I mean, how could you look at yourself and say I'm running half the amount of a guy who's missing two to three toes on each one of his feet and falls down a couple of times per week because of a balance thing from missing both of his big toes?" Brian asks, somewhat bewildered.

Brian and Harold have a lot in common: they're both relentless workers. Brian tore his calf muscle in two right after Carrier announced that jobs were leaving. Despite the betrayal and his physical pain, Brian was out on the floor working when he did not have to. T.J. also broke his finger while working at Carrier. "I've bled in there. I've sweat in there," he recalled. And yet the good work of Brian, Harold, and T.J. is undermined by lazy employees.

It's a combination of bad trade deals, an unwillingness to adapt to automation, corporate greed, and worker irresponsibility that have caused a hemorrhaging of American manufacturing jobs. But while the solution is just as complex as the problem, there is one remedy that rests in the American spirit.

As T.J., Brian, and I discussed the fate of American manufacturing over dinner and a beer, a bystander who recognized me from CNN approached us. When the woman inquired about Carrier, T.J. explained that oftentimes production will move to Mexico for a while, and although the product comes back cheaper, quality goes down. Just

With Brian (left), and T.J. at Charbonos in Avon, Indiana. *Courtesy of author's collection*

that week, the Carrier factory had to temporarily cease production because of issues with Mexican-made control boards. Companies will move production back to the U.S. only to have the next guy in line that gets promoted say, "We're paying too much to produce this. Let's move this back to Mexico."

"It's a vicious cycle," T.J. told the woman.

"I'll pay more for USA made," she said. "I care about that. I'll pay more just to buy local in Hendricks Country than to do something on Amazon."

"I could never buy a foreign car," T.J. said.

"Oh, no!" she retorted.

★   ★   ★   ★

For now, T.J. and Brian are both safe in their Carrier manufacturing jobs, but it will never be the same. February 10, 2016, changed everything. For Brian, "it's very hard, even still, to go to work and feel dedicated. I mean, you go to work and do your job, but it's still not that good feeling if you do a little extra. It still feels like you're going through the motions." He described to me how he relished those days when everything went wrong that possibly could, but he found a way to make it right and get his product to the line without shutting it down. "Some of the best days I can say I had at work are also some of my worst days." But not anymore. "I'm still doing it, but there's no passion in it," he said.

"It's hard to come in and put in 110 percent," T.J. said.

"It's like a marriage," Brian said.

"You know it's ending," T.J. continued the analogy.

"The love is just gone. It's over, and you're just going through the motions."

"You're together for the kids. Because the company's already stabbed you in the back once," T.J. said.

Management is still breathing down their necks. Workers are expected to give 110 percent, but the feeling of having been betrayed lingers. "There's some days you're shooting screws and you might have one that's in there crooked and you're, like, 'Well, it's not going in my house,'" T.J. said. "You know I don't like having that thought, but there are some days."

Despite a loss of passion for their jobs, T.J. and Brian still manage to add some life to their work. "Me and T.J., we sit and play cards together every day," Brian told me. "We play euchre at lunch together every day. He's anti-Trump. I'm pro-Trump,"

"But we get along," T.J. added.

"We might dig at each other here or there, but it's never the typical 'Hey, man, you're an idiot.' It's nothing like that."

"It's not hard to get along with people you have disagreements with."

"Common respect," Brian emphasized.

Two hardworking factory workers. Two different political parties. United in betrayal.

THE STAKES

Health Care

"There is nothing I dread so much as a division of the Republic into two great Parties, each arranged under its leader and concerting measures in opposition to each other. This, in my humble apprehension, is to be dreaded as the greatest political evil under our Constitution."
—JOHN ADAMS

Talan's Story

Stan Summers and his son, Talan, drove through the sprawling farmland of Northern Utah just behind the Wasatch Range, when they encountered traffic. With the passenger's seat slightly reclined and oxygen tubes draped across his body, Talan turned to his father and commented, "Dad, at least we get to be together a little longer." The twenty-six-year-old had spent his whole life in and out of doctor's offices, but he always managed to see the glass as half-full, no matter the circumstances. Today was no exception.

As the father and son progressed slowly along I-15, the conversation took a more serious turn. Leaning back in his white T-shirt, black sunglasses, and gray Under Armour hat, Talan urged his dad, "If I die, please don't be sad. I know where I'm going." As a strong person of faith, Talan knew exactly where he was going, but he still had one reservation: "It just makes me nervous who's going to meet me there."

Stan broke down in tears, assuring his son that there would be plenty of loved ones on the other side waiting for him. The affectionate father then shared an extraordinary moment in life that he had never mentioned before. Two months earlier Stan had turned fifty-two years old, making him the same age as his mother when she lost her battle with cancer. Even though Stan's mom had passed when he was just a teenager, that didn't stop her from reaching out when Stan needed her most.

Talan was born prematurely at just twenty-two weeks and weighed a meager 2 pounds 10 ounces.[1] He had multiple holes in his lungs and underwent heart surgery at just ten days of age. Talan spent a full two and a half months in the hospital with Stan and his wife, Jennifer, at his side every step of the way. Filled with grief over the condition of his newborn son, Stan dropped to his knees and began praying. "I can't go through this alone," he told God, pleading with his maker to save his son. As Stan prayed, he remembers clearly hearing the voice of his mother, "What makes you think you're going through this alone?"

"I didn't realize I never told Talan that," Stan disclosed. After relating the story, Stan told his son, "From the day you were born I knew that there were great things involved. I had no idea how long you were going to live, but I knew your life was here for a reason. You have no idea how many lives you've touched." Talan and his family had indeed touched the lives of many, through his dad's public advocacy and Talan's Facebook page—"Talan's Fight—Never Give Up"— which gets up to ten thousand views per post.[2] Stan often puts religious material on Talan's widely read page and receives criticism for doing so. But in the face of disapproval, something told Stan that one particular photo needed to go up: a picture of Talan kneeling by his bedside, praying for his mom.

In addition to Talan being sick, Stan's wife also suffered from health problems. She went for a run-of-the-mill root canal, but the dentist drilled into her sinuses, which became infected. "My boy wasn't doing good, and she wasn't. I almost lost both in a small amount of time," Stan recalled. During that difficult period, Stan snapped a picture of Talan kneeling by his mom. With oxygen tubes protruding from his body, Talan prayed out loud for her recovery.

Torn over whether to post the picture, Stan said, "I listened to that small voice." Two weeks later Stan received a message from a local woman on Facebook. "I just want you to know that I came home and was about to commit suicide," she wrote. "Then I saw that post about Talan praying for his mom, and I thought if Talan could do it and worry about someone else, then I can do it too." Astounded by the revelation, Stan told me, "Usually you don't see the answer to your actions come back that quick . . . Now I pass her in the grocery store and she winks at me because she knows that I know."

Talan has helped many through his outward profession of faith, but it doesn't always feel that way. "Dad, I just don't feel like a hero," Talan told with his dad during that car ride home. Talan's rare disease—IgG4-related disease, or scleroderma—presented few visible symptoms. While many individuals with chronic disease display physical evidence of their illness, Talan does not: no hair loss, no wheelchair, no outward indications of sickness, leading his peers to question his very real ailment.

Growing up, Talan would call his dad and ask to be picked up from school. Despite feeling sick, he could never fully explain what was going on. Talan would return home looking very pale and eventually start throwing up. "We knew something was wrong, very wrong, but could never find it," Stan said.[3] Throughout his adolescent years, Talan tried to overcome the disease, harnessing his natural athleticism on the football field and basketball court despite his physical struggle. "He was teased by friends, school teachers, yes school teachers and coaches that he was always sick and faking it," Talan's mom, Jennifer, wrote on Utah Rare, a support group for people with rare diseases and their loved ones.[4]

Talan's health problems worsened during his sophomore year of high school when he and another player had a head-on collision. "When Talan went to get up he couldn't," Jennifer wrote.[5] He had broken his back and had to undergo intense surgery, having hardware installed and removed a year and a half later. He moved from his local high school to a community high school, where he was still derided by those around him. Teachers accused Talan of being lazy and unmotivated, but his dad knew Talan's struggle was due to illness, not lack of a work ethic. He was right.

For nearly a decade, the Summers family tried to find out what was wrong with Talan. During that time Talan experienced dramatic weight losses and gains and intense recurring pain in his back that kept him from walking. He had raw skin and bleeding for four months that resembled shingles. Talan took part in NIH research and his family went to the Mayo Clinic, seeking answers but finding none. After years of searching, it was Talan's mom who had proposed he might have a type of scleroderma, a suggestion later confirmed by doctors. "The disease actually turns your tissue from the inside out," Jennifer Summers explained.[6] Due to hardening of his lung tissue, Talan needs a constant flow of oxygen and requires extensive medical attention.[7]

As Talan fell victim to this rare disease, his family became enveloped in an insurance nightmare. When Talan was born prematurely, Stan had a minimal $500 out-of-pocket maximum deductible. After Stan reached the deductible, the rest was covered: heart surgery, lung holes, trips in and out of the hospital. It's how the system was supposed to work. Stan's deductible slowly increased over time, but it was still manageable. Just before Obamacare went into effect, Stan's insurance cost him $240 with a $1,000 out-of-pocket maximum. But everything would change in the post-Obamacare world.

Stan received coverage through the Box Elder County Commission, where he served as a part-time commissioner. Even though he was not on an Obamacare exchange plan, the new law caused Stan's health care costs to skyrocket. Stan's deductible initially soared to a $5,000 out-of-pocket maximum and then to $7,500 before hitting a whopping $9,000 in 2017. "I've been married twenty-nine years, and I've met my out-of-pocket maximum deductible twenty-six out of the twenty-nine years," Stan recalled. That meant that Stan had to pay a full $9,000 before his health care coverage would even kick in!

An almost double-digit deductible is a devastating blow to the hard-working school bus driver and part-time commissioner. In 2016 alone, Stan spent $35,000 on health care—the equivalent of some people's salaries. On top of high deductibles, Stan deals with drugs that are not covered, out-of-network doctor costs for Talan's rare disease, and an 80/20 health care coverage scenario after paying thousands of dollars in his deductible.

In addition to high costs, Stan's benefits declined, causing Talan to lose access to vital medicines. "I have something in my fridge that cost me nine hundred bucks," Stan told me in disbelief. His insurance would not cover "compounding," when two separate drugs are mixed together at a pharmacy. His previous insurance had covered this, but not in the new post-Obamacare landscape. "I'm still driving [a] school bus because I can't quit because of my health premiums," Stan said.[8]

Even more problematic, Talan's severe pain can only be treated by an investigational medicine that comes in the form of breath spray. Because Talan's stomach and esophagus were sclerosing, or hardening, at such a rate, breath spray and injections were the only option, because pills could not deliver the benefit of the opioids. "Again, here comes the non-Affordable Care Act, saying that those could only be given out to people with cancer or somebody who was dying," Stan rightfully complained. Without insurance coverage, Stan could not afford the $11,000 medicine. "As soon as they took him off of those almost two years ago, he's basically been down in a spiral," Stan lamented. "The only time I can get him out of the house is maybe for a doctor's appointment, and that's very seldom." Although Talan uses a fentanyl patch and has an internal pain pump, neither offers him the pain management that the breath spray did. With his hands tied by Obamacare, one doctor told Stan, "I would have had Talan on investigational medicine six months ago, but because of Obamacare requirements, I can't without Talan failing a bunch of tests."[9]

On another occasion, Talan entered hospice care because his lungs were functioning at only 55 percent. When Talan started to recover slightly, he was kicked off hospice care because of onerous limitations on those eligible for care.[10] It took Stan a full two months to get Talan on palliative care, a step in between hospice care and pain management.

The pain of the Summers family did not go unnoticed by the Trump administration, which invited Stan and his family to the White House after learning about their situation from Utah senator Orrin Hatch. "I'm a dairy farmer's son from east Tremonton, Utah, in northern Box Elder County, and my hometown had one thousand people in it. We milked two-hundred-plus cows, morning, noon, and night," Stan told me. "And here I am at the table with the President, Vice President, secretary of

Stan at the White House with President Donald Trump. *Courtesy of Stan Summers*

commerce, and secretary of health and human services . . . I was so en-amored being there." The president went around the table, listening to each and every person's story. Stan was the last to go. "I mean every-thing's been said, you know? I didn't even go in there with any talking points," he said, recounting that nerve-racking moment. But Stan, being a religious man, knew that God would give him the right words.

Given the Summers family's experience, perhaps it should come as no surprise that Stan hesitated to even call Obamacare by name. "I'm not going to call it the other word," Stan said, looking straight at President Trump, frustrated by a title that suggested Obama cared. "I call it the last president's health care bill. I don't need to say the name."[11] In his typical lighthearted manner, Trump joked back, "Other than that, you like him a lot?" Taking a more serious tone, Stan remembers the presi-dent saying, "I've been telling all these people to let Obamacare crash, but I look at you guys, and I look at your stories. What's going to happen if we let it crash? Is it going to take two years, three, years, four years, for everything to come around? Is it going to be instantaneous? I'm not willing to let that happen because of people like you."

I asked Stan what he thought of the president's response. "I've met senators and congressmen . . . and there are a lot of them that are inside themselves and obsessed and power-driven," Stan observed. "When I got out of that, I was so amazed at how humble [Trump was] . . . [H]e hung on every word . . . He remembered everything that everybody was saying." Stan's recognition of President Trump's sincerity was similar to Sabine Durden's experience: Trump was the man who sent her a note celebrating the day a portion of a trail at Hidden Springs Park was dedicated to her lost son Dominic. There was nothing in it for him. The cameras weren't there. He did it from his heart.

After the private meeting between Trump and the Obamacare victims, Trump said to his chief of staff, Reince Priebus, "How are we on time?"

Priebus gave him two thumbs-up, and the president asked the men and women before him, "You guys want to go jump across the hall and take some pictures in the Oval Office?"

A young girl from Georgia sitting next to him exclaimed, "Oh, yes, Mr. President, would that be OK?"

The president grabbed her hand in a show of sincerity and said, "Sweetheart, this isn't my house. This is your house."

Stan was equally impressed with Vice President Mike Pence. Upon arriving at the White House, Stan had given the president and vice president a copy of a poem he had written for his two kids called "I Have a Secret." When Stan stood up to go take pictures, the vice president grabbed Stan's arm and said, "Commissioner, you get it, don't you?" The vice president had already read those beautiful words on the pages of Stan's book:

> My secret I tell you nightly before our prayers
> as I ask Father-in-Heaven to keep us safe down here . . .
> Take our hand—we'll guide you through,
> Only God knows what's in store for you.[12]

"Yeah, I do get it. This might be our last best hope," Stan told Vice President Pence.

After the event ended, friends asked Stan, "What did you say? What did you say?"—hoping to learn all about his day with the president.

"To tell you the truth, I can't remember," Stan answered. "We're going to have to watch it together. I was letting my emotions and the things that I've gone through speak for me and for everybody else that doesn't have a voice and doesn't have that opportunity."

The Trump administration continues the arduous task of delivering an Obamacare replacement plan that all Republicans can agree on. Although repeal and replacement stalled in the Senate in the summer of 2017, Republicans work tirelessly to find middle ground and deliver on their promise to the American people. Stan, in the meantime, remains optimistic—optimistic that his son will gain access to the medicine he needs, optimistic that his health care costs will go down, and optimistic they will soon resume their health battle without having to battle over insurance as well.

Melissa's Story

"Where's the money going to come from?" It's a question Rich and Melissa Ackison found themselves asking all too often in 2016. Melissa's 401(k) was empty. Her credit was decimated. The family sold the RV, their middle son's ATV, and the dirt bike belonging to their oldest son— the same son who was about to put on the uniform of this great country and go off into battle. "At one point we were actually rolling quarters in our living room to buy our [youngest] son's prescriptions," Melissa, a mother of four, recalled.[13]

Medical hardship accompanied financial hardship for the Ackison family. Melissa was born with fibrous dysplasia, one of the rarest bone diseases. Scar-like tissue forms in place of normal bone, causing severe pain, swelling, and bone deformity, requiring continuous medical attention.[14] In addition to Melissa's own medical troubles, Royce, one of her four children, also had a preexisting condition called strabismus, in which his eyes would not always look in the same direction. It required him to have surgery at the age of four and requires follow-up treatments and surgeries down the road. In addition to strabismus, Royce also had a minor birth defect, causing fine motor delay. While he did not have a learning disability, he did need occupational therapy, which he received at the Nationwide Children's Hospital. The therapy helped him to thrive in his elementary school environment.

One day Melissa drove her son to the hospital for therapy as she routinely did, only to receive disturbing news. "Melissa, none of these appointments are being covered by your insurance," the staff member regretfully informed her. "No, this is Obamacare," Melissa protested. "We get to keep our providers." She was simply reiterating the promise President Obama had made to the American people many times over.

Melissa had just enrolled in a UnitedHealthcare (UHC) plan through her state Obamacare exchange in Ohio. After her Obama co-op, In-Health, went bankrupt, she was forced to reenter the marketplace and reinsure her family. Co-ops are nonprofit plans created under Obamacare and subsidized by federal loans. In short, they were an unmitigated disaster working right before Melissa's very eyes. As of December 2016, just four co-ops remained in all fifty states, costing taxpayers upwards of $2.2 billion.[15] The Ackison family fell victim to a bankrupt co-op, and they paid a heavy price.

Before InHealth went bankrupt, the co-op stopped paying Melissa's bills without alerting her. Melissa only learned that InHealth had stopped paying many months after the fact when her doctors, not her insurer, brought it to her attention. When she approached the co-op to find out what was going on, InHealth claimed that Melissa had not submitted a "Creditable Letter of Coverage"—a document that the co-op had never asked for during the enrollment process. In fact, InHealth representatives had told Melissa that her application looked good and would be approved during the enrollment period. She even received an approval email.

A few days later Melissa learned that the missing document was not the problem. InHealth was not reimbursing her providers because they had listed themselves as Melissa's secondary provider, noting that Medicare was her first. Medicare? Melissa was not even eligible for Medicare!

InHealth had mistakenly listed Medicare as Melissa's primary coverage, even though Melissa had never mentioned the government-run program. Since several of the outstanding bills were more than sixty days old, they were referred to a collections agency. In all, Melissa had eighty-seven outstanding claims, and her credit was quickly declining through no fault of her own.

When InHealth went bankrupt, Melissa enrolled in UHC, a new Obamacare exchange plan, which proved no better than the bankrupt co-op. Even though Melissa routinely paid her premiums, she was informed that Royce would not have access to care. She received several letters stating that UHC needed proof of citizenship, proof that Melissa had overnighted on three separate occasions. When Melissa called an Obamacare representative to find out the problem, the lady curtly replied, "Ma'am, you did not send his driver's license to us. Yes, you sent yours. Yes, you sent your husband's. You did not send his." Confounded, Melissa replied, "Ma'am, six-year-olds don't drive."

In addition to enrollment complications, the new UHC plan would not cover Royce's follow-up surgery at National Children's Hospital for his preexisting condition. "His doctor is a world-renowned ophthalmologist who did surgery on me over thirty years ago," Melissa explained, but her Obamacare coverage would not cover it. UHC also would not cover Royce's occupational therapy at Nationwide Children's Hospital. He had been on a six-month waiting list for the hospital and was finally being treated effectively, but Melissa was left with a choice: pay out of pocket or her son would lose access to care. "The whole 'You get to keep your plan, you get to keep your provider' Obamacare promises didn't happen," she told me.

When Melissa called a representative and explained that her son needed this therapy, they replied, "We're sorry, but Nationwide Children's occupational therapy clinic won't participate in our program." Melissa explained that this was her only option for therapy. Besides, it was a well-known children's hospital. How could it not be covered? UHC and the Obamacare marketplace both assured her that they would send a list of providers to meet her son's needs, but instead of receiving the names of occupational therapists, Melissa received the names of pediatricians, who just referred her back to Nationwide Children's Hospital. It was a vicious circle with no solution, and there were no alternate occupational therapists in Union County, Ohio, or in the surrounding area.

The marketplace and UHC both continued to give Melissa the runaround, encouraging her to write appeals that never solved the situation. It was time-consuming and it was frustrating, prompting Melissa to finally call the marketplace and say, "You lied to me." Melissa continued to pay out of pocket until she finally had to stop therapy for her son altogether. Eventually, Memorial Health opened, allowing her son to seek care, but the quality level is "no comparison," in Melissa's words.

In November, Royce had a new ailment: constant fevers. Every Monday, Melissa would take Royce to a pediatrician, who would provide fever reducers that had little effect. One night his fever reached 105 degrees. Melissa took him to the doctor, who said he must go to the children's hospital immediately. She explained the problems with their insurance, and the doctor simply replied, "We're beyond that at this point."

After paying out of pocket for her son's treatment, Melissa soon discovered that UHC would not cover his prescriptions, either. Melissa was paying her monthly payment on time, but the Obamacare system had matched her information to the wrong Social Security number, therefore disrupting her coverage. Beyond the incompetent mismatching, they also lost her personal information, which became compromised, forcing the Ackison family to enroll in LifeLock. "You name an issue that came from Obamacare, we had it," Melissa remarked.

In addition to Royce's insurance problems, Melissa incurred problems of her own. Melissa's youngest son, Cross, was considered a high-risk pregnancy because of Melissa's age. As a result, Melissa needed ultrasounds that she cleared with insurance and scheduled months in advance. Upon arrival at the appointment, she once was told, "We're sorry, but we've stopped participating in the Obamacare plans." Melissa countered, "But you're the only hospital with the type of equipment that's going to do this test. I'm not going anywhere without it today. You can put it on my credit, charge me for it . . . but I'm not going anywhere." After her son was born via C-section, Melissa had a stroke within twenty-four hours of leaving the hospital. Melissa was rushed to ICU for treatment—more treatment that would not be covered, since it was not an "emergency service."[16]

Melissa incurred insurance problems as well in treating her rare bone disease. She had been in clinical trials for fibrous dysplasia since she was fourteen years old and had seen the same doctor since she was a kid. Because fibrous dysplasia is so rare, few specialize in treating it, and access to Melissa's childhood doctor was essential. Melissa had undergone nineteen surgeries over her lifetime in controlling the disease. On the left side of her face, her eye socket was removed and her cheek was hollowed out as a result of tumor growth. The surgeries created a large amount of scar tissue, requiring routine maintenance surgery.

In December of 2016, Melissa scheduled a surgery to clean out scar tissue. It was important to have it done in December so that the surgery would be fully covered before the deductible was renewed in January. Two days before surgery, Melissa's surgeon called and apologetically informed her, "We have a problem. Your Obamacare insurance is denying your surgery." Melissa felt that she was losing her mind. In that moment she realized that coverage for a preexisting condition is only as good as your access to specialist doctors. While many rightfully support protections for those with preexisting conditions like Melissa's, these protections are meaningless when you are unable to access needed care.

Forgetting about her own problem for a moment, Melissa rushed to the pediatrician to take Royce in for a follow-up after his fevers finally subsided and to get her newborn, Cross, immunized. When she arrived at the pediatrician, they informed her that Cross's insurance had been canceled. Her only option was to pay out of pocket the shocking amount of $947. "It's right around Christmastime. I'm broke. I don't have the money. He needs to have his shots, though," Melissa pleaded with her doctor. "My son just got out of Infectious Disease."

For two hours Melissa sat in the office calling Obamacare and UHC, all the while telling the doctor, "You know I have insurance. You just treated Royce!" The doctor knew she had insurance but couldn't process it without the Obamacare system resolving the problem. The nurse, the doctor, and Melissa passed the phone around, taking turns talking to Obamacare and UHC. Each entity referred the callers back to the other. "Bottom line, we didn't get his immunization. We went to the health department," Melissa said. "I think Royce only had three Christmas gifts that year because we didn't have the money." The insurance that the Ackisons paid for on time and in full was useless.

Left with no choice, Melissa called her senator, Rob Portman. She detailed her experience to his staff, and they assured her, "We're going to get this resolved." Miraculously, within twenty-four hours, her surgery was approved. "Isn't it interesting the way that works?" Melissa mused. Everything should have been covered: Melissa's surgery, the immunization, everything. After Portman got involved, UHC tried to blame Melissa, claiming they didn't have the prior authorization. The excuse was bogus, since Melissa had copies of the authorization right in front of her.

In all, Melissa calculated that her family paid $40,000 in out-of-pocket medical expenses in 2016. "I'm trying to run a family business. I'm taking care of little kids, living on a farm. I have cows and chickens, and I would be inside on the phone all day long trying to navigate through systems," she recounted. This was despite being fully covered under Obamacare. In addition to draining her 401(k), Melissa's credit was ruined. Although failure to pay medical bills was a result of an Obamacare plan going bankrupt and government incompetence in the enrollment process, Melissa—not the federal government—suffered the consequences. "How much do you think collectors are going to listen to me when I say things like 'I'm sorry, we have Obamacare. Now, that bill wasn't covered, but they're working this out'?" Melissa asked. To make matters worse, the government has not reimbursed Melissa for one dime of her out-of-pocket costs.

Melissa's insurance plan changed for a third time when she enrolled in the 2017 marketplace. Despite being a business owner with a net worth that made health care affordable for her, she was told that she was eligible for Medicaid, since its criteria is based on income only. Melissa explained that "2016 was our only bad year . . . We shouldn't be on Medicaid at all"—she did not need or even want Medicaid—but it was her only viable option. "We come from a long line of military service members, who worked hard for everything," Melissa said. "My grandparents were coal miners and lived in the coal camps of West Virginia until they could leave to go to the military to make a life for themselves. We come from a long line of very hardworking people. I know the difference between right and wrong." Melissa felt that taking Medicaid was wrong, especially considering her total assets.

The only alternative to Medicaid was CareSource, the government-managed plan in the Obamacare exchange, offering high premiums and insufficient coverage. Melissa faced two bad options for her family, both essentially operated by the government. Eventually she accepted that Medicaid was her only real choice. When Melissa enrolled, the caseworker went further in offering her another government-subsidized handout: an electronic benefit transfer (EBT) card. "I'm pulling up in an S-Class Mercedes-Benz, presenting a welfare Medicaid program. This makes no sense!" Melissa exclaimed, noting that she turned down the EBT card offer. "We are not vulnerable, we are not unable to care for ourselves; we were simply business owners who had a poor year!"

Medicaid and Medicare were intended for people like Melissa's grandparents, who were both diagnosed with dementia and did not have the means to afford health care. "Medicaid was not designed as a safety net to take care of individuals who are not working or choose not to work. That's not what these programs were provided for," Melissa explained. When Democrats talk about millions of Americans losing Medicaid, some of those recipients are individuals like Melissa who do not need Medicaid but are forced on it because there is no other affordable option for health care in the free market.

Although Medicaid works for Melissa, it comes at an immense cost to the taxpayer. "Medicaid is a better deal," Melissa flatly admitted. "Who in their right mind would work hard to get off of this? We know better, because that's how we were raised." Melissa believes that pushing people onto Medicaid or a government-operated plan like CareSource is the ultimate goal of Obamacare, which slowly corrals millions of Americans into the hands of the federal government.

Through the stress and hardship, Melissa relied on faith. In the lead-up to the 2016 election, Melissa and her church met every Sunday at 10:30 a.m. to pray, specifically for the upcoming vote. "We knew that it was the last opportunity we had to turn things around," she said. "And if you think I'm the only one like this, you can talk to all of the farmers, all of the people in the area, anybody who's worked hard for anything: they have felt the exact same way."

The night before the election, Melissa's husband grew nervous about the prospect of a Hillary Clinton victory and the continuation of their Obamacare nightmare. Melissa looked at him and said with confidence, "There's never been a time in our country where we have prayed collectively like we're praying right now . . . There's nothing more powerful than that." I told her that I understood, because my whole church family was praying as well. I have no doubt that it made the difference. "Most people who don't follow the teaching of Christ, they're not going to understand it," she said. "That is the only thing that helped us."

Melissa's prayers were answered in the form of a Trump victory. In July she was invited to the White House to share her story with Vice President Mike Pence. "It was humbling," Melissa said. "It was almost

Rich and Melissa Ackison with Vice President Mike Pence. *Courtesy of Melissa Ackison*

Melissa and her family at the White House, visiting President Donald Trump.
Courtesy of Melissa Ackison

as if you were sitting down with someone who you've known your entire life. He was gracious. He was kind. I believed that he cared." With her husband beside her, Melissa described her situation to the vice president: "Guess whose 401k is empty now? My credit is ruined. At 39 years old, a business owner, I've worked for everything I've had. I wouldn't be able to get a line of credit right now even if I tried. Where's the money going to come from?"[17]

In July, Melissa was invited to the White House again, this time to meet with President Trump amid a stalling Obamacare repeal-and-replace effort on Capitol Hill. A few days after the meeting, when asked what going to the White House was like, Melissa replied, "At this point, this is a job for me. I was honored to be a part of this, but I've been lobbying at Republican dinners, trying to get in front of my congressman . . . I was happy to meet Mr. Trump. I support his efforts . . . But at this point I wasn't really overwhelmed with any of that. I'm more concerned with the legislature."[18] Melissa does have confidence in the Trump administration solving the health care dilemma, but she nevertheless remains frustrated with the Obama-era leaders in Washington who left her family in a perilous situation: "How do you vote for bailouts for large companies? Where's *my* bailout? . . . I've got a son heading to the Middle East. He called us the night before we left to let us know it will be his first tour. We have raised our kids patriotic. We love our country. Why is this happening to us? Why?"[19]

My Story

Every summer I lie facedown on a cold, sterile, uninviting surface. Apprehensive and fearful, I am slightly pulled back into a confining tube, where a magnetic field pulsates around my body. A gentle tap, tap, tap begins, followed by a loud and obtrusive continuous thump.[20] Radio waves dart into my body and contrast is shot into my veins through an intravenous tube, creating a cold sensation internally and a curious metallic taste. "Please try to stay as still as you possibly can," the nurse's voice blares through the speaker in my ear. As I attempt to lie motionless with my face buried in a cushion, I try my best to push out that one haunting question that has crept into my mind constantly over the last decade: Is today the day I will find out I have cancer?

The thirty-minute-long MRI procedure creates hundreds of pictures, showing my breasts in cross-sectional slices that my doctors at Moffitt Cancer Hospital search for any sign of potential malignancy. If my imaging is normal, I return in six months for a follow-up mammogram. But if it reveals new growth I am called back for further testing. In the intervening waiting period, fear can envelop you if you let it. Is it cancer? Will I have to have chemo? What about radiation? Could I lose my hair? What if I have the aggressive, fast-growing breast cancer and it's too far gone? The line of questioning can ravage you.

For eight years, I have dealt with questions like these, trying to cabin them to the far corner of my thoughts. Until December 24, 2009, I was never really cognizant of health. Like most twenty-one-year-olds, I was far more concerned with boys, college, and job offers. But that all changed on Christmas Eve. Instead of waking to the joyous celebration of the impending holiday, I woke to a piercing, foreboding ring and a daunting, life-altering reality. Recognizing the area code but not the number, I answered with a lazy hello. The voice on the other end greeted me with the grim news: "Kayleigh, this is your doctor. We're sorry to inform you that you've tested positive for the BRCA2 genetic mutation."

An unexpected waterfall of tears poured down my face as I tried to comprehend the magnitude of the news: I had an 84 percent chance of getting breast cancer in my lifetime. Days earlier, my mom had undergone a mastectomy. Although she did not have breast cancer, she chose to remove her breast tissue as a preventive measure, since she too was BRCA2 positive and faced a frighteningly high chance of breast cancer. With eight extended relatives plagued by the disease, the choice to take proactive measures seemed like an obvious one for my mom. When I went to visit her in the hospital, she was sick and physically weak, but I recognized profound strength—a certain valor in her decision to take control of her future. I could look at my mom and say with near certainty that she would never die of breast cancer. But could I say the same for myself? No. The recognition of my mom eradicating a disease before it could ever plague her compelled me to get tested for the BRCA2 genetic mutation myself, on the very day of her surgery.

I had casually and somewhat cavalierly taken the BRCA2 genetic mutation test, not expecting to hear a positive result just days later and not prepared for the torrent of emotions that would accompany it. I knew that I was at risk for breast cancer, but now my fate seemed all but certain. I walked downstairs on that Christmas Eve, and my family immediately noticed my teary eyes. My mom and grandmother enveloped me with a supportive embrace, fully understanding my feelings in that moment, and my dad provided those sage words of comfort that I have passed along to so many others. "Kayleigh," he said, "you know your weakness. We all have one in life—cancer, Alzheimer's, heart disease, or some unknown weakness that creeps into our lives—but you know yours. You know your weakness, and you can attack it head-on."

My tears began to subside as I realized that the BRCA2 genetic mutation, instead of being a curse, was really a blessing. It permitted me to take the offensive against breast cancer rather than being on the defensive. That didn't mean there weren't costs to accompany this new awareness. In fact, there were many. Like the time when I got my first mammogram at the age of twenty-two. It was a bewildering, frightening experience. Walking into the cancer hospital, I saw women with scarves on their heads, covering their bald scalps, and feeble patients shuffled around in wheelchairs by family members. Sitting in the waiting room in a light-blue gown, I was the youngest one there. Surrounded by all older women, I was the only girl.

In the mammogram room, a lead pad shield is Velcroed around your waist to protect the ovaries from radiation. A nurse squeezes and positions your breasts into a cold machine, beneath a clear panel that is pressed tightly down. She instructs you to remain as still as possible and hold your breath while X-ray beams shoot through your breasts in search of calcifications, early indications of cancer. After a dozen or so cycles of repositioning, motionless posing, and pictures, you are ushered back to a waiting room to see if you need further testing.

After that first mammogram, I took a seat by my mom, who was talking to another patient. "It's my second battle with breast cancer," she told us. "During my first fight, they took one of my breasts, but I wouldn't let them take the other . . . And it came back." Following a brief period of remission, she now sat before us with a scarf covering her head, undergoing rounds of chemotherapy. "You don't have to worry," she assured me. "You only worry when they come in and call you back for an ultrasound."

Almost instantly, a nurse came in the door. "Kayleigh," she called, looking down at her pad. "We're going to need you to do an ultrasound." Terrified and certain I had cancer, my eyes welled up.

"Can my mom come?" I nervously asked the nurse.

"No, she has to stay," the nurse told me.

I went back to the ultrasound room and lay on a metal table as my mind flooded with thoughts of what chemotherapy would be like and how cancer would affect my postgraduate plans. Trying my best to hide my tears, I turned my head away from the nurse and continued to cry as she squirted gel on my right breast. Picking up a small, handheld wand, the nurse began rubbing the transducer along my skin in a circular motion. Sound waves pulsated beneath the wand and into the breast, creating an odd-looking black-and-white bumpy terrain on a small television screen. Turning my head to the right and peaking beyond the nurse's arm, I saw the landscape shift as she moved the wand. Occasionally she stopped and placed marked dots on four sides of a circular-looking oval specimen. *Was that the cancer?* I wondered. Curious and frightened, I asked her, "Is everything OK?" She replied, "You'll have to wait for the radiologist."

Returning to the waiting room, I found my mom on the phone with my dad, worried that her oldest daughter might have cancer. The lady beside her had left, carrying on her battle against the ugly illness. After thirty minutes of fear and apprehension, I found out that everything was OK. I just had a spot that needed to be continually monitored for change. Constant monitoring for breast cancer and a revolving door of doctors and worry was my new reality.

My twenties have been a blessed decade, free from the ravages of cancer, but not from the prospect of it. There was the time when I found the lump in my breast during my first year of law school. The first year of law school (1L) is notoriously the most difficult one: fourteen-hour days of classes or studying, seven days a week. Although nearly every waking hour of my life that year was devoted to studying, that day I found the lump was entirely devoted to my health. After a worry-filled day of visits with the gynecologist and the radiologist, I was relieved that it was likely just a benign cyst or a hardened lump of fat.

Next was the haunting study I came across: "In carriers of BRCA 1/2 mutations any exposure to diagnostic radiation [i.e., mammography] before the age of 30 was associated with an increased risk of breast cancer . . ."[21] Soon after this study was published, I had a mammogram. A worried radiologist came out after the test and expressed concerns about the procedure. He explained that this new study revealed a risk of accumulated radiation from mammograms in young women. The study confirmed a worrying dilemma: Could my mammograms actually be giving me cancer?

For years I debated the issue and urged doctors to allow me to continue with MRIs only, especially given that almost without fail the nurse conducting the mammogram would exclaim to me, "Wow, your breast tissue is so dense that we can barely see a thing!" Doctors urged me to stick with the current plan. Nowadays, many reputable medical entities do not recommend mammograms for BRCA patients until after age thirty. Yet I have had nearly a dozen throughout my twenties.

As I move forward, I face a permanent, fearful, and final step in my journey: a double mastectomy. Although I have had the first in a series of three surgeries, the second daunting surgery looms: the one where I must remove all of my breast tissue and accept my new self. The tissue that is removed will be replaced with silicone implants, making my appearance virtually unchanged from before, but the procedure is nevertheless frightening, since it cannot be reversed.

As I approach the age of thirty, my decision-making time has arrived. Thirty is the age at which my chances of breast cancer begin to rise significantly above that of the normal population, and it also happens to be the age that I will begin thinking about starting a family. Pregnancy is yet another consideration, since BRCA cancers are estrogen-fed, and during pregnancy a woman's body is inundated with estrogen. Fortunately for me, as of November 2017, I have a new, loving, selfless, and supportive husband to join the incredibly encouraging and supportive family that I already have.

I also have the brave women who have come before me, like my mom, who had the courage to get a double mastectomy before it was popularized as a preventive measure. And strong women like Angelina Jolie, who openly announced her decision to have a mastectomy after learning she carried the BRCA1 mutation. My mom called me on May 14, 2013, and hurriedly urged, "You have to read the *New York Times*, Kayleigh! Angelina has BRCA just like us." I opened my computer to find Jolie's words. "I am writing about it now because I hope that other women can benefit from my experience. Cancer is still a word that strikes fear into people's hearts . . . But today it is possible to find out through a blood test whether you are highly susceptible to breast and ovarian cancer, and then take action," she wrote.[22] With confidence, she could now say what my mom was able to say to me several years earlier: "My chances of developing breast cancer have dropped from 87% to under 5%. I can tell my children that they don't need to fear they will lose me to breast cancer."[23] Jolie's bravery helped to bring BRCA1 and BRCA2 mutations into the mainstream, creating awareness for vulnerable women and bestowing acceptance on mutation carriers who previously felt alone.

As I move forward, I do so in the face of creeping fears but in the knowledge that Jesus Christ is guiding my path, wherever that may lead. I have a special heart for the three hundred thousand women in our country alone who are diagnosed with breast cancer each year.[24] And I have a special empathy for a group of citizens who find themselves at the center of the American health care debate: the 52 million Americans with preexisting conditions.

As a BRCA2 mutation carrier, I am among the roughly one in four Americans who have a preexisting condition.[25] Preexisting conditions come in a variety of forms: genetic mutations, actual cancer, lupus, obesity, and even pregnancy.[26] But unlike millions of uninsured Americans, I am a high-risk patient blessed with continual health care coverage. For a BRCA patient, cancer can often feel like a *when*, not an *if*, and absent the ability to monitor with costly testing, haunting helplessness ensues.

I tell you my BRCA story in vivid detail for a reason, and the reason is this: there are two sides to the health care debate. Yes, Obamacare is beset with flaws: soaring double-digit premiums and one-third of U.S. counties offering just one insurance option in their exchanges. Yes, it should be repealed and replaced. But the Affordable Care Act had an important component that ought to be recognized: in theory, it protected individuals with preexisting conditions from being denied coverage or left with prohibitively expensive insurance options.

Or did it? Melissa Ackison's story revealed a forgotten angle of the preexisting conditions coverage debate. Even though, under the letter of the Obamacare law, Melissa's high-risk pregnancy and rare skin disease and her son's strabismus and fine motor delay in theory amounted to four protected preexisting conditions, none of them were covered in practice. "The myth needs to be debunked as it relates to the general public thinking the words 'pre-existing conditions' are some form of protected class under the Obamacare programs," Melissa wrote to me. "Our examples of pre-existing conditions are a clear example that the Obamacare insurance didn't save us from anything and in fact made our situation worse." She was spot-on, and it is a point that I had never truly considered until I listened to both sides of the health care debate.

One of the several reasons I supported candidate Donald Trump throughout the 2016 primaries and beyond was his willingness to observe the realities of health care and cross party lines when necessary. Although Trump recognized the need to repeal Obamacare, he also acknowledged that patients with preexisting conditions must be protected. Obamacare had to go, but protections for these vulnerable patients must not. "I would absolutely get rid of Obamacare," Trump so often said. "[But] I want to keep pre-existing conditions. It's the modern age, and I think we have to have it."

In addition to protecting this group of patients, Trump vowed to fight for all Americans to have access to health care. When asked on a Republican debate stage whether he espoused views similar to Bernie Sanders's on health care, since he had previously said everyone has got to be covered, Trump replied, "I don't think I am. I think I'm closer to common sense."[27] He went on to say Obamacare must be repealed but that "there were will be a certain number of people that will be on the street dying, and as a Republican I don't want that to happen. We're going to take care of people that are dying on the street."[28] Trump's mix of free-market principles and compassion was a winning combination, and one that must be implemented in practice through a Republican-passed health care plan that ensures those with preexisting conditions retain coverage but that simultaneously lowers costs for everyone else.

Throughout 2016, Republicans proposed a variety of plans to repeal and replace Obamacare. Along with each proposal came media accusations that Republicans were rolling back protections for those with preexisting conditions. But Republican efforts from the so-called Skinny Repeal to Graham-Cassidy's state-centric model did nothing of the sort. Like Obamacare, Republican plans barred insurers from rejecting customers due to preexisting conditions. Some of the Republican plans, however, altered Obamacare's blanket mandate that insurance plans cost the same for those with preexisting conditions as those without— a regulation that has helped cause premiums nationwide to skyrocket by $3,000 on average. These Republican proposals allowed states to opt out of this regulation *if* and *only if* they have another, working means of providing affordable coverage to those with preexisting conditions. In other words, the states were empowered to find localized solutions to a failed Obamacare regulation. By the letter of the law, those with preexisting conditions were protected—a nuance lost upon much of the media.

Ultimately, a solution to American health care will take bipartisan recognition of the valid concerns on both sides of the aisle. While Trump acknowledged the real concern of Americans losing coverage, few on the left have recognized the horrors of Obamacare: mothers like Melissa who are just trying to afford health care for her family, and fathers like Stan whose son cannot access drugs vital to his well-being. These Americans are real. Conveniently ignoring those plagued by the policies you purvey, whether Democrat or Republican, only takes us further from the answer. We must listen to one another. The stakes are simply too high.

★ PART TWO ★

The President

Coach Kennedy lost his liberty. Brian Easton lost his job. And Dominic Durden lost his life. All at the hands of unjustified government intrusion or avoidable government inaction. The American government, purporting to represent these Americans, instead forgot them. The stories of these resilient citizens are the stories of millions of Americans who have lost hope in government. Together they explain the making of a powerful, unforeseen populist movement and the eventual election of Donald Trump as president of the United States.

While Part I of this book explored the making of a movement, Part II recounts the manifestation of it. After years of betrayal, frustration with the governing class turned into a deep-seated anger that should have been discernible to anyone who took the time to listen to what the people were saying. But the media wasn't listening and neither were the politicians. Ensconced in a Northeast Corridor echo chamber, few took the time to speak directly to the American people: the factory workers, the first responders, the small-business owners. If they did, they would fully understand the motivating emotions and rationale that sent Donald Trump to 1600 Pennsylvania Avenue. Voter contempt for the governing elite and irritation with the politically correct confines of our society fueled the rise of Trump and the era of outsiders.

THE BEGINNING

"During this course of administration, and in order to disturb it,
the artillery of the press has been leveled against us, charged with
whatsoever its licentiousness could devise or dare. These abuses of an
institution so important to freedom and science are deeply to be regretted,
inasmuch as they tend to lessen its usefulness and to sap its safety."
—THOMAS JEFFERSON

On June 14, 2015, then-citizen Donald Trump called his family over for dinner. The day marked his sixty-ninth birthday, but it also marked the start of a life-changing journey that would end at 1600 Pennsylvania Avenue. "Guys, I want to do it. I want to run for president," one family member remembered him saying. "What does everyone think? It's not going to be easy. Our family will become a target." Donald Trump had the foresight to know a candidacy intent on changing Washington, not conforming to it, would be controversial, subjecting his whole family to unfair and unsubstantiated media attacks.

His reluctance to drag his family into the national spotlight comported with what he had told Oprah nearly three decades earlier: "I just don't think I really have the inclination to do it. I love what I'm doing . . . but I do get tired of seeing what's happening with this country, and if it got so bad, I would never want to rule it out totally."[1] America had finally gotten to the point where Trump knew he had to sacrifice and make a bid for the nation's highest office. "If you run, you'll win," his wife, Melania, assured him.

With the full-fledged support of his family and two thumbs-up,

Trump descended that Trump Tower escalator on June 16, 2015, with his wife by his side, departing the world of business for the realm of politics. Cameras flashed and Trump signs shot into the air as Trump took the stage, joining his oldest daughter, Ivanka, who stood waiting to introduce her father to an exuberant crowd of onlookers. The words he prepared to say would begin the process of changing the political landscape forever, setting the country on a promising trajectory but not without consequences for his family. In the years leading up to Trump's announcement, the media celebrated Ivanka Trump, the young, successful businesswoman, whom Trump now proudly embraced onstage.

"Thank God: Ivanka Trump Is Redefining the Idea of the 'Working Woman'"[2]

"Ivanka Trump Celebrates #WomenWhoWork with a Bold New Business Venture"[3]

"Ivanka Trump knows what it means to be a Modern Millennial"[4]

The media lauded the innovative female CEO, entrepreneur and inspiring role model with headlines like these. *Fortune* magazine awarded her a coveted spot on their "40 Under 40" list, recognizing "the most influential young people in business"; and *Vanity Fair* listed her on their 68th Annual International Best-Dressed List.[5] But in the months to come, many of these same media outlets would take a vicious turn in cutting down the thirty-three-year-old businesswoman and the rest of her family simply because of their last name.

Standing before eight American flags in his signature red tie and American flag pin, then-citizen Trump began, "Our country is in serious trouble. We don't have victories anymore ... [W]hen is the last time anyone saw us beating China in a trade deal? ... When did we beat Japan at anything? ... When do we beat Mexico at the border?" After posing these questions to the crowd, Trump proceeded to lay out a fresh set of ideas foreign to many Republicans. His message was anti–unbridled free trade, anti–Iraq War, anti-globalism, and—perhaps most important—antiestablishment. "Politicians are all talk, no action. Nothing's going to get done. They will not bring us—believe me—to the promised land. They will not," Trump declared. "I've watched the politicians. I've dealt with them all my life . . . they're controlled fully by the lobbyists, by the donors, by the special interests."

Near the conclusion of Trump's forty-five-minute speech, the New York businessman emphatically stated to roaring applause, "Ladies and gentlemen, I am officially running for president of the United States, and we are going to make our country great again!" In that moment, citizen Trump became candidate Trump, offering voters a new type of Republicanism, imbued with conservative principles but tempered with populist concern on issues like trade, foreign policy, Medicare, and Medicaid.

At the time, few recognized the potency of a Donald Trump candidacy. The media dismissed it out of hand. The day before Trump's announcement, MSNBC's Lawrence O'Donnell quipped, "He is obviously never going to be president. He is obviously never going to be the Republican nominee for president."[6] Chris Matthews agreed, erroneously predicting, "It still looks like Hillary is the next president."[7] The *Washington Post*'s Philip Bump described Trump's campaign launch as "spectacular, unending, utterly baffling, often-wrong."[8] He wrote, "If nothing else, let his candidacy serve as a reminder that no matter how rich or powerful you are, it's useful to have someone around who can say 'no.'"[9] CNN's Chris Cillizza warned his media peers, "Trump has every right to run . . . But what he should not get is covered as though this is an even-close-to-serious attempt to either win the Republican nomination or influence the conversation in GOP circles in any significant way. It's not."[10]

By June 30, 2015, the Huffington Post was already touting "The Super-Quick Implosion of Donald Trump's Candidacy."[11] Even Nate Silver's FiveThirtyEight, which prides itself on accurately calling elections, ran an article called "Why Donald Trump Isn't a Real Candidate, in One Chart," predicting "Trump has a better chance of cameoing in another 'Home Alone' movie with Macaulay Culkin—or playing in the NBA Finals—than winning the Republican nomination."[12] CNBC's Ben White went so far as to make a wrongheaded bet with rather grave consequences for his physical health, stating confidently, "Donald Trump is not going to be the next president of the United States. This reporter is already on record pledging to eat a bag of rusty nails if the real estate tycoon . . . manages to snag the GOP nomination."[13] It is unclear whether White ever made good on that promise.

The so-called analysts that fill our TV screens were not just off base in their 2016 analysis; they were dead wrong. Although these political analysts were hired to predict accurately the political will of the people, they instead made it their mission to malign the future president. In most professions, perennial failure to do your job would cost you that job, but in political punditry the never-Trump resistance is rewarded. "They were constantly saying we had no chance of winning," Jared Kushner said. "They were looking at our campaign through a traditional lens and were just talking to each other."

The political pundits just didn't seem to get it. Their failure to recognize the powerful movement of frustrated Americans and their continual underestimation of Trump's candidacy would become somewhat of a trend. Consider the long litany of false narratives spun by the media throughout the primary alone:

First, we were told Donald Trump would never run for president.

"Stop pretending—Donald Trump is not running for president," said the *New York Post*.[14]

"Donald Trump says that he's forming an 'exploratory' committee for president. And mermaids have been spotted near Atlantis," a *Newsday* editorial quipped before continuing, "The perennial game Trump plays with the American electorate, and with the media, where he pretends to run for high office to get his name back in the headlines, has become more than just disingenuous. It's downright insulting at this point, not to mention undignified."[15]

A piece in *Time* magazine echoed the "Trump's not running" narrative, pointing to all of the previous times Trump had teased about running before ultimately concluding, "[He] sounds pretty serious, unless you have a memory of what he has said before . . . The echoes of past feints haunt Trump's latest tease like a poker tell."[16]

Trump, of course, did run for the highest office in the land, but that didn't stop the next flawed media narrative:

"Trump will drop out." Convinced that Trump would never throw

his hat in the 2016 arena, the media couldn't help themselves in predicting a quick and embarrassing exit for the New York businessman.[17]

In listing three "truths" about Trump, the *Atlantic* offered, "We
know *what* will happen—that Trump will drop out—even though we
don't know exactly when. We know too that each day spent covering
his alleged 'campaign' means a day of lost time for the Republicans in
choosing their real candidate."[18]

GOP strategist Stuart Stevens predicted that Trump would exit the
race before primary votes were even cast, telling CNBC, "I don't see that
Donald Trump has the temperament to subject himself to the voters in
Iowa and be judged."[19]

In a *New York Times* article called "From Donald Trump, Hints of
a Campaign Exit Strategy," another Republican strategist erroneously
predicted, "[Trump] would not leave himself to have his destiny settled
by actual voters going to the polls or the caucuses."[20]

But voters perceived Trump's seriousness a bit differently, with the
Times article concluding, "In Iowa, people 'think he's in for the dura-
tion,' said Doug Gross, a Republican strategist. But, he added, 'I think
he's peaked.'" Republican voters saw Donald Trump as not just serious
but necessary—a needed fighter to take on the Republican establishment that had betrayed them. It's why after just seven days in the race,
Trump quickly shot up to number one in the Republican primary field.
According to the media, though, Trump's upward trajectory would
soon hit a ceiling.

"He has shot up like a rocket since his June announcement but likely
has a low ceiling and short staying power," wrote Peggy Noonan in the
Wall Street Journal.[21] The "ceiling" talk was pervasive:

"He will probably hit a natural ceiling on his support."[22]

"Instant-runoff polls would highlight Trump's very low ceiling of
support."[23]

"His support has a relatively low ceiling."[24]

"The favorability number might actually show Trump's ceiling."[25]

The flawed "ceiling" talk could not have been more off base. Trump's
so-called ceiling rose from 10 percent in July to 20 percent in August to
30 percent in September.[26] His "ceiling" continued to grow to the point

where he earned 44.9 percent of Republican primary votes, amounting to some 13.3 million votes—more votes than any candidate has won in Republican primary history by a long shot.[27]

I remember one Florida voter asking me, "How did you predict Trump's victory so early in the primary?" Well, the key was simple: you had to immerse yourself in the people, not the punditry. My frequent weekend trips home to Florida revealed a change-oriented electorate with severe distrust of institutions: the media, big business, and certainly the politicians.

In July of 2015, about a month after Trump declared his candidacy, *CNN Tonight* host Don Lemon asked for my thoughts on the *Des Moines Register* editorial board calling Trump a "bloviating sideshow" and "unfit to hold office" before ultimately recommending that "the best way Donald Trump can serve his country . . . [is by] terminating this ill-conceived campaign."[28]

"What's your reaction, Kayleigh?" Don asked.[29]

"You know what the problem is with that, Don?" I replied. "The *Des Moines Register* is reacting to the fact that Donald Trump is not your typical politician. And if you ask me, that is a good thing. Donald Trump is the anti-politician. He's coming off very refreshing . . . not rehearsed. He's not poll testing every word coming out of his mouth."[30] White House press secretary Sarah Huckabee Sanders said it well when she told me: "He says what he thinks instead of thinking about what you want to hear."

In addition to offering fresh, unadulterated, realspeak, Donald Trump had the added attribute of being a fighter—a necessary attribute in combating mainstream media misrepresentation. As they so often do to Republican candidates generally, the media did not just misunderstand Trump and underestimate his electoral prowess; they intentionally mischaracterized him. Anything and everything Trump did would be construed entirely negatively.

Take, for example, the June 6, 2016, call that I and a few surrogates were on with then-candidate Donald Trump. Although most candidates do not take the time to get on the phone with their surrogates, leaving the task to a low-level staffer, Trump spent almost an hour on the phone with his supporters. It was a calm and positive discussion in which Trump thanked us and did something most politicians would not do: he listened. Yes, he explained his point of view on the issues of the day, but, as I recall, Trump spent most of the hour listening to his surrogates' input, fielding questions and comments.

Hours later, news of the so-called red-hot call broke in the news.[31] The media began wall-to-wall coverage, alleging that Trump was "irritated" and had issued "orders" and "mandates" for his surrogates to say certain things. Perplexed by the off-kilter tone of the media coverage, I told CNN's Erin Burnett, "This is an example of media selective listening. I was on the call. This was a positive phone call where he thanked supporters . . . [This is] a complete example of why the American people do not trust the media. It's one of the least trusted institutions in this country . . . They spin things the way they want to spin them."[32] Here was the media characterizing a phone call they were never even in on.

"I wasn't surprised by the media backlash," Michael Glassner, former deputy campaign manager of Trump 2016 and current executive director of Trump 2020, said. "Trump was able to go outside their channels. He was a threat to their monopoly of getting a national political message out."

Only a fighter like Donald Trump could stand up to the media mischaracterization.

From the very beginning, the media and the left maligned Trump, falsely labeling him racist, misogynistic, anti-Semitic, xenophobic, and any other label they could contrive. But as the left formulated their strategy, there is one factor they failed to take into account: the intelligence of the American people. Unable to be easily manipulated, the American people recognized the Trump accusations for the baseless smears that they were. The math just didn't add up.

Trump was called anti-Semitic even though he has a Jewish daughter and son-in-law whom he elevated to important positions in his administration. Democrats dubbed him misogynistic even though the Trump Organization executives are disproportionately female.[33] Likewise, they egregiously labeled him "racist" with no facts to support this horrendous charge.

Ask yourself whether you heard any of the facts to the contrary. Did you hear that Jesse Jackson once praised Trump as a "friend" who "served the underserved communities"?[34] Did you hear that Trump's Palm Beach club, Mar-a-Lago, was the first club there open to African-Americans and Jews?[35] Did you hear that the Anti-Defamation League praised him for shining "the light on Palm Beach. Not on the beauty and the glitter, but on its seamier side of discrimination"?[36] Did you hear the media lavish praise upon Trump for calling for the removal of the confederate flag from the South Carolina capitol or for acknowledging the other side of the police debate in calling what happened to Sandra Bland "terrible"?[37] You likely didn't hear any of that.

Pointing to this disconnect between facts and reality, Ivanka told me, "Critics try to define my father, to label him, but the reality of what he does defies the stereotypes. People see through it." As president, Trump honored the Jewish people, standing at the Western Wall wearing a yarmulke with his hand humbly placed in peaceful reverence. He was the first sitting president to visit the wall. Trump signaled his respect for Islam when he gathered fifty-four Muslim leaders in Riyadh, uniting them in the common goal of denouncing extremism and hate. He stood shoulder to shoulder with King Salman of Saudi Arabia, the Custodian of the Two Holy Mosques. And in a final stop on his first foreign trip, he recognized his own Christian faith by visiting Pope Francis at the Vatican. Trump's actions continue to defy the accusations of those intent on demonizing him.

The effort to define Trump negatively is not too distant from the effort to mischaracterize another American president. In September of 1980, a Democratic congressman said, "I'm going to talk about a man who has embraced a platform that . . . the Ku Klux Klan said couldn't be better if they'd written it themselves . . . [a man] who seeks the presidency of the United States with the endorsement of the Ku Klux Klan."[38] The secretary of health and human services said this presidential candidate raised the "spectre of white sheets."[39] Another Democratic congressman said that this man was "trying to replace the Bill of Rights with fascist precepts lifted verbatim from *Mein Kampf*."[40] And a columnist for *Esquire* posited that voting for him was akin to acting like "good

Germans" in "Hitler's Germany."[41] That man who was widely decried and widely misconstrued is now widely hailed as one of our greatest presidents: Ronald Wilson Reagan.

"The American people are incredibly savvy, inquisitive, and thoughtful," Ivanka told me. They are fully capable of thinking for themselves as they did in November of 1980 and November of 2016. In reality, Donald Trump the man is far different than Donald Trump the media creation. "I got to know him backstage," Governor Mike Huckabee told me. "The thing that was so impressive about him was his relationship with his family . . . It's the relationship that every father could hope to have with children . . . The Trumps backstage had the warmest, most loving and respectful kind of relationship, and those were the things that really told me, boy, the public really doesn't know this guy."

"I've seen on a personal level how he cares about people," Trump's daughter-in-law, Lara, said. "His connection with the doorman. His connection with the man who cleans the floor. He stops and talks to them and asks about their lives." Echoing this sentiment, Governor Huckabee observed, "The loyalty of his staff and his team, people that had worked for him for twenty years and adore him, would take a bullet for him because there was a side of him that people didn't see. The generosity. The kindness. Being willing to stand up for people who made a big mistake." Citing an example, Huckabee noted that Trump stood with the speechwriter for Melania Trump, who echoed lines from Michelle Obama's speech at the Republican National Convention, causing Melania to receive widespread scrutiny from the media. Even though the speechwriter had made a grave mistake, Trump picked up the phone and urged her not to worry. "She made a mistake . . . we all make mistakes," Trump told ABC News.[42] "That says a lot about his character," Governor Huckabee said. "So when people say he doesn't have any, I'm thinking, 'Well, from what I saw, he has a whole lot more than the politicians I've dealt with.'"

"He's a person who cares particularly about people who he thinks are being taken advantage of," Secretary Ben Carson told me. "He doesn't necessarily demonstrate the soft part because you need to be sort of a tough guy to get through all of this morass in the swamp, but he actually is a very kindhearted person." As Ivanka noted in her Republican National Convention speech, her father is the man who would "tear stories out of newspapers about people whom he had never met, who were facing some injustice or hardship."[43] Upon hearing their stories, he would pick up his "signature black felt tip pen" and invite them to Trump Tower, where he would "draw upon his extensive network to find them a job or get them a break."

This is the Donald Trump you may not know. The man who offered Darnell Barton, a city bus driver, $10,000 when he heard that Darnell had pulled his bus over and persuaded a woman not to jump off an overpass.[44] And the man who stepped up and bought jerseys for a Harlem basketball team when he heard that their benefactor had died. That is the Donald Trump some are lucky enough to meet but few will ever hear about. Nevertheless, it's the Donald Trump whom the American people recognized and elevated to the highest office in the land.

THE OUTSIDERS

"The spirit of resistance to government is so valuable on certain occasions, that I wish it to be always kept alive . . . I like a little rebellion now and then. It is like a storm in the Atmosphere."
—THOMAS JEFFERSON

You likely remember the moment.

"Let's welcome the candidates for the Republican nomination for president," David Muir of ABC announced as he prepared to welcome seven candidates to the debate stage in Goffstown, New Hampshire.[1]

"New Jersey Governor Chris Christie," Muir stated, signaling to Governor Christie to emerge from the blue curtained hallway.[2]

"Dr. Ben Carson," Martha Raddatz said amid very loud cheering in an effort to cue Dr. Carson to walk out.[3]

Not hearing his signal, Carson stood still backstage as the camera zoomed in on him. After a few moments, Carson moved forward, only to stop when he heard Muir say, "Texas Senator Ted Cruz."[4]

Carson looked back as Senator Cruz passed by him with a shrug.

"Businessman Donald Trump," Raddatz continued as the crowd began to murmur and whisper, wondering why Carson had not taken his podium.[5] Trump slowly walked out, taking notice of Carson, who stood alone. Well within the camera's angle, the nation watched as Carson stood by as the other presidential candidates passed. Rather than walking out on the stage, Trump made his way over to Carson and patted him on the arm. The two stood alone together as Senator Marco Rubio and Governor Jeb Bush walked by.

The mishap made for an awkward moment, with Muir finally announcing, "And Dr. Ben Carson, please come out on the stage . . . ," echoed by Raddatz saying, "And Donald Trump."[6]

While all the politicians had passed by, waving at the crowd as they took to the stage, just one—Donald Trump—opted to skip his walkout and stand in solidarity with his fellow outsider, Dr. Carson. Dr. Carson told me that the moment was one of several that factored into his decision to endorse President Trump. He recognized that there might be more to the man than the mainstream media portrayal.

The optics of the moment were indeed a fitting symbol for the 2016 election: Donald Trump and Ben Carson alone backstage as the politicians cruise by them one by one. It's how the establishment politicians and the mainstream media pictured the 2016 race playing out. In their narrative, Trump and Carson were not serious contenders. They had never held office. They had never campaigned. They were, well, outsiders.

As it turns out, while the media saw their outsider status as their greatest flaw, it was in fact their greatest attribute. Being outside the Beltway is the very reason that Donald Trump and Ben Carson were the only two candidates in a field of sixteen that ever topped national polls in the early days of the primary. The American people were sick and tired of the political class.

"It was obvious to me out there on the campaign trail early on that [the political climate] was not normal," Governor Mike Huckabee told me. "The voters weren't angry. They were in a seething rage and what they wanted was not someone to fix it. They wanted someone to burn the place down." Huckabee was right.

On the set of CNN nearly every primary or caucus night, I pointed my co-panelists to one indicator: polling charting the anger of the electorate. While many of my colleagues breezed over this, it jumped out at me as yet another red flag that something very big was going on, something uncontainable. Indeed, it was.

The American people wanted to take their government back, and that meant dethroning the political elite. Tired of broken promises and public service becoming personal enrichment, Republican voters mur-

mured their discontent with government in the 2014 loss of the second-ranking congressional Republican Eric Cantor, but they screamed it unmistakably in the nomination and eventual election of President Donald Trump.

Polling confirms Huckabee's observations. In every single one of the twenty-seven states where CNN conducted exit and entrance polls during the Republican primaries, more than 80 percent of the Republican electorate felt angry or dissatisfied with the federal government. In total, just shy of 90 percent of Republican voters overall expressed a negative view of the federal government.

The faces of dissatisfied rallygoers expressing profound distrust for institutions like the Justice Department and FBI were not cabined to a few. They were far and above the majority of Republican voters. "It didn't matter what state I was in or what city I was in. Everyone had the exact same complaint even though they had not spoken to each other," former Trump campaign spokesperson Katrina Pierson said. "There was this intrinsic feeling that something is wrong with our system. And whether a person could pinpoint exactly what it was or not, they were very unhappy and things needed to change."

The undeniable anger at the governing class, however, did not legitimate the false media caricature of Trump voters as brawling, violent, and irrational. "That was not the case at all," Michael Glassner told me, who attended hundreds of Trump rallies. "There was a tremendous feeling of hope, and there was a lot of love in the room. There really was this feeling of banding together to take the country back." Frustration and disenchantment turned into a unified hope among Trump voters.

But something deeper than conservative suspicion of government was at play. There was an unnoticed, ignored anger among Democrats as well. It took its form in the unsuccessful candidacy of the anti-establishment Bernie Sanders. "Bernie was a parallel to the left of what Donald Trump was to the right because Bernie was the ultimate throw-a-match-in-the-gasoline-can-and-blow-it-up," Governor Huckabee said.

There were few in the media who recognized this bipartisan frustration. In a profession dominated by establishment voices, only a handful

With Van Jones at the second presidential debate. *Courtesy of author's collection*

of outsiders existed. Despite deep ideological differences, one of Bernie Sanders's key surrogates and I often found ourselves commiserating with each other in the greenroom, griping about the establishment and discussing our constant battle to empower the people. Beyond Bernie surrogates, Van Jones and I had occasional moments of agreement amid our characteristic jousting commentary. Both outsiders from our respective party establishments, we understood the climate of the electorate.

"I just got back to the one statistic that has stuck out to me this entire election," I said after the third presidential debate. "Sixty percent feel the economy is rigged against them."

"Sure," Van replied in a rare moment of agreement.

"'Rig' is an important word in this election. Donald Trump used it tonight and by using that word he might have just played into that feeling that a lot of Americans feel at home that the deck is stacked against them. And that's unfortunate," I continued.

"You know who else used that? Bernie Sanders used that word," Van noted.

"He did."

Polling indeed confirmed that Van and I were in good company, for there was not just anger among Republicans but a bipartisan discontent with government. In all seven states where CNN polled Democrats on their feelings toward the federal government, a solid majority reported anger or dissatisfaction, with 61.4 percent of Democrats expressing discontent with government. One Democratic voter described it this way: "I was all for Obama the first time around . . . and he let me down. I feel that he was a pushover, and he let people behind the curtain pretty much lead him."[7] Interestingly enough, among Democrats, the highest levels of frustration were recorded in Michigan, a state that would turn red after thirty years of going blue. In Michigan, 69 percent of Democratic voters felt disappointment with the federal government, and it was Donald Trump who was able to defy polling, speak to the anger of voters, and peel off states like Michigan that Republicans had not won in three decades.

Democrats and the Trump Base

Donald Trump prevailed, in large part, because of his profound understanding of the Republican base. While conventional politicians on the left and the right did not understand the base, Trump formed a deep and strong connection with this powerful voting bloc. The left, for its part, painted the Trump voter as narrowly and as negatively as possible: in their arrogant view, the Trump supporter was white, male, and low-income at best, and racist, bigoted, and sexist at worst. In lockstep, the media echoed this portrayal. Headlines like these were pervasive:

"Donald Trump Gives White Men Permission to Be Sexist and Racist"[8]

"The Republicans Are Now Officially the Party of White Paranoia"[9]

"Donald Trump's Victory Was Built on Unique Coalition of White Voters"[10]

A *Cosmopolitan* piece condescendingly summed up the Trump voter this way: "Large numbers of Americans are voting for Donald Trump because large numbers of Americans are racists and sexists, perturbed that their long-standing dominance in American life is slowly waning . . . What they see is the most vulgar, obvious version of many of the values the Republican Party itself has been stoking for decades now: white supremacy and male entitlement."[11]

Hillary Clinton, the Democratic nominee for president, echoed this line of attack in astonishing remarks she would later claim to regret. "You know, to just be grossly generalistic," she said. "[Y]ou could put half of Trump's supporters into what I call the basket of deplorables. Right? The racist, sexist, homophobic, xenophobic, Islamaphobic—you name it . . . they are irredeemable."[12]

For some in the media, her comments did not go far enough. In an NBC article titled "Hillary Is Wrong: 100 Percent of Trump Voters Are Deplorable," the author wrote, "Hillary Clinton far undershot her estimate that only 25 percent of Trump supporters were deplorable. There are two easy facts about Trump supporters that are beyond dispute; they are either racist misogynists, or they are willing to vote for a racist misogynist."[13] A Slate author agreed in a piece called "There's No Such Thing as a Good Trump Voter."[14] "People voted for a racist who promised racist outcomes. They don't deserve empathy," the author contended.[15]

The left, in sum, actively demonized Trump's base of support and underestimated them as a narrow, minority cohort. In their view, Trump would be trounced in the general election. On CNN's set, I was continually rebuked by my colleagues with the admonition that "elections are a game of addition, not subtraction, and Trump has done nothing to add to his base of support." Convinced that they had sufficiently painted Trump as a racist and misogynist, the left was confident Trump would find no support among blacks, Latinos, and women. My Election Day exchange on CNN's set just hours before the results came in revealed this confident but wrongheaded attitude.

Responding to a consensus among the panel that Latinos could ruin Trump's chances of winning Florida, Democratic commentator Kirsten Powers warned, "I think in terms of the Republican Party, the problem that they had before this was that they were not attracting or appealing to women and Latinos . . . [A] lot of Latinos and a lot of women stood by and watched these other Republican leaders sort of tarnish themselves by not standing up against Trump."[16]

"I do think we are writing the headline of 'Latinos Deliver Victory for Clinton' a bit prematurely," I responded.[17]

"Of course," Jake Tapper interjected. "We're just saying *if, if.*"[18]

"I don't necessarily believe all of these Latinos that have turned out can just be given to Hillary Clinton," I continued. "I think there are a number of Latinos who care deeply about the economy . . . who realize some of the threats to democracy we see coming from the other side. They have an aversion to totalitarian rule, some of the executive power issues we have seen come out of President Obama. And I think there are going to be Latinos who do show up for Trump . . . I think there will be at least 20, 30 percent that will vote for Donald Trump."[19]

Just hours later, Trump would indeed win 29 percent of the Hispanic vote, leaving the left and the media in shock. He outperformed Mitt Romney, the 2012 Republican nominee, among Hispanics by a full 2 percent.[20] And, among black voters—a group with whom Trump was supposed to underperform, according to the media—Trump again beat Romney by 2 percent.[21] Finally, Trump won roughly the same percentage of the female vote as did Romney and McCain, his two Republican predecessors.[22]

Reflecting on the left's tactics, Jared Kushner said, "The president's real message was an economy and safety message." The left had made a severe miscalculation in making slanderous race and gender accusations the cornerstone of Hillary's botched campaign. The sexist, racist, misogynist narrative of the left had failed in achieving its end.

More than that, Election Night 2016 debunked the myth of the Trump voter as a homogeneous, white, blue-collar base of support. In reality, the profile of the Trump voter was far more nuanced than the one the media constructed. Yes, it's undeniable that Trump won by large margins among blue-collar workers. In fact, he performed better among this group than any presidential candidate since 1980.[23] But there was another type of unseen, underreported Trump voter.

"There's a Trump supporter you rarely see at rallies, but whose existence has been affirmed, again and again, through polling," wrote one perceptive member of the characteristically tone-deaf media.[24] "Call her the Ivanka Voter. She lives in the suburbs . . . She might be middle-aged, with kids in high school or college, or a stay-at-home mom; she might be an up-and-coming professional, not yet married."[25] BuzzFeed's Anne Helen Petersen wrote this prescient and highly predictive analysis just days before the 2016 election.[26]

The *New York Times Magazine* reflected on this very phenomenon following the election in an article called "Why Did College-Educated White Women Vote for Trump?"[27] The author, Emily Bazelon, interviewed three female Pennsylvania voters, Palma Frable and her two daughters, Abigail and Lauren. All three women voted Trump.

"Trump's business record—the fact that he bounced back despite the ups and the downs—initially attracted Frable and her daughters," Bazelon wrote.[28] But there was another reason this unlikely group of voters pulled the lever for Trump. "Frable also admires Ivanka Trump and felt she was one of the campaign's 'top three assets.' She sees Ivanka as a role model for Abigail in her own entrepreneurial interests," Bazelon wrote.[29] "It's not Hillary's 'Gloria Steinem feminism,' as Frable put it, that she values. It's Ivanka's sleek version of female success, which commentators have labeled 'commodity feminism'—branding to sell products."[30] Indeed, this new age feminism—perfectly embodied in the success of Ivanka Trump—is one that was celebrated on my Harvard Law School campus. All throughout the primaries, female classmates would stop me and express their admiration for Ivanka and her brand of feminism.

For a younger generation, old-wave feminism had been supplanted by a newer, less victim-, more victor-oriented feminism. In the eyes of some women, including myself, Hillary Clinton played victim in a way that was ultimately counterproductive to women trying to climb the corporate or political ranks. This victimization strategy was on ready display during Clinton's years on the debate stage.

In her infamous 2000 New York Senate debate with Rick Lazio, Clinton took on a stunned countenance when her male competitor left his podium and walked toward hers. The *Washington Post* painted Lazio as "bullying and inappropriate," an image that those in the Clinton world gladly hyped up by calling Lazio "menacing" and "personally insulting."[31] Labeled as one of the "worst debate moments ever," the encounter is widely pointed to as a reason for Lazio's loss and Clinton's victory.[32]

Victimization again took center stage in Clinton's 2016 Flint, Michigan, primary debate with Bernie Sanders. In a fiery exchange, Sanders firmly told Clinton, "Excuse me, I'm talking!" Predictably, the media asserted sexism.[33] The Clinton team played into the sexism narrative, with Clinton-friendly Correct the Record tweeting, "That was rude."[34] The next day Clinton's campaign spokeswoman appeared on CNN alleging that Sanders was "at times a little disrespectful."[35] The media echoed the sexism storyline with an illustrative *New York* magazine headline blaring, "Sanders Tells Clinton: 'Excuse Me, I'm Talking' in Arguably Sexist Debate Exchange."[36] After writing an extensive historical research paper on gender dynamics in debates, I concluded this in a CNN article: "Clinton said 'excuse me' to Sanders three times in the Miami debate three days later, and the press did not take notice. A perusal of the 2016 primary debate transcripts shows that 'excuse me' has been leveled in a caustic manner 22 times. Nevertheless, outside of the time a male directed it to a female, the 'excuse me' interjection never graced a single headline."[37]

Clinton continues to use the "victim" strategy even in her post-election life. In promoting her memoir, Clinton released this book excerpt to the media in August of 2017 recounting the moment during the St. Louis debate when Trump allegedly stood too close to her: "It was incredibly uncomfortable. He was literally breathing down my neck. My skin crawled . . . Do you stay calm, keep smiling and carry on as if he weren't repeatedly invading your space? Or do you turn, look him in the eye and say loudly and clearly, 'Back up, you creep. Get away from me. I know you love to intimidate women, but you can't intimidate me, so back up.'"[38] In reality, Donald Trump was several feet away from Clinton, though the camera angle made it appear otherwise. Nevertheless, that didn't stop Clinton from again using the moment to play victim—a tactic that many women recognized and resented.

On CNN's *New Day*, I was asked to respond to a clip of Donald Trump from the primary saying, "Did you know [Clinton's] playing the women's card?"[39] I knew exactly what he meant, leading me to later respond, "In debates, she often defaults to playing the victim which I think is insulting to women. I don't think it's empowering. . . . I think it does a disservice to women who are strong who are out in the workforce, who can compete with their male counterparts without acting like a victim on a debate stage or in the midst of confrontations."[40]

For me and many other women, new age feminism meant emphasizing our strength and our progress, not our weaknesses. It's why Hillary Clinton's gimmicky sale of physical, pink "woman cards" on her Web site fell flat. Asked about this on CNN, I observed, "Most of my colleagues don't feel like they need to walk around with the woman card in their pocket . . . I think this falls on deaf ears for young women," particularly in light of the fact that millennial women are earning degrees and high-paying jobs at higher rates than our male peers.[41]

In the end, Clinton's appeal to female voters went unanswered. Though many predicted women would show up in droves to elect the first female president, Clinton earned 1 percentage point *less* of the female vote than Obama did in 2012 and 2 percent *less* than he won in 2012.[42] The so-called Ivanka voter existed and showed up for Trump.

But the media would nevertheless sum up the Trump voter as an angry white male. BuzzFeed's Petersen acknowledged this in writing, "Many college-educated liberals cling to them [the angry white men at Trump rallies] as proof of just how different, how *Other*, the Trump voter is: He lives somewhere else, he acts like someone else, he believes something else."[43] "Other-ing" of the Trump voter occurred repeatedly in election coverage. I heard it in the snide snickering of peers in reaction to Trump voters interviewed on the airwaves and saw it in the wide-eyed disbelieving stares as they watched throngs of voters in red hats crowd into Trump rallies. They just didn't understand the Trump base.

Republicans and the Trump Base

While the left and the media misunderstood, demonized, and underestimated the Trump voter, establishment Republicans tried to lay claim to this base of support. These establishment Republicans thought they knew the base that they desperately wanted to own. But when establishment Republicans threw around the word "base," they were conceiving it in a classical Republican sense that, in truth, no longer existed. Certain of the modus operandi of GOP primary voters, establishment leaders thought these voters would flirt with outsider candidates like Ben Carson and Donald Trump but ultimately settle on someone "electable" with governing experience, soaring rhetoric, and poll-tested policies. Just as voters had flirted with Mike Huckabee in 2008 and with Newt Gingrich and Herman Cain in 2012, this flirtation with Donald Trump was a mere fleeting fascination that would soon pass. In short, establishment leaders thought the base was highly predictable and easily winnable.

Just before declaring his candidacy, Jeb Bush said, "I kind of know how a Republican can win, whether it's me or somebody else—and it has to be much more uplifting, much more positive, much more willing to be, 'lose the primary to win the general' without violating your principles."[44] But the Republican base had changed. They felt betrayed by their leaders and expressed intense dissatisfaction with Washington.

The spontaneous rise of the grassroots Tea Party was evidence of this, but the GOP Establishment just couldn't see it. To them the Tea Party was a fringe element, a tiny offshoot of the Republican Party. In reality, the dissatisfied conservative voter was far and above the majority of the electorate, and so too was the angry Democrat.

If establishment Republicans had listened to their voters, they likely would not have been surprised by Donald Trump's success. After all, he was a creature of their own making, and signs of discontent among voters were prevalent long before the 2016 Election.

Consider the events of June 10, 2014. The summer night was quiet in American media—that is, until the clock struck 7:00 p.m.

"This is a huge, huge moment in the Republican Party. It's also a huge moment in politics," *Special Report* anchor Bret Baier said, interrupting the night's coverage.[45] News stations and online news outlets alike all abandoned their rundowns and editorial agendas, racing to keep up with the late-breaking story.

"One of the biggest upsets in modern American politics."[46]

"A 10 on the political Richter scale."[47]

"An OMG day in American politics."[48]

"The biggest electoral political shock of at least a generation."[49]

Not a single television outlet was covering the little followed Republican primary race in Virginia's Seventh District. But as the prime-time hours hit, it became increasingly clear that House Majority Leader Eric Cantor—a seven-term congressman and the second-highest-ranking congressional Republican—was on course to lose his primary election to a little-known professor named David Brat. As Cantor watched his congressional career vanish, the political and media worlds exploded into chaos, much as they did on November 8, 2016, when Donald Trump pulled off a shocking victory.

Stunned and staggered at this incredible political upset, the political and punditry class could not explain the shocking turn of events. How could the second-ranking Republican member in Congress who was poised to become the next Speaker of the House lose his primary to a political novice? How could an unknown private citizen who had spent $123,000 during the entirety of his campaign, less than his opponent had spent at lavish steakhouses, beat a polished politician who had hemorrhaged $1 million in the weeks before the election?[50] How could the polling, which showed Brat losing by a full 34 percentage points, be off by a 45-point margin?[51]

Sound familiar? It should. For the questions being asked on the night of June 10, 2014, were much the same as those being asked on May 3, 2016, the night that it became clear that Donald Trump had secured the Republican nomination, and on November 8, 2016, the night he won the presidency. Trump broke every rule in the political playbook. He spoke off the cuff. He resisted spending money. He resisted the traditional campaign structure.

Describing his meeting with campaign manager Corey Lewandowski in May of 2015 (a month before Trump entered the race), Mark Serrano said, "I was surprised. It was him and a desk and a phone." Where were the throngs of campaign staffers? The elaborate campaign headquarters? "I learned very quickly that they were going to run a very lean operation," Serrano said. "Donald Trump was a businessman that wasn't going to spend a dollar more than he had to, and I gained a real appreciation and respect for that."

Trump's primary opponents outspent him, with three outspending him by a 2-to-1 margin. He dismissed the traditional grassroots ground game, resorting instead to overflowing rallies. And he threw out the conventional tactics of focus groups, polling, and telepromptered speeches, opting instead for real, raw, politically incorrect dialogue.

Nevertheless, he prevailed.

"There's never been anything like it before," Michael Glassner told me. "Trump was changing the political model." And this, Michael explained, was what drove the so-called Never Trump movement, which in truth only existed among Washington bureaucrats and TV news commentators. As you may recall, Trump won nearly 90 percent of Republican voters, a metric on par with his predecessors.[52]

"Trump was a threat to the political consultants, who charge huge amounts to do very little," Michael revealed, reflecting on his three decades in politics. "There's a whole machine, political industry complex that built over the decades, and Trump threatened all of it. Trump did his own message rather than engender enthusiasm through fake means. He was a threat to the business model, and they [the Never Trump consultants] cared about money. Elections are a billion-dollar enterprise every four years."

In Virginia's Seventh District, a familiar dynamic was at play, the same one that framed the 2016 presidential election: it was the insider versus the outsider, the establishment versus the novice, and ultimately the political elite versus the people. Eric Cantor, who once posed as a rogue conservative outsider, had changed during his fourteen years in Washington. While Dave Brat was out knocking on doors and shaking hands, Cantor was hobnobbing and elbow rubbing with Washington's most powerful. When he did return to the district, he hosted "invitation only" events with "GOP bigwigs."[53] Comfortable among the chattering class, Cantor would contently take a seat on sets like MSNBC's *Morning Joe*, appearing "with a security entourage larger than most governors'," according to Joe Scarborough.[54] He had become a political poster boy of sorts. Fittingly enough, his Election Day defeat began, not in his district with his voters, but at a Starbucks on Capitol Hill, schmoozing with lobbyists and fund-raisers and assuring them of his impending victory.[55]

As Eric Cantor remained insulated in the bubble of Washington, DC, David Brat immersed himself in the bastions of the people, listening to their concerns and speaking directly to them. He managed to paint Cantor as the typical politician, a characterization that proved toxic in 2014 and beyond. "Eric Cantor singlehandedly changed the language on [the Stock Act] to allow family members of Congress to still do insider trading," Brat would announce to the sound of audible gasps and resounding boos. "It's an impeachable offense," he would continue. "Money just goes to their head."[56] Using Main-Street-not-Wall-Street lines like "Gazillionaires are taking cream off the top," "corporate interests get the ear of Congress and you don't," and "big business wants amnesty," Brat's populist brand of conservatism managed to win him a congressional district that skews seven points Republican.[57]

For me, June 10, 2014, was a wake-up call. I was fascinated by the toppling of entrenched establishment Washington operative Eric Cantor. It defied every political maxim. To the media and political classes, the events transpiring on our television screens were a one-off, an exception. To me, it was a harbinger of what was to come.

Not everyone was blind to the significance of Brat's victory, though. Mike Rubino, David Brat's finance director, told me, "I was not as surprised as I should be." When I asked him whether Brat voters were just frustrated or angry, like the Republican primary voters who propelled Trump to victory, he quickly replied, "Angry. Those same people that turned out to vote Dave came out to vote Trump two years later."

David Carr, writing a media column at the New York Times, astutely warned, "Beltway blindness that put a focus on fund-raising, power-brokering and partisan back-and-forth created a reality distortion field that obscured the will of the people . . . [T]he big miss by much of the political news media demonstrates that news organizations are no less a prisoner of Washington's tunnel vision than the people who run for office."[58] He noted that the punditry class might want "to wipe the egg off their face" before playing the blame game. Had they wiped it off, perhaps they might not have been hit with another unforeseen egg in 2016.

At the time of Brat's victory, Bernie Sanders was a little known senator from Vermont. He was not a nationwide figure, although his looming and surprisingly strong presidential bid was on the horizon. In 2014, Bernie had the foresight to see Cantor's defeat as a rejection of the status quo. In an article the *Huffington Post* titled "Bernie Sanders Thinks Hillary Is Eric Cantor," Sanders told Howard Fineman, "Everyone was shocked by Eric Cantor. My guess—my experience—is that when you go out and you talk to working people, there's a lot more dissatisfaction with the status quo and status quo politics than you think."[59] An observation that would prove all too true two years later as Bernie Sanders posed a formidable challenge to the status quo candidate, Hillary Clinton.

But perhaps none described the impending political landscape better than conservative talk radio. "The Republican Party leadership better wake up," Mark Levin, who along with Laura Ingraham had endorsed Brat, told Sean Hannity just hours after Brat's victory. "People want a new Republican Party with fresh faces, vigorous leadership, and they're not getting it."[60] In Brat's final political rally, Laura Ingraham echoed this same sentiment. "There's going to be a realignment," she predicted. "I would rather work with some people on the left today than some of the people in the GOP establishment." The GOP establishment would of course become the chief target of Donald Trump in the primaries, a tactic that worked to great avail. Betrayed by their party leaders, the American people looked to an outsider. They found it in Donald Trump.

The age of the outsider was upon us, and it had been in the making for quite some time. Michael Glassner, who has worked in politics for 30 years, recognized a transformation of the Republican base going all the way back to 2008 when he served as the head of John McCain's vice president operation. "I underwent a political epiphany," described Michael. "There was a movement in the country that manifested itself initially in the Sarah Palin phenomenon." Palin was routinely packing rooms full of 15 to 20,000 people who were new to the political process, far more than the number McCain—the presidential nominee—was able to draw.

Michael described the throngs of Palin supporters as disaffected Americans with a lot of energy. The Tea Party, he told me, was a direct outgrowth of the activism that Palin instigated. The Great Recession, which rocked Election 2008 and devastated the economic reality of so many, exacerbated this disaffection. "Incomes were stagnant or declining. Jobs were fleeing overseas," Michael noted. "I became one of those disaffected people myself, disillusioned by the power structure in Washington . . . I never lived in DC. I live in a small town in New Jersey and could see what was going on around me. My neighbors were losing homes, jobs. There was no recession among the DC political class. They were insulated by government and detached from reality."

The stark divide between the blindness of the political class and the reality of the American citizen led Michael to align with Trump in July of 2015 long before his decisive primary win. Eighteen months before Trump's victory had blindsided so many, Michael told the New York businessman that he would indeed be victorious. "The traditional operatives didn't understand the significant change in the base of the party," Michael said. "Trump was able to give voice to the voiceless and give a platform to the concept of the American worker being forgotten and ignored."

Benjy Sarlin at NBC News points to a rather revealing 2016 primary exchange.[61] Standing before a town hall audience, Jeb Bush—thinking he knew the crowd of Republican voters gathered around—said, "Donald Trump's view is that the end is near . . . His pessimistic view is 'let's close the borders, let's create tariffs, let's do this, let's do that' all based on negativity and the net result is that all of us will suffer if that philosophy gains favor."[62] As Sarlin noted, immediately following Bush's remark, a voter jumped up and replied, "We are pissed off right now."[63] The GOP establishment misjudged Donald Trump's intense connection with the base, while the left sought to marginalize it. In the end, it was a billionaire living on Fifth Avenue who understood the base and knew how to speak to it.

The Trump Message

Uncharted levels of anger among the American people meant that the fault lines of the 2016 Election were different. It was not necessarily Republican versus Democrat or right versus left but insider versus outsider. Outsiders like Donald Trump and Ben Carson smartly distanced themselves from insiders like Jeb Bush and Hillary Clinton, who touted government experience. Ironically, the farther you were from Washington, the more likely you were to get the most coveted job in the town.

"People had seen for decades what the insiders were doing, be they Democrats or Republicans. Didn't matter. They all seemed to be going the same way," Secretary Ben Carson explained. "They were ready for a change of direction, and they were also ready for somebody who thinks more like they do as opposed to Washingtonthink, which is very different than average-Americanthink."

Anger at the governing class explains why a little-known senator named Bernie Sanders gave the challenge of a lifetime to Hillary Clinton, who narrowly won the nomination with the full backing of the supposedly neutral—and thanks to the bombshell Donna Brazile allegations, admittedly biased—DNC.[64] It likewise explains why established politicians like Jeb Bush never took off and only outsiders like Donald Trump and Ben Carson topped primary polling.[65]

"In Washington, it didn't matter if you were Republican or Democrat," White House press secretary Sarah Huckabee Sanders told me. "If you were controlled by special interests, it was a problem." That meant the traditional model of touting governing experience simply would not work. Governor Huckabee explained that many governors entered the race, planning to sell themselves to voters with a pseudo-outsider message: "I'm not from Washington, but I've governed and I know how to fix the problem," they planned to say. "They [voters] were way past that," Huckabee noted. "They didn't believe anybody."

In addition to challenging the maxim "Experience matters," Election 2016 defied another political truism: "Ideological purity is essential." In a Republican primary, candidates typically position themselves as far right as possible in an effort to appeal to the base of Republican voters who are staunchly right-wing and very likely to vote. Donald Trump disregarded this political axiom and replaced it with another one: "Be yourself." It was a strategy embraced by his campaign manager, Corey Lewandowski, who had a "Let Trump Be Trump" sign hanging in his Trump Tower office.

As the crop of 2016 Republican primary candidates stumbled over one another to sound more right-wing than the person next to them on the debate stage, Trump was not afraid to speak from the heart. On trade, Trump maintained that trade deals like the Trans-Pacific Partnership (TPP)—typically celebrated by Republicans—in fact hurt the American worker. On the issue of women in the workplace, it was then-candidate Trump who urged companies to provide free child care for employees, and nominee Trump who became the first Republican nominee to propose paid family leave.[66] On health care, when other candidates proposed a straight repeal of Obamacare, it was Trump who retorted, "I will not let people die on the streets if I'm president."[67] His fellow Republicans immediately pounced. "Have you said you're a liberal on health care?" Ted Cruz asked.[68] "This is a Republican debate, right?" Marco Rubio echoed.[69] "Call it what you want," Trump boldly doubled down. "[P]eople are not going to be dying on the sidewalk."[70]

Throughout the entirety of the 2016 primary, Trump acted authentically, not strategically. For example, in April of 2016, Trump was closing in on the Republican nomination but still faced a formidable challenger in social conservative Ted Cruz, but the high stakes didn't stop Trump from saying transgender Caitlyn Jenner was welcome to use his bathroom at Trump Tower. He spoke from the heart when the average politician would not.

"He was pragmatic and had authenticity. He made decisions that were right for the American people. He was unafraid to transcend party lines," Ivanka explained, reflecting on her father's candidacy. "Voters responded to his fresh perspective on foreign policy. He would say things that would drive the media crazy, like refusing to share specifics of intended military strategy [and] noting the value of unpredictability when dealing with our enemies, but it made sense to the American people." In a nutshell, Ivanka succinctly described what I mean when I speak of Trump's new "conservative populism"—a term that conservative thought leaders such as

Laura Ingraham have used for years. When I use this term, I do not mean that Trump came in and changed what it means to be conservative or Republican. Rather, I mean that Trump was doctrinally conservative, but when facts clashed with his ideology, he showed a willingness to evolve. For instance, when unbridled free trade hurt the American worker, he advocated for a reassessment of this aspect of the Republican platform.

That was populism: looking out for the American people. It's a principle that Trump had used for decades in crafting his political views. Although some around him have attempted to take the credit, this new brand of Republicanism was unique to Donald Trump. He had proffered these populist views on trade and foreign policy going back to the early 1980s. "In the mid-1980s, while Reagan was extolling the virtues of freer trade, Trump was positioning himself in a vocal minority that believed the United States had been the big loser from global trade liberalization," *Politico* magazine rightly noted.[71]

In a 1988 *Oprah* appearance, Trump said, "I do get tired of seeing the country ripped off."[72] He expressed his frustration with our trade imbalance, explaining, "We let Japan come in and dump everything right into our markets. It's not free trade. If you ever go to Japan right now and try to sell something, forget about it . . . it's almost impossible . . . They come over here they sell their cars, their VCRs. They knock the hell out of our companies." During that same 1988 appearance, he stated that oft-repeated 2016 campaign trail refrain, "I'd make our allies pay their fair share." One year prior, in 1987, Trump even took out a full-page advertisement in the *New York Times*, criticizing Japan for depending on the U.S. for military protection.[73]

In a 1990 interview, Trump highlighted our trade troubles again, saying, "First they [Japan] take all our money with their consumer goods, then they put it back in buying all of Manhattan."[74] And ten years later, in 2000, Trump wrote, "[If I became president], I would take personal charge of negotiations . . . Our trading partners would have to sit across the table from Donald Trump and I guarantee you the rip-off of the United States would end."[75]

Not only were Trump's trade views consistent for decades, so too were his foreign policy ones. Trump regularly expressed a reticence toward foreign policy adventurism and a negative view of the Iraq War, although the media tried to muddy his long and consistent record. In an effort to cover for Hillary Clinton's flip-flop on the Iraq War, a liberal "fact checker" reported, "We have found no evidence of [Trump's] early opposition to the invasion. Trump expressed lukewarm support the first time he was asked about it on Sept. 11, 2002."[76] Apparently, the so-called fact checker did not dig deep enough.

In January of 2003, two months before the war began and two months after Hillary Clinton and a bipartisan coalition voted for the war, Trump expressed doubt, saying, "Perhaps [we] shouldn't be doing it yet . . . I think the Iraqi situation is a problem. And I think the economy is a much bigger problem as far as the president is concerned."[77] Trump continually expressed skepticism toward Iraq in the years to come, long before Hillary Clinton and many others renounced their votes. In March of 2003, he called the war "a mess" and in September of that same year he said, "I would have fought terrorism but not necessarily Iraq."[78] Trump's criticism of the decision to invade Iraq was consistent and continual, falling in line with his long history of advocating for a more inward-oriented, America-first foreign policy.

But this wouldn't stop the mainstream media from repeatedly pointing to that September 2002 interview, six months before the Iraq War began, where Trump replied, "Yeah, I guess so," when asked whether a war with Iraq was advisable.[79] The media constantly cited this one early and casual statement as evidence of Trump supporting the war, casting aside or perhaps deliberately concealing the seven other times Trump expressed skepticism of the Iraq War on the record.[80]

Trump's thirty-year history of populist views on trade and foreign policy made his message uniquely his own. While the media is constantly in search of the "mastermind" behind the Trump presidency, Trump all the while was his own mastermind, and voters responded to his authenticity.

Although only Trump should be credited with his unique and appealing finely honed message, there were indeed Republican forebears who embraced, to some degree, an outsider type of populism foreign to most Republicans. Mike Huckabee, for example, espoused a type of populist realism during his 2008 bid for the Republican nomination. Like Trump, Huckabee was not afraid to offer alternative ideas. While most Republicans sought to cut Medicare and Social Security, Huckabee rallied against cutting the entitlement programs. I asked him if he received blowback for his defiance. "Oh, yeah," Huckabee replied.

Explaining the issue from a place of practicality, not ideology, Huckabee elaborated: "A person who's seventy years old, they've worked now maybe for fifty years . . . All those years, that money was taken out. It was taken out with the promise that we're setting this money aside so that when you're sixty-five, Social Security and Medicare kick in." Huckabee passionately explained to me the grave injustice of the government then taking that money away. After years of the people paying into the system, they see nothing in return? The government mismanaged the money, and now they could yank the promised payout away? It made no sense. Huckabee continued: "That would be like saying to a child, 'You've saved up your allowance so that you can go to summer camp, but, hey, you know what? Dad went out on a real bender last week and got drunk with the guys at work. Sorry, kid you're not going to get to go to camp because your dad's a drunk.' I don't know of anyone that thinks that's OK." Huckabee's practicality tempered blind ideology.

The soon-to-be White House press secretary, Sarah Huckabee Sanders, recognized her father's pragmatism in Donald Trump. In part, it's what led her to endorse Trump shortly after her father exited the 2016 race. "I identified with his message of economic populism. He was fighting for the middle class. Main Street versus Wall Street . . . I liked the authenticity of the message," she said. "I volunteered to join Mr. Trump's campaign because he is a champion of working families, not Washington Wall Street elite."

Like Trump, Mike Huckabee was a man who always felt more comfortable around the people than the politicians. Before Huckabee entered politics, he spent eleven years as a pastor. "I think it was God's school for me. It was like he said, 'Now I'm going to teach you what life's about.'" As pastor, Huckabee had a front-row seat to people's grief. "You are holding the hand of that eighty-year-old when she takes her last breath and the family is standing around in ICU. You're there when the parents tell the doctor that to go ahead and take the breathing tube out of their sixteen-year-old who's comatose from a motorcycle accident. And there is no filter," Huckabee pointed out. "There is an extraordinary sense in which I think I was better prepared to look at issues with a depth that most people in politics simply don't have because they've never touched humanity at that level."

In addition to Huckabee's understanding and true compassion for the people, his impoverished working-class upbringing made him particularly sensitive to the needs of Americans. "I had to work for anything I wanted. I mean, whether it was a baseball glove when I was seven, I had to go collect pop bottles around the neighborhood, you know, to get the money to go get it," Huckabee remembers. "It taught me to work . . . [to] have a great respect for the people who struggle." By contrast, many politicians have an inability to relate to individuals who are truly scared about their future. "Most American families are one root canal away from total financial disaster . . . A thousand-dollar root canal. They're totally wiped out. They have no savings for that," he empathized.

"I saw a lot in 2008 campaigning with my dad," Sarah Huckabee Sanders explained, reminiscing about a 2008 primary debate moment when her dad helped to expose the out-of-touch politicians. "What helped to propel my dad was talking and connecting with people who felt ignored." While several of his Republican colleagues touted a growing economy, Huckabee stated plainly, "For many people on this stage the economy's doing terrifically well, but for a lot of Americans it's not doing so well. The people who handle the bags and make the beds at our hotels and serve the food, many of them are having to work two jobs, and that's barely paying the rent."[81]

"Others were talking about how great the economy was, but my dad said, 'Guys, what are you talking about?' That was in 2007," Sarah Huckabee remembers. Huckabee's assessment came just months before the 2008 recession wreaked havoc on the American economy. "You could see that gap of people who got it and didn't," Sarah said. Turning to 2016, she remarked, "Donald Trump got it. He was a builder, engaged in everything. He would talk to contractors and plumbers." He was a man outside Washington who understood the people.

The Trump Rally

Support for the outsiders manifested itself in the throngs of voters who crowded into packed arenas to hear Donald Trump speak. "I have been to thousands of these rallies in the decades leading up to Trump's election," Michael Glassner told me. "There was a much higher level of energy . . . It was a larger scale than had ever been done before."

"I was shocked by the crowd. I'd never seen anything like it. Never experienced anything like it," Katrina Pierson said, recounting the time that she introduced Trump at a Dallas rally. "The energy was phenomenal. And in that moment, in that stadium, even though I knew he was going to win, from that point in time, I knew there was going to be nothing that could stop him." Before the rally, Katrina was aware that tens of thousands of RSVPs had been returned, but she explained that in politics—particularly grassroots politics—you never knew just how many would show up. But Trump supporters did show up, consistently throughout 2016, lining the streets as early as 2:30 a.m. to try and get a coveted spot inside the magnetic events.[82]

"There was this feeling of hope among people who had been forgotten. They finally had a voice," White House political director and former Trump campaign national field director Bill Stepien told me. Stepien, a campaign veteran who had worked on the campaigns for Christie, Giuliani, McCain, and Bush, joined the Trump campaign just after Labor Day in 2016. "I'd never seen anything like this," Bill said. "I was always envious of the Obama movement in 2008 and 2012. He had given Democratic voters a voice." He explained to me that the electoral map and the path to 270 had been getting harder and harder for Republicans. "We needed to change the script, and Trump did for Republicans what Obama did for Democrats in 2008. He created a movement."

And it wasn't just Republicans crowding in to see the future president of the United States: it was Democrats too and many first-time voters. When Mike Huckabee and Rick Santorum joined Trump at a Des Moines veterans' event he attended, Sarah Huckabee Sanders immediately took notice. "A lot of people in the room liked the soon-to-be president, but they weren't registered to vote. They didn't know the caucus process," Sanders observed. Lara Trump distinctly remembers crossing paths with a World War II veteran in North Carolina. "He had never voted in his whole life," Lara said. "He could barely walk, and he stood there the whole time and came to shake my hand." The man proudly told her, "I really want Donald Trump to know that people fought for this country, and he's our only hope."

Rallygoers like this veteran attended rallies with the hope of hearing Trump speak, yes, but also with the hope of a brighter future. Katrina remembered one occasion when another veteran, who had lost both of his arms, approached Trump clad in camo and grinning from ear to ear. Trump reached out and gently touched the man's face and gave him a kiss, Katrina recalled. Trump truly cared.

Donald Trump's genuine spirit is partly what led him to receive endorsements from devout Christian men like Ben Carson and Mike Huckabee. Just after Super Tuesday, Ben Carson dropped out of the Republican presidential race, leaving just four candidates in the running.[83] "At that time, things were getting quite confusing. It looked like we might be heading for a brokered convention in which case we would not only have lost the presidency, we would have lost the Senate, and the House would have been in jeopardy," Carson recalled. "So I had to ask myself of the people who are left running: Who would be the best person?" An endorsement from Ben Carson was a coveted get. Besides Trump, he was the only other candidate to briefly become a front-runner in the 2016 Republican primaries.

"I had gotten a chance to know [the candidates] all pretty well over the preceding months, and there were a lot of things that I had seen in Trump that really were different from anyone else," Carson told me. He recounted how Trump was the only candidate who complained to the debate hosts that Carson was not getting any questions. And Trump was again the only candidate to stand with Carson when he didn't hear his name called at that New Hampshire debate. "Everybody else walked by except for him. He stood there with me until they straightened it out," Carson recalled.

A little more than a month later, as Carson pondered his endorsement options, he remembered these interactions with Trump. "I decided

I would go over and have an in-depth conversation with him first and make sure that my impressions were correct, and they were," Carson said. Standing beside Trump in Palm Beach at a critical moment in the 2016 primaries, Carson declared his support for the next president. "It's not about me. It's not about Mr. Trump. It's about America," Carson said in announcing his endorsement. "I have found in talking with him that there's a lot more alignment philosophically and spiritually than I ever thought that there was . . . that actually surprised me more than anything. Because I do recognize how a person's image can be greatly distorted, having been a victim of that."

As Ben Carson came to know Trump, he recognized in him a kindred Christian faith and an interest in growing closer to God. "[I] asked him [Trump] if he would spend some time talking to someone from the faith community that I had a lot of confidence in, and that was James Robison," Carson told me. "And you know, he normally only spends fifteen to twenty minutes with people. He spent an hour and fifteen minutes with James. Prayed with him. Did everything." As America began its journey through Election 2016, Carson recognized a journey of another sort, a faith journey for then-candidate Trump.

When the *Access Hollywood* tape came out, Trump not only apologized to the nation, he privately asked God for forgiveness. The morning before the second presidential debate, Trump prayed with Carson's friend James Robison, the well-known pastor.[84] Trump "is coming ever closer to the Lord," Carson said at the time. He still believes that today. "If you listen to his speeches at the beginning of this process versus now, you know, you'll hear faith enter a lot more now than you did back in those days," Carson said.

Throughout Trump's presidential bid, the retired neurosurgeon told Trump that God was using him. I asked Carson how God has used Trump so far. "I think we were in a situation where we were becoming a godless country . . ." Carson replied. "It needed a pretty powerful force to reverse that slide, and you know the only way I think that was going to happen was God had to select someone who could really put the stake in the ground and not be pushed around. I think [Trump] was the right one."

Governor Huckabee also thought that Trump was the right one for the job. "I think people realized that he was not beholden to the traditional political donor class. It was the reason that for me it was real easy," Huckabee said. Although Huckabee did not endorse Trump until after the Indiana primary—nearly two months after Huckabee had exited the race—Trump had always been his second pick. "I tell people that Trump was not my first choice because I was, but he was my second choice from the beginning," Huckabee told me.

After that crucial Indiana primary, Ted Cruz exited the race and Donald Trump became the de facto Republican nominee for president, although establishment forces would try to stop him all the way up until he officially secured those crucial 1,237 delegates in Cleveland, Ohio. The spring of 2016 progressed, and as it did, it became evident that the 2016 presidential race would be a battle between Hillary Clinton and Donald Trump—the ultimate insider versus the ultimate outsider.

THE DEBATES

"You can fool all the people some of the time, and some of the people all the time, but you cannot fool all the people all the time."
—ABRAHAM LINCOLN

The night had finally arrived. With Jeffrey Lord to my right and Van Jones to my left, I anxiously sat on CNN's glowing outdoor set in the heart of Hofstra University, preparing for a night touted to be one of the most watched nights in television history. With my eyes transfixed on CNN's countdown clock, I tried to take in every detail of the historic moment. Throngs of screaming students crowded behind our set, some foisting Clinton-Kaine signs in the air while others proudly displayed "Make America Great Again" flags. The chanting and cheering were so loud that my seven co-panelists and I had to use earpieces just to hear one another. The much-anticipated first presidential debate and first faceoff between Hillary Clinton and Donald Trump was moments away.

As the two nominees prepared to take the stage, my CNN colleagues and I speculated about what was to come. "Part of the problem is we have the most qualified person ever running [Clinton] against the least qualified and prepared man ever," Van Jones quipped.[1]

As my co-panelists predicted a Donald Trump defeat, I offered a necessary alternative perspective. "You know, I think these debates, they're not about the battle of the 15-point plans. We've heard Donald Trump's 15-point plan. We've heard Hillary Clinton's policy speeches," I reminded them. "This is a battle for the heart of the American people

With Jeffrey Lord (left), Van Jones, and Michael Nutter moments before the first presidential debate. *Courtesy of author's collection*

and the person who can reach through that screen and connect with that person sitting at home wins."[2]

It would soon be clear that my basis for judging the three showdowns to come was very different than that of my CNN peers.

As Lester Holt prepared to introduce the candidates, my fellow panelists departed from the set and huddled around a nearby TV to watch the high-stakes event. Just after 9:00 p.m., Donald Trump and Hillary Clinton walked onstage to energetic cheers and flashing lights. I remained on CNN's *Game Day* set just across campus, feverishly taking notes as the two presidential candidates spent ninety momentous minutes trading barbs and engaging one another on the key issues of our time. As the first presidential debate came to a close, my colleagues returned and took their seats beside me. The cameras soon turned to us, and there appeared to be a consensus.

"He totally lost control of the debate," remarked Gloria Borger.[3]

Throngs of cheering supporters behind the CNN set at the first presidential debate. *Courtesy of author's collection*

"You know, we heard a lot of people from the Trump camp, even some of our friends, say, well, let Trump be Trump," David Axelrod chimed in. "Well, Trump was Trump and it wasn't good for him tonight . . . I think [it was] a terrible night for him."[4]

"I thought early on that he was rattled, and it showed," Nia-Malika Henderson echoed.[5]

"He wore on his sleeve before the debate his lack of preparation, and it caught up with him tonight," Michael Smerconish said.[6]

As my colleagues declared Clinton the unanimous, foregone victor of the debate, I couldn't help but think they had missed what had happened before their very eyes. Donald Trump, not Hillary Clinton, had won the debate by connecting with the American people. "We saw a real person acting viscerally [on one side]," I explained to them. "And what you saw on the other side was a scripted politician . . . [who] was calculating her every single word."[7]

Instead of practicing lines in the mirror the way a typical politician would, Trump just spoke from the heart, like a real person. It was authentic. It was believable. But it was simply unacceptable to the media.

According to Nia-Malika Henderson, Trump's body language revealed himself to be a debate novice. She described it this way: "The split screen image of her, standing there pretty firmly, and him sniffling a lot. He was drinking a lot of water, his facial expressions. [His inexperience] was clear."[8]

Water intake and breathing patterns? Is this really what my colleagues thought the American people cared about? Voters were not scoring candidates like a debate coach; they were assessing who they could trust to make life better for them and their families. But the discussion of optics nonetheless persisted.

"It was interesting to see them both in split screen," Anderson said to me. "Secretary Clinton maybe is more used to being in a split screen, used to being on camera all the time. But she certainly seemed to respond differently than Donald Trump did in their split screen. Did you see that?"[9]

"Of course she did," I replied, "Because she spent two weeks away from the American people practicing at a podium at her house in Chappaqua. Instead of talking to the people, that's what she was doing. So what you saw tonight was a perfect mannequin politician as good as they come versus a real American citizen who took advantage of the American dream."[10]

To my colleagues, anything short of an academic, Oxford-style debate presentation was deemed a loss. Being relatable, being yourself, and speaking like a person, not a politician, was just not the Washington way. Obama-style soaring prose and lavish musical dialogue was what the media expected, but realspeak was what the American people wanted.

Trump "speaks to the people. He's not talking above the people. He's bringing it to a normal person level," Lara Trump told me, reminding me of my comments the night of that first debate. "He's a smart guy," Governor Huckabee said. "[But] he wasn't speaking to the academics. He was speaking to the people in ball caps out there who would fill those bleachers . . . It was never a big shock to me that he was successful."

Trump not only spoke like a normal person, he truly felt most comfortable being around the people, not the politicians. Katrina Pierson remembers that at the close of primary debates, when other candidates would talk among themselves or schmooze with debate hosts, Trump would go right to the people—the place where he felt most at home.

In addition to not recognizing Trump's refreshing style, the media focused on the wrong issues: the sensational over the sensible. After the first debate, my CNN postgame panel was engrossed by what they saw as the key moments of the debate: birtherism and sexism. They were incensed that Trump suggested Hillary Clinton's 2008 campaign had started the allegation that Obama was not born in America (the birther movement did indeed have roots in the Clinton campaign, as I would point out to them).[11] They were equally upset that Trump had challenged Clinton on whether she had the stamina for the highest job in the land—a jab that was surely misogynistic and sexist in the eyes of my CNN peers. As I heard them analyze the more irrelevant moments of the debate, I couldn't help but think they had missed the moments most important to American viewers.

Exasperated by the obsession with discussing birtherism, I finally interjected, "I think we are all overlooking one of the key moments of tonight's debate, when we saw the prosecution of a politician live before our eyes."[12] Trump had pushed Clinton to admit that she had done a convenient 180 on so many issues, like calling the Trans-Pacific Partnership "the gold standard" before later coming out against it.

Trump had exposed Hillary's promises as empty and her words as hollow. He showed her elaborate plans to be little more than empty rhetoric. "She's been doing this for thirty years," he repeatedly reminded viewers. "Typical politician. All talk, no action. Sounds good, doesn't work. Never going to happen."[13] The moment was huge. As Trump exposed the political class, he reflected the anger of the American people onstage. It resonated. But my peers nevertheless saw more significance in the superfluous.

In yet another effort to move my co-panelists toward substance, I repeated my previous statement once more. "I agree with Donald Trump when he said, let's move on and talk about ISIS and jobs, because it does a disservice to the American people and he wants to move on [from] this," I pointed out before the panel moved back to discussing birtherism.[14]

The dramatic, more gossipy story lines would dominate after each of the three presidential debates. The dominant discussions following the second debate centered around whether Trump had actually apologized for the *Access Hollywood* tape and whether he had acted like "dictators in Africa, or Stalin, or Hitler" in threatening to jail his opponent for her transgressions.[15] Neither of the leading post-debate narratives were rooted in fact.

Several of my peers erroneously asserted that Trump had refused to apologize for the *Access Hollywood* tape.[16] They said this despite the fact that Trump had clearly apologized before the debate and then again just minutes into the debate. Trump had plainly stated, "I apologize to my family, I apologized to the American people. Certainly, I am not proud of it."[17] Their assertion that he had not apologized truly baffled me, leading me to actually cross-check the transcripts and news articles before countering, "I'm not sure that we watched the same debate, because when I read the transcript, Donald Trump issues three more apologies. He's now up to issuing five. That's enough for most of the American people. I'm still waiting on the media to call for an apology for Hillary Clinton lying to the families of Benghazi when she told them their relatives are dead because of a video, which is not true."[18]

Mark Serrano accurately summed up what was bothering so much of the media. "Your classic, conventional, establishment Republican would curl up in the fetal position and hide under a desk," Serrano said. "The soon-to-be president apologized and he restated his apology, but he didn't cower. He didn't crumble. He didn't curl up into a fetal position. He just resumed the fight."

Equally unfounded was the panel's claim that he would act like a dictator and jail Hillary upon taking office. During the debate, Trump vowed, "If I win, I am going to instruct my attorney general to get a special prosecutor to look into your [Hillary's] situation."[19]

In response, Clinton said, "It's just awfully good that someone with the temperament of Donald Trump is not in charge of the law in our country."[20]

The CNN panel at the second presidential debate. *Courtesy of author's collection*

Trump sarcastically retorted, "Because you'd be in jail."[21]

It was a clever and humorous quip that was met with roaring applause. But several of my CNN co-panelists jumped on this line, with CNN's Dana Bash noting that "what makes this country different from countries with dictators in Africa, or Stalin, or Hitler, or any of those countries with dictators and totalitarian leaders, is that when they took over, they put their opponents in jail."[22] They had clearly missed the sarcasm of the comment, which was not lost upon the applauding audience.

In rehashing Trump's statement, Jake Tapper claimed that Trump had said, "I will tell my attorney general to appoint a special prosecutor *to lock her up.*"[23]

"That's not what he said," I replied. "He said I will appoint a special prosecutor *to look into it.* I just checked [the transcript]."[24]

Appointing a special prosecutor *to lock someone up*, of course, is a lot different than appointing one to *look into something*.

A panelist told me, "Yes, and then later in the same exchange, he said if he were in charge of the government, she'd be in jail."[25]

"I know the media doesn't get satire and humor," I replied. "But that was a humorous line and [a] retort. And to compare him to Hitler and Stalin locking people up, when he said, 'I would appoint a special prosecutor—' "[26]

"I don't think anyone mention[ed] Hitler or Stalin," Tapper cut in.[27]

Thirty minutes earlier Bash had indeed mentioned Hitler and Stalin. Check the transcript.[28]

The final debate's post-analysis proved as sensational as the rest, with the key takeaways being Trump's use of the term "bad hombres" and, ironically, whether he would accept the results of the election. The "bad hombres" exchange on CNN's set clearly demonstrated the politically correct culture that Donald Trump was targeting.

During the debate, Trump said, "One of my first acts will be to get all of the drug lords, all of the bad ones. We have some bad, bad people in this country that have to go out . . . We're going to secure the border. And once the border is secured, at a later date, we'll make a determination as to the rest. But we have some bad hombres here and we're going to get them out."[29]

Trump's statement had clearly delineated who these "bad hombres" or "bad men" were. They were not all illegal immigrants. Of course not. Most illegal immigrants are good people just trying to live the American dream. The "bad hombres" were the drug lords, the bad people, but the media nevertheless distorted Trump's words.

"[There's] one thing we haven't talked about and we need to talk about, which is for the first time Donald Trump used Spanish," Van Jones said. "He spoke a Spanish word only to insult and smear and stereotype Latino immigrants . . . He said we have some bad hombres . . . I thought that was horrible."[30]

"This is certainly get[ting] into this politically correct—" I tried to interject.[31]

"No, it's not political[ly] correct," Jones shot back.[32]

"This is nonsense," I continued.[33]

"It is," Lord echoed.[34]

"This is America . . ." Jones said.[35]

"Let me finish my point," I insisted. "Let's put context here instead of bringing two words. Context. Sabine Durden lost her son at the hands of an illegal immigrant. He would still be here today if the laws were enforced . . . [I]s this man a bad hombre?"[36]

I never received an answer to whether Juan Zacarias Lopez Tzun, the man who had killed Dominic Durden in a hit-and-run, was a "bad hombre," a "bad man." As I suspected, my CNN co-panelists would avoid the question. There was so much concern about Trump using non-controversial Spanish lingo, but where was the concern for the substance of what he was saying, for the men and women who have been victimized by drugs crossing our border or violent crime wreaking havoc on America's citizenry?

"Americans have the right to life, liberty and the pursuit of happiness . . . And no one should die at the hands of an illegal immigrant," I said.[37]

"No one should die at the hands of anybody," Jones said.[38]

"Unless they're a baby," Lord inserted, making an obvious reference to Democratic support of abortion.[39]

"Oh, come on," Patti Solis Doyle said, later addressing me directly. "Kayleigh, my father emigrated into this country from Mexico illegally twice. Was deported twice. Came back the third time legally," she said. "To me, I was born here. I'm an American citizen. To me, that was very offensive. You heard me when we were watching it in the green-room. I—I was aghast at it. That was just offensive. It's offensive to Hispanics."[40]

"To say what?" asked Jeff.[41]

"To Mexicans. Bad hombre," Doyle said.[42]

"Come on, Patti," Lord persisted. "Patti, you're an American. I'm an American. I've heard that phrase all my life. That has nothing to do with Donald Trump."[43]

After more ridiculous discussion, Nia-Malika Henderson asked Lord, "Jeffrey, why do you think he used that phrase? Why didn't he just say bad dudes? Why didn't he just say bad dudes?"[44]

"Because there are dudes that would be offended if he said dude," Jeff said.[45]

"Why specifically use Spanish in that instance?" Henderson pressed.[46]

"Well, what's wrong with it? There's nothing wrong with it," Lord said.[47]

"So why do you think he did it, though? I mean . . ."[48]

"Because it's in colloquial. It's in the American language."[49]

"No one says that. No one says that, Jeffrey."[50]

"You don't know enough people," Jeff quipped.[51]

"Donald Trump has defended the language he uses and says about women," Gloria Borger said. "I don't say things like that. That's not what I do. Well, tonight, Patti [Solis Doyle] was very offended."[52]

"Patti, I love her to death, but she's being politically correct," Lord observed.[53]

"I think she has a lot more credibility than I do on that," Borger replied.[54]

"Right," Henderson agreed.[55]

"And if she's offended, I'm offended," Borger said.[56]

"I can't even believe what I'm hearing," I marveled out loud. The PC police were out in full force and apparently Donald Trump was now barred from using the Spanish language.[57]

"My goodness," echoed Lord.[58]

"I'm sorry," Borger sarcastically replied.[59]

I was seeing the high-offense, politically correct culture Americans were so frustrated by play out before my very eyes. I decided to expose it. "We're in such a high-offense culture [that] when you call someone who killed American citizens a 'bad hombre' we're going to critique the language [you] use. Two words you chose to use—this is such a high-offense culture," I said. "And this is why Donald Trump won this nomination because Americans around this country are fed up."[60]

"He offended women. He offended other minorities. How did he expand his base tonight? How is he going to win the presidency?" Doyle asked.[61]

Well, Trump would go on to win the presidency partly because of discussions like the one we had on CNN's set after the third debate. Americans were tired of a culture of political correctness. Ben Carson observed this high-offense culture in the viral speech that brought him to prominence at the 2013 National Prayer Breakfast.[62] "The PC police are out in force at all times," Carson announced. "And we've reached the point where people are afraid to actually talk about what they want to say because somebody might be offended. People are afraid to say Merry Christmas at Christmas time."[63]

Four years after those remarks, I asked Carson whether this politically correct culture primed the electorate to want someone like Trump. "Without question," he replied. "You know, I gave a lot of speeches. I would say, 'Let me apologize in advance. I'm not politically correct.' . . . That set the tone." The audience always responded with raucous applause after Carson's announcement. Carson continued: "[P]eople were so tired of that because our ancestors fought and died so that we could have freedom of speech. And here we allow the PC police to impose, you know, something different."

Our panel's post-debate discussions were a microcosm of the challenge I faced in advocating for Trump publicly on television. The headlines and topics of choice would always be sensational story lines used to smear the soon-to-be sitting president. It's a challenge he would continue to face during his time in office. Even though nearly 60 percent of the country wanted the media to move on from covering the Russia collusion conspiracy theory, they would continue to cover it—obsessively, devoting 353 minutes of network coverage over a five-week period to Russia and less than a minute to tax cuts.[64] With 80 percent of media coverage being negative toward Trump, according to a Harvard study, the president would have to fight to make his positive achievements known.[65]

But, fortunately for Trump, the American people are fully capable of seeing through the media narrative of negativity. It's what led one Nevada cameraman to tell me, "I didn't vote for the president, but this unfair media scrutiny compels me to give him a chance." The discernment of the American people is the very reason Trump became president despite a slew of negative coverage. He became president and few were capable of seeing it. It's a phenomenon I recognized and pointed out to my co-panelists in the aftermath of the third debate as they marveled over Trump's statement that he would wait until after the election to determine if he would accept the result.

"What I'm saying is that I will tell you at the time. I'll keep you in suspense, okay?" Trump stated.[66]

"That's horrifying," Clinton responded to him. "This is not the way our democracy works. We've been around for 240 years. We've had free and fair elections. We've accepted the outcomes when we may not have liked them, and that is what must be expected for anyone standing on a debate stage during a general election."[67]

It was an ironic statement indeed. For one thing, the confident Clinton would go on to lose the election. Not only would she lose, but she would proceed to blame her loss on twenty-four different reasons: the FBI, James Comey, the Russians, anti-American forces, low-information voters, misogynists, and so many others.[68]

Echoing Clinton in the postgame analysis, Gloria Borger chastised Trump for his response, remarking, "Good or bad . . . this is a role of a leader . . . Part of the responsibility of being a leader is if you don't succeed and you lose, you accept responsibility for the loss."[69]

The assumption that Donald Trump was the inevitable loser of the 2016 election perturbed me. "I just have to say," I responded. "Rush Limbaugh said this today and I think it's so true. He said no matter what station you turn on, everybody is operating on the premise that Donald Trump is about to lose." I offered several recent polls showing that Trump was just a few points behind Hillary Clinton, then asserted that no one knows the future. "We were sitting here 23 days ago, and the momentum was going in Donald Trump's direction. We have 19 more days," I said. "None of us know where we're going to be 20 days from now . . . We shouldn't operate under the premise that, one, he's going to lose."[70]

"I'm not," Gloria insisted.[71]

"And two, that he's not going to accept the result. He said maybe, he'll look at what happens. None of us know what's going to happen," I said.[72]

"If I can just tell you," Axelrod said to me. "I've been involved in campaigns for a long time and presidential campaigns for a long time. No one has in modern history recovered from a deficit like this. Tonight was his opportunity to try and turn that around, and he's just dug himself into a bigger hole. And frankly the arguments you guys are making is also digging him into a deeper hole."[73]

"But, David, no one in modern history has won a primary spending only half of what three of their opponents spent," I protested.[74]

"Kayleigh, God bless you. I appreciate your . . . undying commitment. I'm just telling you what the facts are," Axelrod said.[75]

The fact was Donald Trump would go on to become the forty-fifth president of the United States.

THE ELECTION

A year and a half of caustic debates and outnumbered panels had all come down to this moment. All of the pontificating, the predicting, the imagining different scenarios, would be over, ultimately culminating in a Donald Trump victory.

Over the last few months I had encountered two clashing realities, one that I met in America's heartland and another I faced in the far-off perches of DC and New York. When I would leave the confines of these metropolitan hubs and travel through the rural back roads of my home state of Florida, the signs that Trump would prevail on the night of November 8, 2016, were visible and undeniable. My two-hour drive through rural Florida just two weeks before the election displayed dozens and dozens of Trump signs but not one Clinton sign. As I drove along the two-lane Route 98 and through the tiny west coast towns of Homosassa Springs and Crystal River, I stumbled upon a flea market. Drawn to the colorful array of Trump signs, I pulled over to the side of the road and discovered an array of small-town folk, all avid supporters of then-candidate Trump. It was yet another real-life encounter that defied what the pundits were saying.

My occasional experiences outside the Beltway during Election 2016 comported with the experiences of Lara Trump and Katrina Pierson

out on the campaign trail. Both women, along with other notable female Trump supporters, spent months driving across the country and
campaigning as a part of the Trump-Pence Women's Empowerment
Tour. "For three months, I didn't see my husband," Lara told me. "But
I would call Eric at the end of the day and tell him about the hundreds
of people I saw supporting the president. 'We can't lose,' I would tell
him. There was a feeling in the country." Occasionally returning to New
York City for 12-hour periods, Lara would hear the ominous media predictions of an inevitable Donald Trump defeat. It was the reality I lived
in from day to day on the sets of CNN as I was told again and again that
Donald Trump could never be president. But it just didn't correspond
with what Lara was seeing before her very eyes.

"In Pennsylvania, we drove for miles right outside of Philadelphia.
There was not one Clinton-Kaine sign," she told me. "People paid
with their own money to put up billboards." Lara went on to describe
swaths of people who would come up and tell her they were first-time
voters or lifelong Democrats but now on team Trump. She recalled
the whispered confessions she heard from Trump voters who were
not ready to declare their support out loud. It happened to me too—in
airports, at restaurants, everywhere I went. The hidden Trump voter
was real.

But the continuous media drumbeat of negativity was pervasive.
In one of the more favorable postelection predictions, famed predictor
Nate Silver gave Clinton a 2-to-1 chance of victory.[2] Most dubbed his
prediction far too optimistic for the Trump team. On Election Day, all
twelve of the *Washington Post*'s opinion writers predicted a Clinton victory, and half of them predicted she'd win in a landslide by more than
100 electoral votes.[3]

On my *Anderson Cooper 360* panel the night before the election, my
co-panelists endeavored to write the story of the election before it began.
Sitting on the roof of the U.S. Chamber of Commerce Building with
the glimmering White House as our backdrop, my seven colleagues
and I watched Hillary's final rally in Philadelphia. Standing tall with
unbridled confidence, Clinton stood alongside Presidents Obama and
Clinton before throngs of supporters. John King described the moment

as "torch passing" for the Democratic Party.[4] David Axelrod echoed the sentiment: "We've had 43 presidents, all white men, and on that stage, you have the first African-American president and potentially the first woman president. Pretty extraordinary."[5]

The expected Clinton victory story line was a culmination of the "Trump doesn't have a chance" chorus echoed again and again leading up to that night. But the media narrative would not alter the confidence of many in the Trump campaign. A local news outlet asked Lara just before the election whether Trump had a chance. "He will win in a landslide victory," Lara remembered telling the host. "It was palpable. I knew that the media had it wrong."

At a final rally in North Carolina, Trump assured the crowd that tomorrow would be "historic."[6] "I think it's going to be Brexit plus, plus, plus. It'll be amazing."[7] Brexit, of course, referred to the surprise vote in the United Kingdom to leave the European Union. Few predicted a vote to leave, but the forecasts were dead wrong. Confident of an American Brexit on the horizon, Trump made his final stops in New Hampshire, predicting, "We're hours away from once-in-a-lifetime change."[8]

Trump's focus on a Rust Belt Brexit was as realistic as it was strategic, though the political class simply couldn't see it. One Michigan strategist described Trump's play for Michigan as a "Hail Mary" pass and a discussion of Trump winning Wisconsin in the days before the election was virtually nonexistent.[9] No Republican had won Michigan and Pennsylvania since 1988, and Wisconsin had not gone red since 1984. According to the mainstream media, Trump would not change that. But the Trump campaign had a different mind-set all together.

Sitting across from White House political director and former Trump campaign national field director Bill Stepien, I asked Bill how he was able to pinpoint these long-lost blue states as winnable. Bill quickly popped up from his chair and walked toward a wall covered with colorful maps from floor to ceiling. "Do you see that dark green color?" he asked me, gesturing toward a map of the United States. "And that lighter green area." The map—filled with a sea of different colors—had a very clearly delineated green portion right in the center. Michigan and Wisconsin, in particular, were covered in green. "The green portions are areas where Trump outperformed former Republican nominee Mitt Romney by 10 percent or greater," Bill told me.

Internal campaign data clearly showed these states as winnable. It's why they deployed Trump to Michigan, causing the Clinton campaign to go on the defensive by sending Clinton and Obama to the state, while in the days before the election Mike Pence went to Wisconsin, a state that Clinton ignored entirely. "It was the numbers and the data," Bill said. "But the numbers don't tell the whole story. There's also a human element. There was this *feeling* on the ground at rallies." Something was happening—a Brexit of sorts.

Reflecting on the final Clinton and Trump rallies, Anderson Cooper remarked to our final preelection panel, "He [Trump] also says that whatever the polls say, the country should get ready for the kind of surprise Great Britain had when voters chose to leave the European Union, what became known as Brexit."[10]

Dismissing the comparison, Axelrod replied, "Yeah, one thing, there's a difference in polling here."[11] He went on to explain how our polling is more sophisticated, and early voting numbers lend U.S. polling more credibility.

Van Jones—to his credit—warned, "The data is only as good as the polling sample. And I do think that there are a lot of people who are off the grid, both for Trump and against Trump, who may come pouring in."[12]

Convinced that there was something to this so-called Brexit effect, I chimed in, "When we talk about this Brexit effect, what does it look like? One of the most interesting facts I read today was that in North Carolina, there's a 42 percent surge of independent voters. That is striking . . . Independent voters, we know, are breaking for Donald Trump in most national polls to the tune of 12 to 15 percent . . . I think if we see a Brexit effect, it's going to come in this swing of independents. We know 1.2 million unaffiliated voters turned out in Florida."[13]

Axelrod countered, "Actually [it's] not true that independents are breaking by those numbers. In fact . . . Hillary Clinton was winning among independents in some other polls that just came out in the last few days."[14]

But independent voters did cast their ballots for Trump. In fact, in several of the states key to Trump's victory, independents broke for him by double digits, just as I had speculated.[15] Independents were indeed a huge part of his election night win.

Summing up election eve coverage and Trump's alleged dismal chances of winning, John King concluded: "For 98 straight days, Hillary Clinton has been on top of this race. There's been one or two or three national polls showing Donald Trump ahead . . . That's why a lot of people, the technical people, the people that do this for a living say it's not a Brexit situation."

Well, the so-called technical people who "do this for a living" could not have been more off base. In the aftermath of the election, the "technical people" went back to their cozy jobs in media, in think tanks, and in lucrative consulting firms. Lloyd Gruber, a British academic, was one of the few candid enough to admit his mistake. "As a political scientist, I feel I owe you an apology," Gruber wrote.[16] "To say my discipline has been behind the curve this electoral season would be putting it too charitably. We haven't missed one curve yet. We're speeding through all of them—backwards."[17]

Meanwhile, the Trump campaign was ahead of the curve, barreling forward with a sophisticated data operation that outperformed the political pollsters by wide margins. Bill told me that the Trump operation had zeroed in not just on specific states but also counties and precincts, all the way down to the individual voter. Stepien grabbed a large notebook from a bookshelf of many others. Flipping through the pages, he showed me how voters had been mapped on a spectrum from those most opposed to Trump to those solidly planted in the Trump base. Rally locations and ground operations were selected based on the number of winnable voters. The Trump campaign wanted to truly know the voters—what drove them, what they cared about, and how their campaign could best serve the people. President Trump was a man of the people and his campaign was to be a vehicle for them.

Although the Trump campaign was optimistic, on election eve, the unanimous liberal mainstream media consensus was a Trump defeat. After the final pre-election panel, I joined my mom and grandmother in our DC hotel room, and my relatives expressed the ultimate consensus of the American people that my CNN co-panelists were completely blind to: "He's obviously going to win." The liberal media had already written the conclusion of Election 2016, but the American people had other plans.

★　★　★　★

When the day of decision arrived and millions of Americans went to the polls to cast their ballots, I prepared to go into CNN and face whatever choice the American people made. Leaving my hotel around 2:00 p.m., I told my mom and grandmother that when I returned many hours later and in the early morning, we would know if Donald Trump was going to be the next president of the United States. Huddled together, the three of us said a prayer, urging for God to guide our nation's future.

When I met Lara Trump in Trump Tower, she told me, "God played a role in this election without a doubt . . . the number of people praying. There's something in that."

As she spoke, it gave me chills.

Prayer was my animating principle on Election Day, as it was for so many others. It's what gave me peace. Two weeks earlier the pastor of my hometown church had urged the congregation to "pray, pray, pray" that God would guide the hearts and minds of the voting public. It wasn't so much praying *for* a candidate but *about* a God-ordained outcome that was best for America's future. I, like Lara, am convinced that people of faith praying made a difference. It's an incalculable variable that for some helps to explain an otherwise inexplicable election. Despite my uncertainty about what lay ahead, there was one thing I was completely certain of: the power of my prayer.

When I arrived at CNN that afternoon, the mood could only be described as upbeat. High-spirited colleagues bustled through the halls. An array of food had been ordered. It appeared as if there was an impending celebration of some sort.

Taking my seat on one of our final Election 2016 mega-panels, Jake Tapper asked me, "Kayleigh, are there any specific areas that you're going to looking at tonight as the results start to come in to give you an indication . . . about how well Donald Trump is going to do?"[18]

I explained that my analysis of state polling averages led me to believe that Trump had several viable paths. First, he could get to 265 electoral votes by winning Nevada, Florida, Ohio, and Iowa. He was winning narrowly in each of those states, according to polling.[19] Then he would just need to flip one state: Michigan, Pennsylvania, Wisconsin, or New Hampshire plus Maine's second congressional district would do.

"Pennsylvania is always kind of that elusive state that Republicans think they can get and it's never quite within reach," I told Tapper.[20] "Donald Trump, though, I think he is a different kind of candidate. He has more of a populist streak. He might get it."[21]

Although Trump would not win Nevada as I predicted, his populism would win him not just Pennsylvania, where he was down by 1.9 percent, but Michigan, where he was down by 3.5 percent; Wisconsin, where he was down by a whopping 6.5 percent; and Maine's second congressional, where he led by a slim half of a percentage point.[22]

In the end, Trump would win more than 300 electoral votes. He would flip one-third of U.S. counties that voted for Barack Obama, picking up six Obama states and a portion of Maine.[23] While the media has criticized Trump for calling it a landslide, it was indeed a landslide in every sense of the word, especially given the flawed predictions to the contrary.

But in the early hours of election night at CNN, none of my colleagues suspected a Donald Trump victory, much less a landslide one. The biggest fear for many of my CNN peers was not whether Trump would win but whether he would accept the outcome of the election and concede to Hillary Clinton.[24]

More than two hundred miles up the Northeast corridor, there were a variety of emotions at play in Trump Tower as Donald Trump, his family, and his campaign staff awaited the results. They had all seen firsthand the thousands upon thousands of energetic rallygoers all across America's heartland. But now, back in Manhattan and crowded around a television, watching the media naysaying, doubt began to set in.

"We all felt it, but it was so hard to tune out the media," Lara said. It was Lara and Eric's two-year anniversary on November 8, 2016. "It would be the most amazing or not the greatest," she laughingly told me. Jared Kushner revealed that his data team predicted early that afternoon that Trump was going to win. "It was going to be a Rust Belt Brexit," he told me. Nevertheless, "everyone was nervous," Lara said. "The numbers from our polls reflected that he would win, but every news outlet was confident about a Hillary Clinton victory." Michael Glassner, who was also at the campaign headquarters, said to me in our Trump Tower interview, "The mind-set of the status quo political class was that Trump would never win. That was not the sense among his loyalists in the War Room that night."

Anxiously probing for any advance information, all the campaign had to rely on was their internal polling—until the clock struck 6:00 p.m. "The exit polls were brutal," Jared remembered. The pollsters began to predict the worst.

"I'm starting to think Democrats will take the Senate majority tonight," tweeted Frank Luntz.[25] "In case I wasn't clear enough from my previous tweets: Hillary Clinton will be the next President of the United States," he wrote minutes later.[26]

Discussing the differences in their internal data and the exit polling, Bill Stepien, the Trump campaign national field director, assured Jared that the campaign's data would be more reflective of the actual results. The exit polls had erred in using the old 2012 Obama-Romney turnout model, Stepien noted. This model underestimated the number of low-propensity voters who would show up and vote Trump, just as the Brexit model had underestimated the number of voters who would vote to leave the European Union. Trump would over-perform among evangelicals, union members, and Hispanics, ultimately delivering him a victory.

The mainstream media's exit polling missed the hidden Trump voters, who concealed their support in the hostile environment of Election 2016. Trump supporters had been called deplorable by Clinton. Their houses were egged,[27] their signs, in one case, pierced with bullet holes.[28] "Supporter Who Painted a Trump 2016 Sign on the Side of His House

Has His Home Egged, His Truck Damaged and One of His Walls Vandalized with Graffiti—Before His Front Yard Gets Set on FIRE," read one *Daily Mail* headline.[29]

"The left didn't make it easy to be a Trump supporter," Stepien noted. Recognizing this is what led Stepien to seek out the hidden Trump voter. The Trump campaign included a question in its polling to mine this information, asking voters whether they liked some of Trump's policies even though they might not agree with him all the time. Questions like this led him to the hidden Trump voter. "Eight to 12 percent gave Trump their quiet support," Bill noted. The methodology of the exit polls was just wrong, Stepien explained to Kushner as election night approached.

Although the 6:00 p.m. exit polls looked discouraging, the Trump campaign would not give up. Family and close friends hurriedly called into dozens of drive-time radio shows, knowing that they could still impact last-minute voters. Eric, Lara, Rudy, and Don Jr. all picked up the phone and made an eleventh-hour push to advocate for the Republican nominee. Don Jr. called in to twenty-seven shows, and Trump himself called in to seven. If the Trump campaign went down, they were not going to go down without a fight.

At CNN, word about Hillary Clinton's internal polling began to trickle out. One Clinton ally loudly pronounced in the greenroom, "Clinton wins. It's over. She's got Florida. It's done." My heart sank as I shared with my fiancé and family what I had heard. "That's ridiculous. The polls haven't even closed yet, and you're telling me Hillary won?" my fiancé responded.

The confidence of the Clinton campaign stood in stark contrast to the reserved humility of the Trump world. "That contrast between the glass ceiling at the Javits Center [that Hillary was supposed to break through] and the small ballroom at the New York Hilton [where Trump had his election watch party] was by design," Mark Serrano told me. "The [soon-to-be] president didn't want a mammoth ballroom. He wanted it to be a small event, because he didn't want to take anything for granted." By contrast, Hillary Clinton's campaign planned an elaborate fireworks display in front of thousands of supporters on election night, an event she called off just one day before the election.[30] "He wasn't assuming he

With my co-panelists on the CNN 2016 election night set. *Courtesy of author's collection*

was going to win," Mark told me, "whereas Hillary Clinton assumed she was going to win."

Adding to my nervousness, I crossed paths with former Trump campaign manager Corey Lewandowski as I walked onto the CNN set. As we exchanged seats, I anxiously whispered to him, "What do you think? Is he going to win?" The exit polls were about to come out, and they can be highly predictive of whether any given candidate will win or lose.

"We will know in thirty minutes whether Trump is going to be the next president of the United States," Corey told me.

"Please text me when you know," I said to him.

I anxiously took my seat on CNN's final election night panel with Jeffrey Lord on one side and Van Jones and Paul Begala on the other. The results began to roll in as the clock struck 7:00 p.m. Trump won Indiana and Kentucky, while Clinton won Vermont. Georgia and Virginia were too close to call.

As the hour progressed, I never heard back from Corey, adding to my unease. Then a new bit of CNN reporting completely killed my optimistic spirit. "Jake, a senior advisor from Donald Trump's inner circle is sizing up the GOP candidate to me this way," Jim Acosta reported.[31] "Quote, 'it will take a miracle for us to win.' This adviser went on to say that Trump was in such a deep hole after the release of that *Access Hollywood* tape. It was viewed inside the campaign that he was going to lose this race by a wide margin."[32] Only now do I know—after interviews with many people who were in Trump Tower on Election Night—that this was not the view inside the campaign. In fact, it was just the opposite. Many loyal Trump campaign officials had unbridled confidence that Trump would prevail. This "anonymous source" could not have been more off base.

Even in the face of this new reporting, I did not lose hope. Several times on CNN's set I closed my eyes and quietly said a prayer: *God, let your will be done. Whatever it may be.* The outcome was out of my hands and in God's. That gave me peace.

More polls closed, revealing a tighter-than-expected race. My co-panelists and I quietly zoned in on our computers and our notes, scouring data, maps, and social media for any updates we could find. One fact was certain: all roads to the White House passed through Florida, a state that jockeyed back and forth between Clinton and Trump as vote totals came in. CNN's Jeff Zeleny nevertheless reported, "The Clinton campaign is increasingly confident about Florida . . . [O]ne senior Clinton adviser I just talked to said the Hispanic numbers are rising through the roof. That is why we'll win Florida."[33] For a time that seemed to be the case.

"Hillary Clinton has now taken the lead in Florida and North Carolina," I heard Wolf Blitzer announce from across the room. "Let's look at Florida first, 72 percent of the vote in. That's a big chunk of the vote. Hillary Clinton is now ahead by an impressive almost 172,000 votes . . ."[34] But, in truth, Hillary led by just over 1 percent of the vote.

No prob. Panhandle will make that up, my dad texted me, perhaps sharing some local wisdom lost upon the CNN crew.

At Trump Tower, Bill Stepien was standing right next to then-candidate Trump when the first batch of Florida numbers came out. Recognizing that the Panhandle had not yet come in, Stepien told Trump, "It's going to be a long night, but it will get better." Confident in the campaign's data, Stepien distinctly remembers telling the soon-to-be president, "The pathway still exists."

As 8:00 p.m. approached, Hillary Clinton's prospects of becoming president continued to look promising. In addition to CNN reporting a significant lead for her in Ohio, Wolf Blitzer exclaimed, "Look at all these wins we're projecting for Hillary Clinton right now."[35] Illinois. New Jersey. Massachusetts. Maryland. Rhode Island. District of Columbia. *No surprise there,* I thought.

But in the short course of an hour, the Hillary Clinton momentum would slow. As our colleagues seemed to hint at a Clinton win, Jeff Lord and I—to my knowledge, the only Trump supporters in the room—closely monitored our home states of Pennsylvania and Florida. To two locals, the numbers didn't seem to tell the whole story. We knew our states intimately, and we both predicted that Trump would prevail.

Seemingly out of nowhere, everything changed. In a matter of mere seconds, Hillary Clinton's lead in Florida shrunk from 15,000 votes to 11,000 votes to a mere 700. "You have a tug of war here," John King noted.[36] Remarkably, Trump quickly took the lead by 918 votes in my key home state of Florida. His lead continued to grow. "We have a key race alert right now," Blitzer said.[37] "In Florida right now, 29 electoral votes are at stake, 91 percent of the vote is in and Donald Trump is building up a sort of impressive lead, 63,297 votes."[38]

Wolf later noted, "It's a lot closer, Dana, than so many people thought in these key battleground states. This is going to take a while."[39]

Completely focused on my Mac computer, I stared at a map of Florida divided by county. I pressed the "refresh" button over and over and over again, glued to the second-by-second updates of vote percentage totals by county. "That was me," Stepien told me, sitting alongside a huge map on the floor, pressing "refresh" constantly. "Nothing could've happened without Florida. We never took our eye off of the state."

As the various county totals slowly ticked upward, two counties, Miami-Dade and Broward, didn't seem to budge an inch. Trump had taken the lead, but these two slow-reporting and more liberal counties could deliver the state for Hillary. I pressed the "refresh" button for what seemed like hundreds of times, but Miami-Dade and Broward never seemed to move. In the end it would be Florida's panhandle that delivered the state for Trump, just as my Floridian father had predicted.

As the polls tightened in several states, optimism built over at Trump Tower. "Everyone was on edge, but it was electric," Lara recalled. "Joy and confidence built with every state." The clock struck 9:00 p.m., and Donald Trump had taken the lead in a host of coveted battleground states: Florida, Ohio, Virginia, Georgia, and North Carolina.

We win Florida, I texted Corey. *98% of Broward is in, 99% of Miami, 95% of Palm Beach in. That means no more blue for Clinton to gain.* I was sure of it.

I agree, he answered.

"There are some happy campers over here at Trump campaign headquarters, Wolf. It is very clear, every time the returns are flashed on the screens here from the state of Florida, this place erupts into cheers," Jim Acosta described.[40] "We're hearing a lot of, you know, pessimism and some people sounding very glum inside this campaign, inside this operation earlier today. That mood has done a 180, Wolf."[41]

"Everything we felt on the campaign trail was literally coming true on the screen before us," Lara told me. "The Florida rally that was so huge was coming to fruition on our screen."

By contrast, at the Clinton headquarters, Brianna Keilar reported, "There are a number of anxious faces, the faces I'm looking at here in the crowd."[42]

In a candid admission, Jake Tapper said, "Look, if this night ends up being the way that Donald Trump and his advisers think and hope that it will be, boy, I mean, it's going to put the polling industry out of business . . . I don't know of one poll that suggested that Donald Trump was going to have this kind of night."[43]

Dad—Are you watching this? I texted, well aware that he was usually in bed by this time. *Is this Brexit? Knock on wood,* I cautiously added.

YES, he replied in all caps. *Win Fla. And we got a fight!*

As the minutes passed, the victory that few had predicted was playing out in real time. Trump began to pass Clinton in states that Republicans had not won in years if not decades. Places like Michigan, Pennsylvania, and Wisconsin. Something was going on. Something unexplainable.

As people in the Trump campaign crowded around nearby televisions, Bill Stepien remained in his chair, zoning in on his maps. "At first, we didn't seem likely to win Pennsylvania. We lost Philadelphia and its collar counties by more than Romney, but we drove up numbers in northeast Pennsylvania, in Scranton, for example, and in places like the Lehigh Valley." This was cause for optimism. "That's the Rust Belt. Coal country. Once we began to build momentum in Pennsylvania during the late stages of the campaign, we hoped the rest of the Rust Belt would fall like dominos—and they did."

"We scheduled the last ten days in all the right places," Jared told me. "It was not an accident that we were in Michigan as a last stop. New Mexico was a head fake, and we knew Wisconsin would be close." The campaign suspected that winning Wisconsin would be a long shot, but unlike Hillary, who never visited the state, the Trump campaign didn't count the people of Wisconsin out. Not considering America's Dairyland completely out of reach, the campaign called Paul Ryan and organized an appearance with him and Mike Pence in the days leading up to the election. "We gave it a shot," Jared noted. An aura of optimism began to develop at Trump Tower. "We started to feel good about Pennsylvania," Jared said. "The voting was in line with our empirical model. It was a suburban Brexit based on turnout."

As the mood at Trump Tower brightened, the one at CNN dimmed. Jeff Lord and I began to perk up and sit tall with an excited rejuvenation while my Clinton counterparts slumped down with distressed expressions. Although it was difficult to contain my jubilation, I recognized and empathized with the defeated look on my colleagues' faces.

"Those early exit polls show that there were a lot of angry voters out there in the United States," Wolf observed.[44] It was the point that I had tirelessly reiterated throughout the entire election. It fell on deaf ears

Jeff Lord and I growing increasingly optimistic on CNN's 2016 election night set.
Courtesy of author's collection.

until tonight. All of a sudden our colleagues began to repeat the points that Jeffrey Lord and I had offered for more than a year.[45]

David Axelrod noted that "there was a hunger for change among a lot of Americans and . . . Those who were angered and disenchanted with government overwhelmingly were supporting Donald Trump."[46]

Gloria Borger described the "massive outpouring among voters who perhaps didn't vote before, who perhaps were hidden, and they came out tonight."[47]

Michael Smerconish remarked that the star-studded event with Bill Clinton and Barack Obama on election eve might have "boomerang[ed]" and had "the complete opposite impact because it reinforced who really represented the establishment."[48]

As Trump pulled ahead in states like Michigan and Wisconsin—places he was not even expected to be competitive in—CNN projected a win in North Carolina. In the Trump headquarters, the win was hugely significant.

"My father-in-law was right to the front left of me when they called North Carolina for him," Lara said. Back in August, Donald Trump had looked at his daughter-in-law, Lara, a North Carolina native, and said to her after a rally in the state, "I want you in charge of North Carolina." The next day she went to her boss at *Inside Edition* and informed her that she would need to take three months off to run the state. "I was there once a week during the campaign," Lara explained. "It was so close one hour after the polls closed . . . I've never been as nervous as I was then." After North Carolina was placed in the Trump column, the soon-to-be president-elect turned to his daughter-in-law and said, "We won because of you." Lara said, "I will never forget that moment."

While the media remained in denial, the Trump world began to internalize that Donald Trump would be our next president. According to two family members, people in that room in Trump Tower began to approach the next commander in chief and say, "How does it feel to be the next president?"

He would quickly reply, "Wait, don't jinx it."

"Let's just wait," he told another family member.

"He was superstitious," they recalled.

But as the hour closed in on midnight, the facts continued to suggest just that: Trump was going to win. The biggest indicator was his lead in Wisconsin. "She never stepped foot in the state of Wisconsin since winning the Democratic nomination," Dana Bash noted. "That's how confident they were."[49]

Just after 11:30 p.m., CNN made a major projection: "Take a look at this. And CNN projects Donald Trump will carry the state of Florida."[50]

Still sitting on CNN's set, I sent a quick and simple text: *Corey . . .*

He knew exactly what I meant.

We won, he answered.

After a few brief messages, he sent me the familiar refrain that Trump famously touted on the campaign trail: "I never get tired of winning."

The media was increasingly befuddled by what was transpiring. Tapper noted, "It's just remarkable because I mean—I don't think we can overstate this. Not only Democrats in the Clinton campaign, not only pollsters in the mainstream media but Republicans did not anticipate that this night was going to be this way . . . Very, very few people who were actually running these races anticipated that this night was going to be so strong for Donald Trump."[51]

A few minutes later the cameras shot over to our side of the CNN studio. Anderson Cooper said to me, "Kayleigh, I mean, all along in the face of all these polls . . . you were saying that there were hidden Trump voters out there."[52]

"Yes. It's looking increasingly like we have a Brexit on our hands," I replied. "[T]here were these voters out there that were afraid to talk to pollsters. And Anderson, I think the American people right now are sending a loud, clear, unmistakable message. They want their government back. This is supposed to be a government of, by and for the people. It's increasingly become one of, by and for the elite. This is the people rising up saying it's time to listen to us . . . Donald Trump [ran] against Republicans. He ran against Democrats. He ran against the elite. He ran against the government. He ran against the media, but he was an unmistakable voice for the people."[53]

And the people showed up. All across the nation, hidden Trump voters traveled to their polling locations and silently voted for Donald Trump. Concealing their support from friends, neighbors, and certainly inquiring pollsters, they nevertheless cast their ballots. "They hated Washington and wanted to see change. They felt government was not working for them," Jared told me. He was right, and my night at CNN proved just that, at least anecdotally.

Just before 1:00 a.m., I left the CNN set and was asked to remain in the greenroom in case I needed to rejoin the panel. Sitting alone on the couch, I paused to take in this historic moment. But I wasn't alone for long. As I processed the realization that Donald Trump would be the next president of the United States, a cameraman who I had never met approached the entryway. Before he entered the room, he looked both ways and scurried in. "I can't say this too loud, but I am a Trump supporter. I have to keep it quiet, but I just want you to know how excited I am," I recall him saying. After talking and silently celebrating together, he left the room, only to be followed by another CNN worker. This time a makeup artist joined me, delivering a similar whispered confession of support for our new president. It was rather astounding. These were the hidden Trump voters, and their silent admissions of support were reflective of the hidden Trump voter who delivered him the presidency.

As Donald Trump's path to victory crystallized, disappointment beset the Javits Center, where Clinton had planned to give her victory speech. "Wolf, the scene here is so different than it was a few hours ago when people were happy and relaxed," Brianna Keilar reported. "I have been looking around the room at people who are stone-faced. Some of them have been crying."[54]

Meanwhile, jubilation filled the New York Hilton, where Donald Trump would eventually speak. A sea of red hats chanted, "USA! USA! Donald Trump. Drain the swamp." The mood was electric.

As America watched the contrasting images, Jake Tapper offered this: "If Donald Trump wins . . . in addition to his celebration and the victory lap that he has every right to take . . . I really hope that the victor does actually take that opportunity to try to unite the country after this extremely brutal election."[55]

What Tapper, the media, and the public were unaware of what was transpiring behind the scenes at Trump Tower. Donald Trump eventually left the campaign headquarters and crowded into a small downstairs kitchen with his family, Hope Hicks, Kellyanne Conway, Stephen Miller, Dan Scavino, and Keith Schiller. At this point all the analysts were saying Trump was going to win.

"It really took a while to absorb," Ivanka said.

"This was a distinct line in life," Lara said. "Things were never going to be the same in my life. I could help to make things better in this world."

"When we realized my father would be president, all attention turned to what to communicate for the first time," Ivanka told me. The Trump campaign had prepared two speeches, an A version and a B version, one a victory speech and the other a concession. This was widely reported that evening, but here is what was not reported.

As the president-elect reflected on his first words to an attentive nation, he took notice of the images that came across his TV screen: half images of crying Clinton supporters contrasted with images of jubilant Trump voters. Reflecting on the sight of Clinton voters, Trump picked up the previously planned victory speech and ripped it up. The speech hit the elites and the establishment. It just wasn't right for the moment. "I want to bring the people together. I want to speak to those people too," Ivanka Trump remembered her father saying as he watched the distraught Clinton crowd and set the torn paper aside. "I see their pain."

Trump began to plan his remarks as he waited for a call from Hillary Clinton. "Until she concedes, it's not official," Trump said. After waiting what seemed like forever for the call, the Trump family and team of advisors finally decided to head to the New York Hilton.

Before Trump received the call from Clinton, there were indications that the Clinton campaign knew the race was over. "Wolf, there is still a crowd behind me here at the Javits Center . . . They have turned off the election coverage early for the last several hours," Jeff Zeleny reported.[56] "I am told that campaign chairman John Podesta is on his way here to the Javits Center from the Peninsula Hotel, where he has been with the Clintons . . . He is going to be giving some type of an announcement or message. I'm told Secretary Clinton is not going to be coming here, at least not now at this moment."[57]

Shortly after the announcement, Podesta took the stage to address a crowd of disappointed supporters. "Well, folks, I know you've been here a long time and it's been a long night, and it's been a long campaign . . . They're still counting votes and every vote should count. Several states are too close to call. So we're not going to have anything more to say tonight . . . Everybody should head home. You should get some sleep. We'll have more to say tomorrow."[58]

The announcement was striking on two levels. National media outlets were clearly about to call the election for Trump, and a concession was in order. And didn't her distraught supporters deserve to hear from her directly, not her campaign manager?

Corey Lewandowski, who had taken my place on the CNN panel for the remainder of the night, observed, "Hillary Clinton is going to lose tonight. She should call Donald Trump immediately . . . We have 99.9 percent of these ballots counted. We're waiting for a small fraction . . . which will not materially change the outcome of this election. I think this is, exactly to Van's point, not bringing the country together."[59] Corey continued to point to Hillary Clinton's hypocrisy. She had admonished Trump about his potential unwillingness to accept election results, and here she was doing just that. Corey's allegation was widely rejected by the panel, although Anderson did acknowledge his point.

"I think Corey raised an interesting point," Anderson said.[60] "There was a lot of criticism of Donald Trump, what would you do on Election Night? If the roles were reversed . . ."[61] It's a point on which Dana Bash and Jake Tapper agreed.

After much speculation about Hillary's next move, Dana Bash was finally able to inform viewers around 2:40 a.m., "CNN can report that Hillary Clinton has called Donald Trump to concede the race. She has called Donald Trump to say that she will not be president."[62]

"Everyone in the room was stunned when it happened," Michael Glassner told me. "After Podesta came out publicly instead of Clinton, our assumption was that Clinton would not concede. There was still tremendous uncertainty."

"President-elect Donald Trump," Blitzer chimed in.[63] "If Hillary Clinton has conceded, that is dramatic; that is a dramatic development, Dana. And to hear the words 'president-elect,' we haven't yet projected that."[64]

Donald Trump received the call just before he emerged from behind the curtains to address a divided nation. His whole family hugged, embraced, and congratulated the new president-elect. "I tried not to cry," Lara said. It was finally official.

Vice President elect Mike Pence came out just before the new president-elect. In between the two speeches, CNN finally reported, "Now a historic moment. We can now project the winner of the presidential race, CNN projects Donald Trump wins the presidency . . . Donald J. Trump will become the 45th president of the United States, defeating Hillary Clinton in a campaign unlike anything we've seen in our lifetime . . . History has been made."[65]

They were words that, just hours earlier, almost no one had expected to hear.

Taking the stage after "one of the most stunning political upsets in recent American history" in one CNN reporter's words, a fractured nation looked to their new president.[66] Slowly walking out to the sound of victorious music, Trump appeared with his family just behind him.

"I've just received a call from Secretary Clinton," he said.[67] "She congratulated us—it's about us—on our victory and I congratulated her and her family on a very, very hard-fought campaign . . . Hillary has worked very long and very hard over a long period of time and we owe her a major debt of gratitude for her service to our country. I mean that very sincerely."[68]

It was a gracious, heartfelt nod to a broken opponent. Now it was time to do the same for a half-broken nation.

"Now it is time for America to bind the wounds of division, have to get together," Trump continued.[69] "[T]o all Republicans and Democrats and independents across this nation, I say it is time for us to come together as one united people. It's time. I pledge to every citizen of our land that I will be president for all of Americans and this is so important to me."[70]

Before Trump went on to thank his family and friends, he thanked the people who had stood behind him all along. "It's a movement comprised of Americans from all races, religions, backgrounds and beliefs, who want and expect our government to serve the people and serve the people it will."[71]

Trump delivered his brief speech and left that stage as the soon-to-be forty-fifth president of the United States. The media was speechless. The political world was rocked. The people had spoken.

CONCLUSION

As you flip through the final pages of this book, the second year of the Trump presidency begins. For me, Trump's inaugural year in Washington was a memorable one. I spent the first six months in two alternate realities: one at CNN and the other among the American people, writing this book. As big executives in our nation's metropolises filled the headlines with stories about Russia and White House palace intrigue, the real story of America was being written on the rickety, church-dotted roads of South Carolina, the sprawling knolls of Texas's Hill Country, and the blighted but still hopeful streets of Flint, Michigan. These are among the many forgotten cities and states whose inhabitants rarely make headlines but daily contribute to the lifeblood of this country with little notice or fanfare. In the end, they will write the story of the Trump presidency.

The media is sure to use these opening weeks of January 2018 to reflect on the first year of Trump's presidency, and as they do, let me share with you some things you likely won't hear much about. As I write these words in September of 2017, there is cause for optimism among forgotten factory workers. Foxconn announced it will build a new factory in Wisconsin, providing jobs for thousands of new workers.[1] The Keystone XL and Dakota Access pipelines, which languished in the approval process for years during the Obama administration, have been approved, creating another forty-two thousand jobs.[2] As President Trump promised, he has withdrawn from the job-killing Trans-Pacific Partnership, estimated to eliminate hundreds of thousands of U.S. jobs.[3] Unemployment is at a sixteen-year low, and consumer confidence is at a sixteen-year high as American incomes rise.[4]

Veterans like the late Barry Lynn Coates are finally being given the top-of-the-line treatment and attention that they deserve. The Veterans Affairs Accountability and Whistleblower Protection Act will make it easier to terminate employees who fail to do their job. Already, the VA has fired five hundred people. President Trump created a VA hotline in the White House and has poured billions into the Veterans Choice Program, permitting veterans who live far from VA facilities to access care. And the Veterans Appeals Improvement and Modernization Act expedites the process for the nearly half million veterans with pending appeals.[5] Under the Obama administration, appeals took up to six years for a final decision![6]

In the fight against ISIS, we finally have a president willing to call the enemy by name: "radical Islamic terrorism." Although President Obama claimed ISIS was "contained"—only to be contradicted by his own Joint Chiefs of Staff—in the Trump administration, ISIS is truly being contained as the US has retaken one-third of its territories in Iraq and Syria.[7] Iraqi forces have retaken Mosul, and the president dropped the so-called Mother of All Bombs (MOAB) on a circuit of ISIS tunnels.[8] And in an act widely hailed by the international community, Trump decimated an air base in Syria used by Bashar al-Assad to gas the innocent and vulnerable civilian population.

On immigration, President Trump has reduced border crossings by an eye-opening 52 percent. In the first half of 2017, ICE removed 2,798 criminal gang members, a rate on course to more than double the removals of these violent criminals in 2016. Immediately upon taking office, President Trump redirected $100 million in unused DHS dollars to go toward building a wall along the southern border. The VOICE office for victims of immigration crime was created to help innocent American victims like Sabine Durden.

And in what was perhaps President Trump's biggest achievement of all, Supreme Court Justice Neil Gorsuch was nominated and confirmed by the United State Senate, ensuring a lifetime of conservative decision-making on the Court that will honor our Constitution and protect men and women of faith.

These are just a few of President Trump's achievements. As it stands in September of 2016, I am hopeful that Republicans—and perhaps even some Democrats—will come together in passing bipartisan tax cuts that put more money in the pockets of hardworking Americans. I am likewise hopeful for a renewed effort to repeal and replace Obamacare, which has had devastating consequences for the Ackison and Summers families.

I would be remiss if I didn't add an important footnote to the Trump administration's 2016 achievements: they come amid resistance—resistance from the mainstream media, the left, liberal judges, and even Establishment Republicans. In Trump's early days in office, Trump's *temporary* travel pause from *terror hotbed countries* was widely misconstrued as a *permanent* travel ban from *Muslim nations*. Never mind that more than forty Muslim-majority countries were not even affected by the temporary pause![9] A handful of liberal judges issued a nationwide ban on Trump's travel pause only to be rebuked by the Supreme Court, which reinstated the majority of it in a unanimous—yes, a unanimous—decision.[10] That means that even liberal justices like Ruth Bader Ginsburg upheld the Trump travel pause!

But as I mentioned, there has been obstinacy from Trump's own party as well. While the House did their job in passing $1.6 billion in funding for the wall, the Senate—as of September 2017—has yet to do their part in approving the measure.[11] On healthcare too, Republican resistance has meant that Obamacare repeal and replace is a mere dream, not a reality—an unfulfilled promise to the American voter. It is my wish that as you read this you will find my words dated and supplanted by a tangible health care replacement bill.

As President Donald Trump continues on the journey of his first term, I know he does so with an eye for the people, not the politicians. It's why he said this during his first speech before the United Nations General Assembly: "The greatest [words] in the United States Constitution [are] its first three beautiful words. They are: 'We the People.'"[12] The media might tell you otherwise, but I can assure you of the president's first, guiding principle. It's you, the American people, who ignored the fallacies of the mainstream media and instead safeguarded the values of liberty, constitutional order, and sovereignty that make America the greatest nation on earth.

Although I often grew concerned and disconcerted by the narratives of negativity concocted by the press, Election 2016 and my travels across America instilled in me a hope, optimism, and realization that the American spirit rests in its citizens. Grassroots movements like the Tea Party and the Trump rallygoers were not top-down orchestrated efforts by the political class but bottom-up organic movements of the people.

What's the New American Revolution, you ask? It's the American people's effort to take their government back, not by force but by ballot. It is, in essence, "the great task" that President Abraham Lincoln bestowed upon us all in those beautifully crafted words of his famous Gettysburg Address: "that this nation, under God, shall have a new birth of freedom and that government of the people, by the people, for the people, shall not perish from this earth."[13]

Where does the revolution go from here? Only time will tell. As Alexis de Tocqueville, the nineteenth-century Frenchman who wrote of American greatness, so wisely observed, "In a revolution, as in a novel, the most difficult part to invent is the end."

NOTES

TWO BRIGHT LIGHTS

1. Kim's speech.
2. "Celebration of Life."
3. "Pamplona, Spain: Running of the Bulls," *Rick Steves' Europe*, YouTube, Jan. 5, 2011, http://bit.ly/2jLApd0.
4. Ibid.
5. "The Bull Run," http://bit.ly/2ujfBPs.
6. Sasha Goldstein, "Family of American Student Severely Injured by Bull in Spain Shocked by Goring Pictures," *New York Daily News*, Feb. 17, 2015, http://nydn.us/2uE7wEE.
7. "Celebration of Life."
8. Ibid.
9. Ibid.
10. Ibid.
11. Eun Kyung Kim, "Kim Copeland Talks Grief—and Berlin Truck Attack—5 Months After Losing Son, Husband in Nice," *Today*, Dec. 20, 2016, http://on.today.com/2sAqRKi.
12. Kim's speech.
13. "Nice Terror Attack News Coverage 14.07 (2016)," CNN International, YouTube, July 16, 2016, http://bit.ly/2tjOzYj.
14. Ibid.
15. Bill Keveney, "French President Hollande: 'Horror Again Has Struck France,'" *USA Today*, July 15, 2016, https://usat.ly/2tGeT0K.
16. "8 New Arrests in Nice, France, Truck Attack That Killed 86," Associated Press, Sept. 20, 2016, https://usat.ly/2tKCY7J; Alissa J. Rubin, Lilia Blaise, Adam Nossiter, and Aurelien Breeden, "France Says Truck Attacker Was Tunisia Native with Record of Petty Crime," *New York Times*, July 15, 2016, http://nyti.ms/2sAlESF.
17. Tarek Amara, "Brother of Nice Attacker Says He Sent 'Laughing' Photo Amid Crowds," Reuters, July 17, 2016, http://reut.rs/29SttbI.

18. Nadine Bonewitz, "Hundreds Fill Church for Candlelight Service to Remember Copeland Family," KXAN, July 18, 2016, http://bit.ly/2skpnjc.

19. "Texas Woman: 'Nightmare' Terror Attack in Nice Killed My Husband, Son," *Today*, YouTube, Aug. 4, 2016, http://bit.ly/2uEmtGy.

20. Kim's speech.

21. Ibid.

22. Tim Lister, "One ISIS Attack Every 84 Hours' Spurs Dread and Anger in Europe," CNN, July 31, 2016, http://cnn.it/2amFK4K.

23. Jason Hanna, Ralph Ellis, Saeed Ahmed, and Emanuella Grinberg, "Terror Attack in Bangladesh: The Victims," CNN, July 6, 2016, http://cnn.it/29EFGyN.

24. Tim Hume, Elliott C. McLaughlin, and Margot Haddad, "Hollande: Deadly Church Attack in France Carried Out in Name of ISIS," CNN, July 27, 2016, http://cnn.it/2aqAmSk.

25. Ibid.

26. Dominic Casciani, "London Attacker: Khuram Butt Showed His Extremist Colours," BBC, June 5, 2017, http://bbc.in/2ujDeaz.

27. Ibid.

28. Aurelien Breeden, "Attacker in Nice Plotted for Months and Had Accomplices, French Prosecutor Says," *New York Times*, July 21, 2016, http://nyti.ms/2tjXLvH.

29. "Full Speech: Donald Trump Addresses Radical Islamic Terrorism," *Hill*, Aug. 15, 2016, http://bit.ly/2xlIwaj.

30. Ibid.

31. Rowan Scarborough, "Islamic State Finds Success Infiltrating Its Terrorists into Refugee Flows to West," *Washington Times*, Jan. 29, 2017, http://bit.ly/2nEsTmz.

32. Judson Berger, "Anatomy of the Terror Threat: Files Show Hundreds of US Plots, Refugee Connection," Fox News, June 22, 2016, http://fxn.ws/28PH0Su.

33. "San Bernardino Shooting Victims: Who They Were," *Los Angeles Times*, Dec. 17, 2015, http://lat.ms/1Rq8yLZ; "Fiance Visa Used by San Bernardino Terrorist Under Scrutiny," Fox News, Dec. 9, 2015, http://fxn.ws/2wRiRDx.

34. Scarborough, "Islamic State Finds Success Infiltrating Its Terrorists into Refugee Flows to West."

35. Ibid.; C. Eugene Emery Jr., "Donald Trump Says Hillary Clinton Wants to Let 500 Percent More Syrians into the U.S.," PolitiFact, June 13, 2016, http://bit.ly/1XncCjX.

36. "Celebration of Life."

37. "In the Spirit of Family: Sean & Brodie Copeland Memorial Endowment for Texas Baseball," Longhorn Foundation, http://bit.ly/2tKtE3u.

38. Bob Ballou, "Lakeway Family Honors Father, Son Lost in Terror Attack

by Giving to Future UT Athletes," CBS Austin, Feb. 16, 2017, http://bit.ly
/2taZJjz.

39. "In the Spirit of Family."
40. Ballou, "Lakeway Family Honors Father, Son Lost in Terror Attack by Giving to Future UT Athletes," CBS Austin, Feb. 20, 2017, http://bit.ly/2taZJjz.
41. Ibid.
42. Ibid.
43. Ibid.
44. Ibid.
45. Andres Sosa, "Fresh Faces on the Forty," Longhorns Network.

THE WINNER

1. Barry Lynn Coates, Letter to Congress, http://bit.ly/2uE0Vtz.
2. Barry Coates, Testimony before Congress, April 9, 2014, http://bit.ly/2skEhWq.
3. Scott Bronstein, Nelli Black, and Drew Griffin, "Veterans Dying Because of Health Care Delays," CNN, Jan. 30, 2014, http://cnn.it/1edUSSc.
4. Coates, Testimony before Congress.
5. Ibid.
6. Ibid.
7. Bronstein et al., "Veterans Dying Because of Health Care Delays."
8. Ibid.
9. "Arizona VA Boss Accused of Covering Up Veterans' Deaths Linked to Previous Scandal," Fox News, April 24, 2014, http://fxn.ws/2uDVqv2.
10. Snejana Farberov, "'Don't Let Me Die': Veteran's Tearful Plea Before He Succumbed to Cancer Without Ever Receiving Treatment as It Emerges That 'Phoenix VA Kept up to 1,600 Patients on a Secret Wait List,'" *Daily Mail*, April 24, 2014. http://dailym.ai/2tFYsSj.
11. C. J. Ciaramella, "VA Director at Phoenix Hospital Got $9K Bonus," *Washington Free Beacon*, April 24, 2014, http://bit.ly/1nt3bNO.
12. Coates, Testimony before Congress.
13. Ibid.
14. Ibid.
15. Senator Tim Scott, "Remembering Barry Lynn Coates," *Congressional Record*, March 17, 2016, http://bit.ly/2ujgcAZ.
16. Stephen Collinson, "Obama Comes Face to Face with Burdens of 9/11 Generation," CNN, Sept. 28, 2016, http://cnn.it/2xP7NY1.
17. Ibid.
18. Ibid.
19. Ibid.
20. Ibid.
21. Ibid.

22. Curt Devine, Drew Griffin, and Nelli Black, "Report: Deadly Delays in Care Continue at Phoenix VA," CNN, Oct. 4, 2016, http://cnn.it/2tG2I47.
23. D'Angelo Gore, "Fiorina's Unsupported Claim About VA Deaths," Fact-Check.org, Sept. 23, 2015, http://bit.ly/1jOIAVg.
24. "Compensation: Exposure to Contaminated Drinking Water at Camp Lejeune," VA.gov, http://bit.ly/2oeCpwI.
25. "Transcript: Rachel Maddow Interviews Hillary Clinton," MSNBC, Oct. 23, 2015, http://on.msnbc.com/1H074zT.
26. Ibid.
27. Ibid.
28. Ibid.; Ben Kesling, "Republicans Take Aim at Hillary Clinton for VA Remarks," *Wall Street Journal*, Oct. 28, 2015, http://on.wsj.com/2vMElA5.
29. "ICYMI: Sen. John McCain & Rep. Jeff Miller Respond to Hillary Clinton's [*sic*]," GOP, Oct. 28, 2015, http://bit.ly/2xX6lCC.
30. Kesling, "Republicans Take Aim at Hillary Clinton for VA Remarks."
31. "Transcript: Donald Trump's Full Immigration Speech, Annotated," *Los Angeles Times*, Aug. 31, 2016, http://lat.ms/2bEhguL.
32. "Exit Polls," CNN, Nov. 23, 2016, http://cnn.it/2fBsNej.
33. "Transcript: CNN Presidential Town Hall: America's Military and The Commander and Chief," CNN, Sept. 28, 2016, http://cnn.it/2cEC2tx.
34. Donovan Slack and Bill Theobald, "Veterans Affairs Pays $142 Million in Bonuses Amid Scandals," *USA Today*, Nov. 11, 2015, https://usat.ly/2tDtxGL.

THE TRANSFORMATION

1. Sabine Durden, "Who Was Dominic and Was He Really That Funny?," Dom Hugs, April 25, 2016, http://bit.ly/2jDWFpc.
2. Brian Rokos, "Dispatchers Grieve 'Everyone's Plus-one,'" *Riverside* (CA) *Press-Enterprise*, July 16, 2012, http://bit.ly/2qMkizy.
3. Ibid.
4. Brian Rokos, "Sheriff's Dispatcher Killed in Collision with Unlicensed Driver," *Riverside* (CA) *Press-Enterprise*, July 12, 2012, http://bit.ly/2jVBxdu.
5. Allison Graves and Neelesh Moorthy, "Who Were the Victims of Illegal Immigrants Trump Named at the RNC?," PolitiFact, July 21, 2016, http://bit.ly/29XpTLY.
6. Ibid.; Brian Rokos, "Dispatcher Killed: Other Driver Had Two DUI Arrests," *Riverside* (CA) *Press-Enterprise*, July 16, 2012, http://bit.ly/2wRzyi0.
7. Ibid.; Frank Camp, "Immigrant Mother Pens Powerful Letter to Trump—and It's Not What You Probably Think," *Independent Journal Review*, http://bit.ly/2jdcMOI.
8. "Statement of Jessica M. Vaughan," U.S. House Committee on Oversight and Government Reform, Feb. 25, 2015, http://bit.ly/2wRcsZ7.

9. Vivian Yee, "For Grieving Parents, Trump Is 'Speaking for the Dead' on Immigration," *New York Times*, June 25, 2017, http://nyti.ms/2eVTUCc.

10. Brian Rokos, "Dispatcher Killed: Other Driver Had Two DUI Arrests."

11. "Statement of Sabine Durden," AILA.org, http://bit.ly/2gTiR1W.

12. Brian Rokos, "Crash defendant out of Immigration Custody," *Riverside* (CA) *Press-Enterprise*, Aug. 23, 2012, http://www.pe.com/2012/08/23/moreno-valley -crash-defendant-out-of-immigration-custody/.

13. Ibid.; Brian Rokos, "Man Accused of Killing Dispatcher in Court Monday," *Riverside* (CA) *Press-Enterprise*, Aug. 25, 2012; http://bit.ly/2eWzklf.

14. Brian Rokos, "Driver Gets Nine Months in Dispatcher's Death," *Riverside* (CA) *Press-Enterprise*, April 3, 2013, http://bit/ly/2pRnOpw.

15. Ibid.

16. Ibid.

17. Rokos, "Driver Gets Nine Months in Dispatcher's Death."

18. Brian Rokos, "Mother Describes Grief in Letters to Judge," *Riverside* (CA) *Press-Enterprise*, May 10, 2013, http://bit.ly/2wRb2iI.

19. Rokos, "Driver Gets Nine Months in Dispatcher's Death."

20. Ibid.

21. "Man Gets Jail Time, Probation for Causing Motorcyclist's Death," *Valley News* (Fallbrook, CA), April 3, 2013, http://bit.ly/2jelf3V.

22. Rokos, "Driver Gets Nine Months in Dispatcher's Death."

23. Ibid.

24. Ibid.

25. "Statement of Jessica M. Vaughan."

26. Rokos, "Mother Describes Grief in Letters to Judge."

27. Rokos, "Driver Gets Nine Months in Dispatcher's Death."

28. Brian Rokos, "Dispatcher's Killer Could Serve Only 34 Days," *Riverside* (CA) *Press-Enterprise*, April 4, 2013, http://bit.ly/2gSG6sI.

29. "Statement of Jessica M. Vaughan."

30. Rokos, "Mother Describes Grief in Letters to Judge."

31. Ibid.

32. Brian Rokos, "Man Who Killed Sheriff's Dispatcher Deported," *Riverside* (CA) *Press-Enterprise*, March 21, 2014, http://bit.ly/2vX7M6u.

33. Kerry Picket, "Mother of Slain Victim by Illegal Alien Says Some Lawmakers Fell Asleep at Hearing," *Daily Caller*, July 21, 2015, http://bit.ly /1DtvSi7.

34. Michelle Moons, "Exclusive—Grieving Mom's Letter to Obama: 'You Again, Invited a Known Illegal Alien to the White House," Breitbart, July 1, 2015, http://bit.ly/2p7m3u1.

35. Kirsten Powers, "Trump Administration Sets New Enforcement Priorities, Aired 9–10p ET," CNN, Feb. 22, 2017, goo.gl/yZORZ7.

36. "Dreamer: My Family Is 'Scared' of Donald Trump," MSNBC, Sept. 1, 2016, http://bit.ly/2pMRA36.

37. Sabine Durden, "Flying with my very own angel," Dom Hugs, Sept. 15, 2016, http://bit.ly/2jSsOc3.

38. Ibid.

39. Ibid.

THE THIN BLUE LINE

1. Phil Trexler and Katie Nix, "Mourners Recall Fallen Akron Police Officer Justin Winebrenner," *Akron Beacon Journal*, Nov. 24, 2014, http://bit.ly/2r3lVcr.

2. Ibid.

3. Paula Schleis, "Highway to Heaven: Route Chosen to Honor Slain Officer Justin Winebrenner Goes Past His Grave," *Akron Beacon Journal*, June 4, 2015, http://bit.ly/2pPnh8N.

4. "Staff Sergeant Robert C. Winebrenner," Ohio Military Hall of Fame, http://bit.ly/2qZ6a9f.

5. "Kenan Ivery Trial Day 1 09/28/15," posted by LawNewz Network on YouTube, Sept. 28, 2015, http://bit.ly/2pOkZYg.

6. Ibid.

7. Phil Trexler, "Akron Police and Victim Assistance Showered Slaying Suspect's Family with Christmas Gifts," *Akron Beacon Journal*, Nov. 19, 2014, http://bit.ly/2qolWYr.

8. Ibid.

9. Ibid.; Adam Ferrise, "Man Accused of Killing Akron Cop Served Three Stints in Prison, Including Once for Nearly Running Over an Officer," Cleveland.com, Nov. 17, 2014, http://bit.ly/2qJRaw8.

10. Phil Trexler, *Akron Beacon Journal* on Newspapers.com, http://bit.ly/2r9qULr.

11. Ibid.

12. Ibid.

13. Adam Ferrise, "Fiancee of Slain Akron Police Officer Testifies During Trial," Cleveland.com, Sept. 28, 2015, http://bit.ly/2rjky9s.

14. Darcie Loreno and Dave Nethers, "Trial Begins for Man Accused in Shooting Death of Akron Officer," Fox 8 Cleveland, Sept. 28, 2015, http://bit.ly/1FDlfQ9.

15. Betty Lin-Fisherand and Phil Trexler, "Slain Akron Officer Was a Hero, Eyewitness Says; Four Others Shot, Suspect Arrested," *Akron Beacon Journal*, Nov. 16, 2014, http://bit.ly/2riPPJ5.

16. Ferrise, "Fiancee of Slain Akron Police Officer Testifies During Trial."

17. Ibid.

18. Ibid.

19. "Kenan Ivery Trial Day 3 Part 1 09/30/15," posted by LawNewz Network on YouTube, Sept. 30, 2015, http://bit.ly/2pPs8ac.

20. Ibid.

21. Tom Beres, "Fallen Akron Officer's Family Remembers His Service," WKYC, Nov. 18, 2014, http://on.wkyc.com/2pQuPbl.

22. Ed Meyer, "Jurors See Videos of Bar Confrontation in Trial of Akron Man Accused of Killing Off-duty Officer," *Akron Beacon Journal*, Oct. 3, 2015, http://bit.ly/2pQznlx.

23. Adam Ferrise, "Man Testifies at Trial to Fatally Shooting Off-duty Akron Police Officer," Cleveland.com, Oct. 7, 2015, http://bit.ly/2xWgWxF.

24. Darcie Loreno, "'You All Probably Hate Me': Man Who Killed Akron Officer Chokes Up, Apologizes in Court," Fox 8 Cleveland, Oct. 23, 2015, http://bit.ly /2xdqE0y.

25. "Man Convicted of Killing Akron Officer Sentenced to Life in Prison Without Parole," Fox 8 Cleveland, Oct. 28, 2015, http://bit.ly/2wQ39e6.

26. Courtney Danser, "Dad of Justin Winebrenner to Killer: 'Last Good Deed He Did Was Getting You off the Street Forever,'" News 5 Cleveland, Oct. 28, 2015, http://bit.ly/2qlKpzk.

27. Beres, "Fallen Akron Officer's Family Remembers His Service."

28. "Department of Justice Report Regarding the Criminal Investigation into the Shooting Death of Michael Brown by Ferguson, Missouri, Police Officer Darren Wilson," Justice Department, March 4, 2015, http://bit.ly/1PV91Rc; Kayleigh McEnany, "A Year After Ferguson Burned," Above the Law, Nov. 24, 2015, http://bit.ly/2qykwN2.

29. "135 Law Enforcement Officer Fatalities Nationwide in 2016," National Law Enforcement Officers Memorial Fund, Dec. 29, 2016, http://bit.ly/2rj QEBl.

30. Will Racke, "FBI Report: Media Narrative Inspires Violence Against Police," *Daily Caller*, May 5, 2017, http://bit.ly/2qptABT.

31. https://www.facebook.com/StepOutInBlueWCPA/?fref=nf.

32. "Clarke: Officers Fear Witch Hunt by 'Cop-Hating DOJ, Led by Race-Obsessed AG,'" Fox News Insider, May 13, 2016, http://bit.ly/1rL23u0.

33. Michele McPhee, "The Hidden Trump Voter—the Police," *Boston Globe*, Nov. 9, 2016, http://bit.ly/2qlDMNU.

34. Danser, "Dad of Justin Winebrenner to Killer: 'Last Good Deed He Did Was Getting You off the Street Forever.'"

35. Ibid.

THE SILENCING

1. Kiera Blessing, "Ferguson Protest Blocks Traffic near Harvard Square," *Boston Globe*, Dec. 1, 2014, http://bit.ly/2rjGeFp.

2. Kiera Blessing, "Harvard Students Stage 'Die-in' to Protest Ferguson, NYC Cases," *Boston Globe*, Dec. 10, 2014, http://bit.ly/2qy8Hqn.

3. Meg P. Bernhard and Samuel E. Liu, "Protest at Primal Scream Leads to Chaotic Exchange," *Harvard Crimson*, Dec. 12, 2014, http://bit.ly/1wEYDKl.
4. Ibid.
5. Charles C. W. Cooke, "Social Injustice Ate My Homework," *National Review*, Dec. 9, 2014, http://bit.ly/1sjMgft.
6. Letter to Dean Minow and Harvard Law School Administration, Coalition at Harvard Law School, Dec. 8, 2014, http://bit.ly/1ulLyiC.
7. Eugene Volokh, "Columbia Law Students Demand Exam Extensions Because of 'Trauma Related to the Recent Non-indictments' (in Ferguson and Staten Island)," *Washington Post*, Dec. 8, 2014, http://wapo.st/2pQ1YsK.
8. Kayleigh McEnany, "A Year After Ferguson Burned," Above the Law, Nov. 24, 2015, http://bit.ly/2qykwN2.
9. "A New Low," Socratic Shortcomings, December 18, 2014, http://bit.ly/1yBhNkD.
10. Calvin Trillin, "The Color of Blood," *New Yorker*, March 3, 2008, http://bit.ly/2q1dr3W.
11. "What Our Trauma Teaches Us," Socratic Shortcomings, http://bit.ly/1yBhNkD.
12. Ibid.
13. Ben Bastomski, "Dogmatic Shortcomings," *Harvard Law Record*, Jan. 2, 2015, http://bit.ly/2qyvXnQ.
14. "Sanctity of Life," Socratic Shortcomings, Feb. 28, 2016, http://socraticshortcomings.tumblr.com/.
15. "Chalk Offensive," Socratic Shortcomings, April 5, 2016, http://bit.ly/1yBhNkD.
16. "'Holy Cow,'" Socratic Shortcomings, April 5, 2016, http://bit.ly/1yBhNkD.
17. "The Jail Bird," Socratic Shortcomings, April 15, 2016, http://bit.ly/1yBhNkD.
18. "'The Framers,'" Socratic Shortcomings, April 1, 2015, http://bit.ly/1yBhNkD.
19. "Legal Profession," Socratic Shortcomings, Jan. 14, 2015, http://bit.ly/1yBhNkD.
20. Bill Barlow, "Fascism at Yale," *Harvard Law Record*, Nov. 10, 2015, http://bit.ly/1MLUiqi.
21. Liam Stack, "Yale's Halloween Advice Stokes a Racially Charged Debate," *New York Times*, Nov. 8, 2015, http://nyti.ms/2rwKrCg.
22. Bill Barlow, "Fascism at Yale."
23. Ibid.
24. "Who We Are," Reclaim Harvard Law School, http://bit.ly/2pYckT5.
25. "Remove Demands That Infringe on Academic Freedom," Responsible Speech at HLS, Dec. 10, 2015, http://bit.ly/2qymxsG.

26. Claire E. Parker, "Student Activists Protest Award Ceremony for Dean," *Harvard Crimson*, Feb. 26, 2016, http://bit.ly/2rwhgzY.

27. Ibid.

28. Randall Kennedy, "Black Tape at Harvard Law," *New York Times*, Nov. 27, 2015, http://nyti.ms/2qyim01.

29. Claire E. Parker, "Law School Activists to Continue Occupation," *Harvard Crimson*, March 9, 2016, http://bit.ly/2q1u0MV.

30. Bill Barlow, "Censorship at Harvard Law," *Harvard Law Record*, April 5, 2016, http://bit.ly/2rwNcU6.

31. Lindsay Church, "Reclaim Harvard Law Removes Critical Posters, Stirring Debate over Academic Freedom," *Harvard Law Record*, March 31, 2016, http://bit.ly/1RNluaQ.

32. Najwa Tannous on Twitter, April 5, 2016, via Imgur, http://bit.ly/2qwyUFm.

33. Najwa Tannous on Twitter, April 5, 2016, via Imgur, http://bit.ly/2qyofKs.

34. "Abridging the Freedom of Speech," *New Society*, Feb. 3, 2016, http://bit.ly/2rwAeph.

35. "What Our Trauma Teaches Us," Socratic Shortcomings, Nov. 17, 2014, http://bit.ly/1yBhNkD.

36. "Disinvitation Attempts," Foundation for Individual Rights in Education, http://bit.ly/2eXkDyu; Kayleigh McEnany, "Conservative Thought Is Silenced on Our Nation's Campuses," *Hill*, Feb. 7, 2017, http://bit.ly/2gWjqbr.

37. Ibid.

38. Ibid.; Jessica Chasmar, "John Cornyn's Commencement Speech Canceled by Historically Black Texas College," *Washington Times*, May 12, 2017, http://bit.ly/2qaSHdz.

39. Kayleigh McEnany, "Conservative Thought Is Silenced on Our Nation's Campuses"; "Statement from President Tim Sands," Virginia Tech, May 5, 2016, http://bit.ly/2gVdAmI; "NYPD Commissioner Ray Kelly Shouted Down at Brown University Lecture," *Guardian*, Oct. 30, 2013, http://bit.ly/2eXkDhK; Katie Reilly, "Texas Southern University Cancels Commencement Address by GOP Senator Amid Backlash," *Time*, May 12, 2017, http://ti.me/2eWjfMs.

40. Kayleigh McEnany, "Why I Am Backing Donald Trump," CNN, May 11, 2016, http://cnn.it/2w9RMe6.

41. Ibid.

THE FORSAKING

1. "Oscar Rodriguez, Jr.," First Liberty, https://firstliberty.org/cases/rodriguez/.

2. "Oscar Rodriguez Removed from Air Force Retirement Ceremony," YouTube, June 20, 2016, http://bit.ly/2bU7MLL.

3. "Air Force Veteran Oscar Rodriguez Assaulted over the Word God," You-Tube, June 20, 2016, http://bit.ly/28IBYmf.

4. "Flag Fold Ceremony USAF Mentions God," YouTube, Sept. 25, 2013, http://bit.ly/2rNrQ5w.

5. "Oscar Rodriguez Removed from Air Force Retirement Ceremony."

6. Ibid.

7. "Senator Landrieu's Shares How a Veteran Lost His Business Due to Serving in the Military," YouTube, June 20, 2016, http://bit.ly/2qSKVp8.

8. "A Reservist's Reward—Bankruptcy," *CBS Evening News*, Nov. 11, 2003, http://bit.ly/2qSS0G3.

9. Ibid.

10. Ibid.

11. Ibid.

12. "Oscar Rodriguez, Jr."

13. Ibid.

14. "Report of Inquiry: Travis AFB 3 Apr 16 Retirement Ceremony," Inspector General of the Air Force, July 2016, http://bit.ly/2vXz1Ox.

15. "Charles 'Chuck' Roberson testifies he invited Rodriguez," YouTube, June 20, 2016, http://bit.ly/2qSFzdC.

16. "Oscar Rodriguez, Jr."

17. "Air Force Draws Secularist Ire After Permitting Religious Expression at Retirement Ceremonies," *Washington Times*, Oct. 13, 2016, http://bit.ly/2qM7XgO.

18. Dianna Cahn, "Flag-Folding Fight Questions Interpretation of Air Force Regulation," *Stars and Stripes*, June 24, 2016, http://bit.ly/2wWfQlk.

19. "Report of Inquiry: Travis AFB 3 Apr 16 Retirement Ceremony."

20. Ibid.

21. Ibid.

22. Ibid., at 37.

23. Ibid., at 37–38.

24. *Sterling v. United States*," First Liberty, https://firstliberty.org/cases/sterling/.

25. Ibid.

26. Alan Dowd, "Finding the Balance," Military Chaplain, Summer 2016, http://67.199.60.145/Articles.aspx?ArticleId=999.

27. William J. Cadigan, "Christian Persecution Reached Record High in 2015, Report Says," CNN, Jan. 17, 2016, http://cnn.it/1OXICpW.

28. "American Views on Intolerance and Religious Liberty in America," LifeWay USA, http://bit.ly/2xecdtp; Bradford Richardson, "Persecution of Christians on the Rise, Americans Say," *Washington Times*, April 5, 2016, http://bit.ly/1q4QQU4.

29. Ibid.
30. Eric Nicholson, "After Years of Wandering, a Dallas Synagogue Finds a Home—and a Chilly Welcome," *Dallas Observer*, April 30, 2015, http://bit.ly/2rNC9qf.
31. Ibid.
32. Ibid.; "Defendants' Motion to Transfer Venue" in *City of Dallas v. Gothelf*, http://bit.ly/2repEXR.
33. Nicholson, "After Years of Wandering, a Dallas Synagogue Finds a Home—and a Chilly Welcome."
34. Ibid.
35. Ibid.; "Congregation Toras Chaim," First Liberty, http://bit.ly/2qSIhj4.
36. Nicholson, "After Years of Wandering, a Dallas Synagogue Finds a Home—and a Chilly Welcome"; "Congregation Toras Chaim."
37. Ibid.
38. Ibid.
39. Paul Strand, "Bellwether? Why This Tiny Synagogue Should Concern You," CBN News, June 16, 2015, http://bit.ly/2qSHP4z.
40. "Alexia Palma," First Liberty, http://bit.ly/2q8PPiv.
41. Kristina Guerra, "Catholic Health Educator in Texas Fired for Refusing to Teach Birth Control," *Chicago Tribune*, Dec. 21, 2016, http://trib.in/2qTnKsI.
42. "RE: Charge of Discrimination Against Legacy Community Health," First Liberty, Dec. 21, 2016, https://firstliberty.org/wp-content/uploads/2016/12/Palma-EEOC-Full-Charge-REDACTED.pdf; "Alexia Palma—Fired for Her Faith," YouTube, April 20, 2017, http://bit.ly/2qTLJIb.
43. Ibid.
44. Guerra, "Catholic Health Educator in Texas Fired for Refusing to Teach Birth Control."
45. Claire Chretien, "Catholic Health Educator Fired for Refusing to Promote Contraception, Attend Class at Planned Parenthood," Life Site News, Dec. 22, 2016, http://bit.ly/2rNxJjo.
46. Ibid.
47. Ibid.
48. "Alexia Palma," First Liberty, http://bit.ly/2q8PPiv.
49. Chretien, "Catholic Health Educator Fired for Refusing to Promote Contraception, Attend Class at Planned Parenthood."
50. Ibid.
51. "Coach Kennedy," First Liberty, https://firstliberty.org/cases/coachkennedy/; Todd Starnes, "A Faithful Coach Wants His Job Back," Fox News, Aug. 9, 2016, http://fxn.ws/2axXwXI.
52. Ibid.

53. "Coach Kennedy: How His Faith Ended His Football Career," YouTube via *Daily Signal*, Jan. 26, 2016, http://bit.ly/2qhupuL.

54. Ibid.

55. Ibid.

56. Ibid.

57. Starnes, "A Faithful Coach Wants His Job Back"; "Equal Employment Opportunity Commission Intake Questionnaire," First Liberty, https://firstliberty.org/wp-content/uploads/2016/01/Kennedy-EEOC-Intake-Questionnaire-and-Supporting-Materials_Redacted.pdf.

58. Bradford Richardson, "Praying High School Football Coach Sues District to Get His Job Back," *Washington Times*, Aug. 10, 2016, http://bit.ly/2qMoMbm.

59. "Coach Kennedy: How His Faith Ended His Football Career"; "Coach Kennedy."

60. Todd Starnes, "Court Rules High School Football Coach Cannot Pray on the Field," Fox News, Aug. 23, 2017, http://fxn.ws/2vqXC9i.

61. Richardson, "Praying High School Football Coach Sues District to Get His Job Back."

62. "Circuit Scorecard—October Term 2016," SCOTUSblog, June 28, 2017, http://bit.ly/2jgOOlD.

63. Starnes, "Court Rules High School Football Coach Cannot Pray on the Field."

64. "Equal Employment Opportunity Commission Intake Questionnaire."

65. "Vintage Church," First Liberty, https://firstliberty.org/cases/vintage/.

66. Todd Starnes, "Church Hit With Criminal Summons for Praising Jesus Too Loudly," Charisma News, Dec. 14, 2015, http://bit.ly/1O0nCtS.

67. Ibid.

68. Ibid.

69. "Vintage Church."

70. "Mary Anne Sause," First Liberty, https://firstliberty.org/cases/sause/.

71. ChristianPost.com, "Kansas Woman Who Claimed Police Told Her to Stop Praying in Her Home Fights Court Ruling," Fox News, Oct. 5, 2016, http://fxn.ws/2rNBFjY.

72. Ibid.

73. *Sause v. Louisburg Police Dept.*, No. 15-CV-9633-JAR-TJJ, at *3 (United States District Court for the District of Kansas, June 17 2016).

74. Ibid.

75. *Sause v. Bauer*, No. 16-3231 (10th Circuit Court).

76. "Mary Anne Sause," First Liberty, https://firstliberty.org/cases/sause/.

77. ChristianPost.com, "Kansas Woman Who Claimed Police Told Her to Stop Praying in Her Home Fights Court Ruling."

78. Gregory A. Smith and Jessica Martinez, "How the Faithful Voted: A Prelimi-

nary 2016 analysis," Pew Research Center, November 9, 2016, http://pewrsr
.ch/2ffve5n.

THE CLEANSING WATER

1. Dr. Sanjay Gupta, Ben Tinker & Tim Hume, "'Our Mouths Were Ajar': Doctor's Fight to Expose Flint's Water Crisis," CNN, Jan. 22, 2016, http://cnn.it /1PkRZSA.

2. Adriana Diaz, "Flint Mother: I'm Worried My Son Will Wake Up Different," CBS News, Jan. 22, 2016, http://cbsn.ws/2gW1eyu.

3. Josh Sanburn, "The Poisoning of an American City," *Time*, Jan. 21,2016, http://ti.me/1nzYtkt.

4. John Hall, "Flint Is the Most Dangerous City in America—but It Has Nothing to Do with the Water Crisis," *Independent*, Jan. 19, 2016, http://ind.pn /2uG1S61.

5. Lisa John Rogers, "What Will Happen with the Flint Water Crisis Once the Cameras Leave?," *Vice*, Feb. 3, 2016, https://broadly.vice.com/en_us /article/9aepw8/what-will-happen-with-the-flint-water-crisis-once-the -cameras-leave.

6. "Even A Bit of Lead Is Bad For Kids' Development," American Psychological Association, http://www.apa.org/action/resources/research-in-action/lead .aspx; Philip Bump, "Lead Contamination Exists Throughout the U.S.— But Flint Has a Special History," *Washington Post*, March 6, 2016, https:// www.washingtonpost.com/news/the-fix/wp/2016/01/19/lead-contamination -exists-throughout-the-u-s-but-flint-has-a-special-history/?utm_term=.c52b 6de7777a.

7. Hertz-Picciotto, "The evidence that lead increases the risk for spontaneous abortion.," *American Journal of Industrial Medicine* 38, no. 3 (Sept. 2000); Janet Contursi, "Poisons That Make Hair Fall Out," LiveStrong, Aug. 14, 2017, http://www.livestrong.com/article/82586-poisons-make-hair-fall-out/; Maggie Fox, "Flint Water Crisis: Here's What Lead Can Do to You," NBC, Jan. 19, 2016, https://www.nbcnews.com/storyline/flint-water-crisis/flint-water -crisis-here-s-what-lead-can-do-you-n499916.

8. Merrit Kennedy, "Lead-Laced Water in Flint: A Step-by-Step Look at the Makings of a Crisis," NPR, April 20, 2016, http://n.pr/1VkVSsZ.

9. Bump, "Lead Contamination Exists Throughout the U.S.—But Flint Has a Special History."

10. Monica Davey, "Flint Officials Are No Longer Saying the Water Is Fine," *New York Times*, Oct. 7, 2015, https://www.nytimes.com/2015/10/08/us /reassurances-end-in-flint-after-months-of-concern.html?_r=0.

11. Paul Egan, "Amid Denials, State Workers in Flint Got Clean Water," *Detroit Free Press*, Jan. 28, 2016, http://on.freep.com/1UtPeg2.

12. Trymaine Lee, "The Rust Belt: Once Mighty Cities in Decline," MSNBC, http://on.msnbc.com/1VrZ6Ik.

13. Ibid.

14. Jiquanda Johnson, "Flint, Detroit Among Nation's Poorest Cities, New Census Data Show," MLive.com, Sept. 17, 2015, http://bit.ly/20H3clP.

15. "Noah," RYOT.org, http://bit.ly/2pB2AO9.

16. Dana Romanoff, "He Grew Up on the Streets, Now He's Making Them a Better Place," *National Geographic* via YouTube, April 30, 2017, http://bit.ly /2uC2viI.

17. Ibid.

18. Ibid.

19. "Noah."

20. Romanoff, "He Grew Up on the Streets, Now He's Making Them a Better Place."

21. Ibid.

22. Ibid.

23. "Noah."

24. Romanoff, "He Grew Up on the Streets, Now He's Making Them a Better Place."

25. Genesis 6:8, New International Version, http://bit.ly/2v1y7iw.

26. "Post-Debate Analysis of Democratic Debate. Aired 11p–12a ET," CNN, March 6, 2016, http://cnn.it/2xsvckD.

27. Timothy Cama, "EPA Official Resigns Over Flint Water Crisis," *Hill*, Jan. 21, 2016, http://thehill.com/policy/energy-environment/266661-epa -official-resigns-amid-flint-water-crisis; Jake Neher, "Director of Michigan Department of Environmental Quality Resigns," WEMU, Dec. 20, 2015, http://wemu.org/post/director-michigan-department-environmental-quality -resigns#stream/0.

28. Alex Swoyer, "Trump: 'Now, the Cars Are Made in Mexico and You Can't Drink the Water in Flint," *Breitbart*, Sept. 14, 2016, http://bit.ly/2c9n61a.

29. Dominic Adams, "Locally Owned Grocery Store Inches Closer to Reality on Flint's North Side," Michigan Live, May 28, 2017, http://www.mlive.com /news/flint/index.ssf/2017/05/locally_owned_grocery_store_in.html.

30. Romanoff, "He Grew Up on the Streets, Now He's Making Them a Better Place."

31. Section 3, HUD.gov, http://bit.ly/2vceuoq.

32. Romanoff, "He Grew Up on the Streets, Now He's Making Them a Better Place."

33. "Noah."

THE BETRAYAL

1. "Anterior Cruciate Ligament (ACL) Surgery," WebMD, http://wb.md/1lenObO.

2. Dr. John E Sherman, "Spinal Fusion Surgery: One to Three Months Post-Operation," Spine-health.com, Oct. 10, 2015, http://bit.ly/2t57BAH.

3. Donald Trump, Twitter, February 13, 2016, https://twitter.com/realdonaldtrump/status/698522430847983616?lang=en.

4. Julia Hahn, "Donald Trump Only Candidate to Address 1,400 Indianapolis Workers Whose Jobs Are Being Sent to Mexico," *Breitbart*, Feb. 13, 2016, http://bit.ly/2tYrDQo.

5. "Timeline: Carrier, 1 Year Since the Announcement," TheIndyChannel.com, Feb. 10, 2017, http://bit.ly/2uy6myd.

6. Noam Scheiber, "Unions Lean Democratic, but Donald Trump Gets Members' Attention," *New York Times*, Jan. 29, 2016, https://www.nytimes.com/2016/01/30/business/donald-trump-unions.html.

7. Ibid.

8. "U.S. Economic Confidence Changed Little in September," Gallup, Oct. 4, 2016, http://bit.ly/2hlN055.

9. "CBS News 2016 Battleground Tracker, Methods: Battlegrounds, . . . ," for Sept.14–16, 2016, Scribd, https://www.scribd.com/document/324406718/CBS-News-2016-Battleground-Tracker-Methods-Battlegrounds-September-18-2016.

10. "Middle-Class Americans Face Biggest Strain Under Rising Obamacare Costs," NPR, Nov. 6, 2016, http://www.npr.org/2016/11/06/500898851/middle-class-americans-face-biggest-strain-under-rising-obamacare-costs.

11. "Remarks by the President on the Economy," Concord Community High School (Elkhart, Indiana), The White House, June 1, 2016, https://obamawhitehouse.archives.gov/the-press-office/2016/06/01/remarks-president-economy.

12. James Gherardi, "Trump Calls Out Carrier in First Presidential Debate," Fox59, Sept. 27, 2016, http://bit.ly/2tYjds0; Steven Greenhouse, " 'Trump Talks a Big Game' on Indiana Factories—but Workers Express Doubt," *Guardian*, Sept. 30, 2016, http://bit.ly/2up4siX.

13. "Indiana Factory Workers Expect Donald Trump to Fulfill Promise on Jobs," NBC News via YouTube, Nov. 14, 2016, http://bit.ly/2t5AU66.

14. "Timeline: Carrier, 1 Year Since the Announcement."

15. Ibid.

16. Chris Isidore and Cristina Alesci, "What's at Stake for Trump, Carrier in Talks Over Jobs Bound for Mexico," CNN, Nov. 29, 2016, http://cnnmon.ie/2th4nOU.

17. Katie Cox, "Trump Administration, Carrier Reach Deal to Keep Nearly 1,000 Jobs in Indiana," TheIndyChannel.com, Nov. 29, 2016, http://bit.ly/2g EkqiE.

18. Donald Trump, Twitter, Nov. 29, 2016, https://twitter.com/realdonald trump/status/803805823503925250?lang=en.

19. Henry Grabar, "Trump Saved Jobs at Carrier by Making the Same Deal American Politicians Always Make," *Slate*, Nov. 30, 2016, http://slate.me/2gH8Wef.

20. "Is Trump's Deal with Carrier a Form of Crony Capitalism?," NPR, Dec. 2, 2016, http://n.pr/2gGXDzJ.

21. "Trump's Carrier Shakedown," *Wall Street Journal*, Dec. 1, 2016, http://on.wsj .com/2uoZNO1.

22. Chris Isidore and Eric Bradner, "How Donald Trump Got Carrier to Stay," CNN, Dec. 1, 2016, http://cnnmon.ie/2gDRTqz.

23. "Full Speech: Donald Trump, Mike Pence Carrier Plant Announcement 12/1/2016 Trump Indianapolis Speech," Based Patriot via YouTube, Dec. 1, 2016, http://bit.ly/2tYm1p2.

24. "T. J. Bray Prompted Trump About Jobs," WTHR via YouTube, Dec. 2, 2016, http://bit.ly/2th1kpE.

25. Ibid.

26. "Full Speech: Donald Trump, Mike Pence Carrier Plant Announcement 12/1/2016 Trump Indianapolis Speech."

27. Ibid.

28. "Carrier Worker: Donald Trump You're My Hero," Rusty TV via YouTube, Dec. 1, 2016, http://bit.ly/2uoGQeA.

29. Danielle Paquette, "He 'Lied His A— Off': Carrier Union Leader on Trump's Big Deal," *Washington Post*, Dec. 6, 2016, http://wapo.st/2h2TVB3.

30. Jon Greenberg, "MSNBC's Ed Schultz: Trade Deals Closed 50,000 Factories," PolitiFact, April 23, 2015, http://bit.ly/2hlTLDQ.

31. Lauren Carroll, "Trump: Since China joined WTO, U.S. has lost 60,000 factories," PolitiFact, March 24, 2017, http://www.politifact.com/truth-o -meter/statements/2017/mar/24/donald-trump/trump-china-joined-wto-us -has-lost-60000-factories/.

32. Matt Turner, "The CEO of United Technologies Just Let Slip an Unintended Consequence of the Trump-Carrier Jobs Deal," *Business Insider*, Dec. 5, 2016, http://read.bi/2gLiWm7.

33. Tom Huddleston, Jr., "Former CEO of United Technologies Left with $195 Million," *Fortune*, Feb. 6, 2015, http://for.tn/2th1BZP.

34. David Jamieson, "Joe Biden Warns the Right Is 'Intent on Breaking' Labor Unions," *Huffington Post*, March 9, 2015, http://bit.ly/2xYlcfW.

35. Ibid.

36. Alexis Boncy, "Paid Family Leave, Explained," *Week*, Aug. 2, 2016. http://bit
.ly/2tZIvoi.

THE STAKES

1. Jennifer Summers, "Our Utah Rare—Talan (Never Give Up!)," Utah Rare,
http://bit.ly/2v1Da2z.
2. "Talan's Fight: Never Give Up," Facebook, http://bit.ly/2tHe9Gb.
3. Summers, "Our Utah Rare—Talan (Never Give Up!)."
4. Ibid.
5. Ibid.
6. Ibid.
7. Robert Gehrke, "Gehrke: Team Trump Is Using a Tragic Utah Story to Gut
a Law Helping Millions," *Salt Lake Tribune*, March 17, 2017, http://bit.ly
/2h6EgEB.
8. Thomas Burr, "Utah Obamacare 'Victim' Meets with Trump," *Salt Lake Tribune*, March 13, 2017, http://bit.ly/2tNCONe.
9. Abby Hamblin, "White House: Share Your Obamacare Horror Stories!," *Salt
Lake Tribune*, March 14, 2017, http://bit.ly/2tH97cp.
10. Paula Span, "Bounced from Hospice," *New York Times*, Jan. 7, 2014, http://
nyti.ms/2vbIi4w.
11. Burr, "Utah Obamacare 'Victim' Meets with Trump."
12. Stan Summers, "I Have a Secret," Square One Printing, http://amzn.to
/2h6Y6zp.
13. "Melissa Ackison and Rich Ackison of Marysville, Ohio," U.S. Department
of Health and Human Services via YouTube, June 30, 2017, http://bit.ly
/2w4ltfG.
14. Mayo Clinic Staff, "Fibrous Dysplasia," MayoClinic.org, http://mayocl.in
/2uGPJO4.
15. Richard Pollock, "Repealing Itself? Only Four of 24 Obamacare Co-ops Remain Open," *Daily Caller*, Dec. 12, 2016, http://bit.ly/2gyPnWh.
16. "Melissa Ackison and Rich Ackison of Marysville, Ohio."
17. Vice President Pence, Twitter, June 27, 2017, http://bit.ly/2uGqWdi.
18. "Melissa Ackison," *Risk and Reward with Deirdre Bolton*, Fox Business, July 27,
2017.
19. Ibid.
20. Mayo Clinic Staff, "What You Can Expect," Mayo Clinic, http://mayocl
.in/2j5r4zB.
21. Anouk Pijpe, Nadine Andrieu, et al., "Exposure to Diagnostic Radiation and
Risk of Breast Cancer Among Carriers of BRCA1/2 Mutations: Retrospective
Cohort Study," *BMJ*, Sept. 6, 2012, http://bit.ly/2w4flns.

22. Angelina Jolie, "My Medical Choice," *New York Times*, May 14, 2013, http://nyti.ms/1l0wAtL.

23. Ibid.

24. "How Common Is Breast Cancer?," American Cancer Society, http://bit.ly/2tDVkTm.

25. Gary Claxton, Cynthia Cox, et al., "Pre-existing Conditions and Medical Underwriting in the Individual Insurance Market Prior to the ACA," Henry J. Kaiser Family Foundation, Dec. 12, 2016, http://kaiserf.am/2sv4tjz.

26. Ibid.

27. "Mary Katharine Ham Questions GOP Candidates During ABC News Debate," Townhall Media via YouTube, February 7, 2016, http://bit.ly/2w3LcF4.

28. Ibid.

THE BEGINNING

1. "Donald Trump Teases a President Bid During a 1988 Oprah Show," OWN via YouTube, June 25, 2015, http://bit.ly/1PcnWKR.

2. Maria Ricapito, "Thank God: Ivanka Trump Is Redefining the Idea of the 'Working Woman,'" *Marie Claire*, March 25, 2015, http://bit.ly/1NbQ26f.

3. Margaret M. Perlis, "Ivanka Trump Celebrates #WomenWhoWork with a Bold New Business Venture," *Forbes*, Dec. 17, 3014, http://bit.ly/2x39S1D.

4. Jonathan Van Meter, "Ivanka Trump Knows What It Means to Be a Modern Millennial," *Vogue*, Feb. 25, 2015, http://bit.ly/2wMqfyy.

5. "Ivanka Trump, 32," 40 Under 40, *Fortune*, 2014, http://for.tn/2h2aE80; "The 68th Annual International Best-Dressed List," *Vanity Fair*, Sept. 1, 2007, http://bit.ly/2vOSm01.

6. "MSNBC Laughs at Trump When He Runs and Then Meltdown When He Wins!," YouTube, Nov. 26, 2016, http://bit.ly/2my9zam.

7. Ibid.

8. Philip Bump, "Donald Trump's Spectacular, Unending, Utterly Baffling, Often-Wrong Campaign Launch," *Washington Post*, June 16, 2015, http://wapo.st/2vKiTLS.

9. Ibid.

10. Callum Borchers, "The Wrongest Media Predictions About Donald Trump," *Washington Post*, Nov. 9, 2016, http://wapo.st/2eQCI16.

11. Andy Ostroy, "The Super-Quick Implosion of Donald Trump's Candidacy," *Huffington Post*, June 30, 2016, http://bit.ly/2wMyuxF.

12. Harry Enten, "Why Donald Trump Isn't a Real Candidate, in One Chart," FiveThirtyEight, June 16, 2015. http://53eig.ht/2gMrM1i.

13. Callum Borchers, "The Wrongest Media Predictions About Donald Trump," *Washington Post*, Nov. 9, 2016, http://wapo.st/2eQCI16.

14. Kyle Smith, "Stop Pretending—Donald Trump Is Not Running for President," *New York Post*, May 30, 2015, http://nyp.st/2eR3juS.

15. William F. B. O'Reilly, "Donald Trump and Mermaids near Atlantis," *Newsday*, March 18, 2015, http://nwsdy.li/2wMAJRt.

16. Michael Scherer, "Forget the Past America, Donald Trump Could Run for President," *Time*, Feb. 25, 2015, http://ti.me/1zJ1iin.

17. Steven Ginsberg and Robert Costa, "'I. Will. Never. Leave. This. Race.,'" *Washington Post*, Dec. 9, 2015, http://wapo.st/2wMLsfK.

18. James Fallows, "3 Truths About Trump," *Atlantic*, July 13, 2015, http://theatln
.tc/2xTwUZs.

19. Daniel Libit, "The GOP's Real Pickle: If/When Trump Bows Out," CNBC, July 29, 2015, http://cnb.cx/2vRfXkU.

20. Maggie Haberman, "From Donald Trump, Hints of a Campaign Exit Strategy," *New York Times*, Oct. 9, 2015, http://nyti.ms/2wdihhw.

21. Peggy Noonan, "Donald Trump's Appeal—and Its Limits," *Wall Street Journal*, July 9, 2015, http://on.wsj.com/2gMCcOB.

22. John Fund, "Trump, the Unhappy Warrior, Woos Angry Voters by Telling Them What They Want to Hear," *National Review*, July 12, 2015, http://bit
.ly/2v2HUmh.

23. Sam Wang, "Donald Trump Is Not the Frontrunner. Smarter Polls Would Prove It," *New Republic*, July 20, 2015, http://bit.ly/2xSXWzZ.

24. Colin Campbell, "Trump on Fire: Dominating Headlines, Rocketing up in Polls," Business Insider, July 1, 2015, http://read.bi/2vK5UKa.

25. Daniel Strauss, "Are Trump's Poll Numbers Too Good to Be True?," *Politico*, June 24, 2015, http://politi.co/2j7aG2w.

26. "2016 Republican Presidential Nomination," Real Clear Politics, http://bit.ly
/2iiYMSZ.

27. "2016 Republican Popular Vote," Real Clear Politics, http://bit.ly/2wN0G4q.

28. "Editorial: Trump Should Pull the Plug on His Bloviating Side Show," *Des Moines Register*, July 20, 2015, http://dmreg.co/1MEo1U7.

29. "Donald Trump Tops New National Poll—Kayleigh McEnany," YouTube, July 21, 2015, http://bit.ly/2vXaIx2.

30. Ibid.

31. Kevin Cirilli, Michael C. Bender, and Jennifer Jacobs, "Trump Orders Surrogates to Intensify Criticism of Judge and Journalists," Bloomberg, June 7, 2016, https://bloom.bg/2eTQxIz.

32. "Trump Tells Supporters to Up Attacks on Judge," *Erin Burnett OutFront*, CNN, June 6, 2016, http://cnn.it/2wXZaK9.

33. Chuck Ross, "Attorney: Trump Companies Employ More Female Execs Than Male," *Daily Caller*, Aug. 17, 2015, http://bit.ly/1RKx09O.

34. Kayleigh McEnany, "Racism: The Left's Last Refuge," *Hill*, Dec. 6, 2016, http://bit.ly/2xg5Lyt.

35. Jacqueline Bueno, "Trump's Palm Beach Club Roils the Old Social Order," *Wall Street Journal*, April 30, 1997, http://on.wsj.com/1S6WFtk.

36. Ibid.

37. Adam B. Lerner, "Trump to Confederate Flag: You're Fired!," *Politico*, June 23, 2015, http://politi.co/1OWvbSZ; "Trump on Bland Arrest: 'I Thought It Was Terrible,'" *Anderson Cooper 360*, CNN, http://cnn.it/1ftbBTZ.

38. Martin Schram, "Carter Says Reagan Injects Racism," *Washington Post*, Sept. 17, 1980, http://wapo.st/2fWDJVF.

39. Ibid.

40. Steven F. Hayward, "The Liberal Misappropriation of a Conservative President," American Enterprise Institute, Oct. 11, 2011, http://bit.ly/2weVcyV.

41. Ibid.

42. Jeremy Diamond, "Trump Aide Offers Resignation in Melania Trump Plagiarism Incident," CNN, July 21, 2016, http://cnn.it/29MatwA.

43. Will Drabold, "Read Ivanka Trump's Speech at the Republican Convention," *Time*, July 21, 2016, http://ti.me/29PBxeH.

44. Jessica Chasmar, "Donald Trump Offers $10,000 to Heroic Bus Driver," *Washington Times*, Nov. 3, 2013, http://bit.ly/2wuCxyG.

THE OUTSIDERS

1. David Muir, "Transcript of the Republican Presidential Debate," *New York Times*, Feb. 6, 2016, http://nyti.ms/2wqwqfH.

2. Ibid.

3. Martha Raddatz, ibid.

4. Muir, ibid.

5. Raddatz, ibid.

6. Muir, ibid.

7. "Why People Vote Donald Trump: The Death of the American Dream," *Guardian*, http://bit.ly/2goC8FW.

8. Jill Filipovic, "Donald Trump Gives White Men Permission to Be Sexist and Racist," *Cosmopolitan*, March 3, 2016, http://bit.ly/1njIt57.

9. Matt Taibbi, "The Republicans Are Now Officially Party of White Paranoia," *Rolling Stone*, Sept. 4, 2015, http://rol.st/1OirxEk.

10. Nicholas Confessore and Nate Cohn, "Donald Trump's Victory Was Built on Unique Coalition of White Voters," *New York Times*, Nov. 9, 2016, http://nyti.ms/2gPLv3W.

11. Filipovic, "Donald Trump Gives White Men Permission to Be Sexist and Racist."

12. Angie Drobnic Holan, "In Context: Hillary Clinton and the 'Basket of Deplorables,'" PolitiFact, Sept. 11, 2016, http://bit.ly/2crTbVL.

13. Stephen A. Nuño, "Opinion: Hillary Is Wrong. 100 Percent of Trump Voters Are Deplorable," NBC News, Sept. 10, 2016, http://nbcnews.to/2eKgAlj.

14. Jamelle Bouie, "There's No Such Thing as a Good Trump Voter," *Slate*, Nov. 15, 2016, http://slate.me/2eX453y.

15. Ibid.

16. Kirsten Powers, "Americans Cast Votes on Election Day; Trump Does Not Commit to Accepting Results; Nevada Judge Rules Against Trump Campaign on Early Voting; People Line Up at Susan B. Anthony's Gravesite; Just Hours Away from First Election Results. Aired 4:30–5p ET," *The Lead with Jake Tapper*, CNN, Nov. 8, 2016, http://cnn.it/2wNY5EC.

17. Kayleigh McEnany, ibid.

18. Jake Tapper, ibid.

19. Kayleigh McEnany, ibid.

20. "Reality Check: Who Voted for Donald Trump," BBC, Nov. 9, 2016, http://bbc.in/2fDp1kB.

21. Amanda Sakuma, "Trump Did Better with Blacks, Hispanics Than Romney in '12: Exit Polls," NBC News, Nov. 9, 2016, http://nbcnews.to/2g8ZMsb.

22. Alec Tyson and Shiva Maniam, "Behind Trump's Victory: Divisions by Race, Gender, Education," Pew Research Center, Nov. 9, 2016, http://pewrsr.ch/2fyPSvu.

23. Ibid.

24. Anne Helen Petersen, "Meet the Ivanka Voter," BuzzFeed, Nov. 2, 2016, http://bzfd.it/2xSCVpb.

25. Ibid.

26. Ibid.

27. Emily Bazelon, "Why Did College-Educated White Women Vote for Trump?," *New York Times Magazine*, Nov. 15, 2016, http://nyti.ms/2ja4BSX.

28. Ibid.

29. Ibid.

30. Ibid.

31. Kayleigh McEnany, "Candidates in Monday's Debate, Beware the Gender Minefields," CNN, Sept. 23, 2016, http://cnn.it/2d7uzma; Rachel Weiner, "The Worst Debate Moments Ever," *Washington Post*, Nov. 10, 2011, http://wapo.st/2wNGRqX.

32. Ibid.

33. Ibid.

34. Marisa Schultz, "'Excuse me!': Bernie Snaps at Hillary During Debate," *New York Post*, March 7, 2016, http://nyp.st/1ptvyzr.

35. David Sherfinski, "Sanders' Adviser: He Wasn't Disrespectful at All; Clinton 'Constantly Interrupted Him,'" *Washington Times*, March 7, 2016, http://bit .ly/1ROZmj7.

36. Margaret Hartmann, "Sanders Tells Clinton: 'Excuse Me, I'm Talking' in Arguably Sexist Debate Exchange," *New York*, March 6, 2016, http://nym .ag/2eKPAlM.

37. McEnany, "Candidates in Monday's Debate, Beware the Gender Minefields."

38. Robin Eberhardt, "Clinton Wanted to Say 'Back Up, You Creep' to Trump at Debate," *Hill*, Aug. 23, 2017, http://bit.ly/2w3luld.

39. "How Will Gender Play a Role Throughout This Election?; Just Over Eight Weeks Until Summer Olympics in Rio; Outrage over Sentencing in Stanford Rape Case. Aired 6:30–7a ET," *New Day*, CNN, June 9, 2016, http://cnn .it/2eKfje1.

40. McEnany, "Candidates in Monday's Debate, Beware the Gender Minefields."

41. Ibid.; Eric Pianin, "Data Shows Millennial Women Are Dominating the Current Job Market, Inc.," May 23, 2017, http://on.inc.com/2qTAboy.

42. Alec Tyson and Shiva Maniam, "Behind Trump's Victory: Divisions by Race, Gender, Education," Pew Research Center, Nov. 9, 2016, http://pewrsr .ch/2fyPSvu.

43. Bazelon, "Why Did College-Educated White Women Vote for Trump?"

44. Benjy Sarlin, "Jeb Bush Leaves Behind Republican Party He Can Barely Recognize," NBC News, Feb. 21, 2016, http://nbcnews.to/2f8qii2.

45. "Dave Brat Beats Eric Cantor in GOP Primary," YouTube, June 10, 2014, http://bit.ly/2wlQ4cF.

46. David Wasserman, "What We Can Learn from Eric Cantor's Defeat," FiveThirtyEight, June 20, 2014, http://53eig.ht/2x3bGbb.

47. Gail Collins, "Putting a Cap on Cantor," *New York Times*, June 11, 2014, http:// nyti.ms/2iinfYA.

48. "Stunned Cable News Anchors React to Eric Cantor Primary Defeat," YouTube, June 10, 2014, http://bit.ly/2ve5Bqb.

49. "Rachel Maddow: Unpopularity Real Reason for Eric Cantor's Downfall," YouTube, June 11, 2014, http://bit.ly/2vUzVbk.

50. Byron Tau and Tarini Parti, "How Big Money Failed Cantor," *Politico*, June 11, 2014, http://politi.co/2hgUhqH; Jon Greenberg, "Rare Feat: Cantor Spent More at Steakhouse Than Opponent Did on Campaign," PunditFact, June 11, 2014, http://bit.ly/1s73b9B.

51. Sean Sullivan, "Cantor Internal Poll Claims 34-Point Lead over Primary Opponent Brat," *Washington Post*, June 6, 2014, http://wapo.st/2x2YYZH.

52. Stanley Feldman and Melissa Herrmann, "CBS News Exit Polls: How Donald Trump Won the U.S. Presidency," CBS News, Nov. 9, 2016, goo.gl/T2q6GC.

53. David A. Fahrenthold, Rosalind S. Helderman, and Jenna Portnoy, "What Went Wrong for Eric Cantor?," June 11, 2014, http://wapo.st/2xgpvCq.

54. "Morning Joe talks About Eric Cantor and His Entourage," MSNBC via You-Tube, June 12, 2014, http://bit.ly/2wlYroQ.

55. Fahrenthold et al., "What Went Wrong for Eric Cantor?"

56. "David Brat Stump Speech Pt. 1," YouTube, March 20, 2014, http://bit.ly/2wu c9oE.

57. Ibid.; Cook Political Report, http://bit.ly/2wlMYpb.

58. David Carr, "Eric Cantor's Defeat Exposed a Beltway Journalism Blind Spot," *New York Times*, June 15, 2014, http://nyti.ms/2eKQxuk.

59. Howard Fineman, "Bernie Sanders Thinks Hillary Is Eric Cantor," *Huffington Post*, June 25, 2014, goo.gl/RhV7f2.

60. Hannah Bleau, "Brat on Hannity: 'We Need to Move away from Cheap Political Rhetoric of Right and Left,'" *Daily Caller*, June 11, 2014, http://bit.ly/2wcR2Uk.

61. Benjy Sarlin, "Jeb Bush Leaves Behind Republican Party He Can Barely Recognize," NBC News, Feb. 21, 2016, goo.gl/Roj6G6.

62. Ibid.

63. Ibid.

64. Aaron Zitner, Dante Chinni, and Brian McGill, "How Clinton Won," *Wall Street Journal*, June 8, 2016; http://bit.ly/1UnZ7Kz; Donna Brazile, "Inside Hillary Clinton's Secret Takeover of the DNC," *Politico*, Nov. 2, 2017, goo.gl/FpP6P1.

65. "2016 Republican Presidential Nomination," Real Clear Politics, http://bit.ly /2iiYMSZ.

66. Jenna Johnson, "Donald Trump Says Companies Can 'Very Easily' Offer Child Care to Employees," *Washington Post*, Nov. 19, 2015, http://wapo.st/2h 2aWM8.

67. Donald Trump, "The CNN-Telemundo Republican Debate Transcript, Annotated," *Washington Post*, Feb. 25, 2016, http://wapo.st/2h0kwmu.

68. Ted Cruz, ibid.

69. Marco Rubio, ibid.

70. Donald Trump, ibid.

71. Edward Alden, "The Roots of Trump's Trade Rage," *Politico*, Jan. 16, 2017, http://politi.co/2jY4YzQ.

72. "Donald Trump Teases a President Bid During a 1988 Show," OWN via You-Tube, June 25, 2015, http://bit.ly/1PcnWKR.

73. Edward Alden, "The Roots of Trump's Trade Rage," *Politico Magazine*, January 16, 2017, http://politi.co/2jY4YzQ.

74. Jonathan Soble and Keith Bradsher, "Donald Trump Laces into Japan with a Trade Tirade from the '80s," *New York Times*, March 7, 2016, http://nyti.ms /2gMabGU.

75. Alden, "The Roots of Trump's Trade Rage."

76. Michelle Lee, "Fact Check: Yes, Trump Did Support the Iraq War," *Washington Post*, Sept. 26, 2016, http://wapo.st/2xQC73d.

77. Eugene Kiely, "Donald Trump and the Iraq War," FactCheck.org, Feb. 19, 2016, http://bit.ly/1MB7NdM.

78. Ibid.

79. Ibid.

80. Ibid.

81. Mike Huckabee, "Oct. 9 Republican Debate Transcript," NBC News, Oct. 9, 2007, http://nbcnews.to/2vSEQuK.

82. "Donald Trump's Nashville Rally: The Photos You Need to See," *Heavy*, March 15, 2017, http://bit.ly/2ilCCj9.

83. David Jackson and Erin Kelly, "Ben Carson Drops Out of GOP Presidential Race," *USA Today*, March 4, 2016, https://usat.ly/2xkCYJo.

84. Hunter Walker, "Ben Carson Says Donald Trump Prayed for Forgiveness Before the Debate," Yahoo News, Oct. 10, 2016, https://yhoo.it/2wgUvVN.

THE DEBATES

1. Van Jones, "Awaiting Historic Clinton-Trump Debate on CNN; Aides: Clinton to Decide 'on the Fly' About Fact Checking Trump; Hillary Clinton Arriving at Debate Hall; Debate Commission Officials Addressing Audience; Debate Commission Chair Explains Format of Debate. Aired 8–9p ET," *Anderson Cooper 360*, CNN, Sept. 26, 2016, http://cnn.it/2xYhv9i.

2. Kayleigh McEnany, ibid.

3. Gloria Borger, "Debate Night in America: Post-Debate Analysis; Clinton and Trump Spar on Their First Presidential Debate; Interview with Mark Cuban; Interview with Kellyanne Conway. Aired 10:40p–12a ET," CNN, Sept. 26, 2016, http://cnn.it/2vSRKXs.

4. David Axelrod, ibid.

5. Nia-Malika Henderson, ibid.

6. Michael Smerconish, ibid.

7. McEnany, ibid.

8. Henderson, ibid.

9. Anderson Cooper, ibid.

10. McEnany, ibid.

11. Kelly Riddell, "Fact checking the media—yes, the Clinton machine did start the birther movement," *Washington Times*, Aug. 22, 2016, goo.gl/5AJqNp.

12. Ibid.

13. Aaron Blake, "The First Trump-Clinton Presidential Debate Transcript, Annotated," *Washington Post*, Sept. 26, 2016, http://wapo.st/2xwgkSs.

14. McEnany, "Debate Night in America."

15. "Clinton and Trump Wrap Up Second Presidential Debate; Post Debate Analysis; Ohio Uncommitted Voters Weigh in on Debate; Interview with Kellyanne Conway; Fact-Checking the Candidates. Aired 10:36p–12a ET," CNN, Oct. 9, 2016, http://cnn.it/2wZOX1L.

16. Ibid.

17. Trump, "Full Transcript: Second 2016 Presidential Debate," *Politico*, Oct. 10, 2016, http://politi.co/2dWghSC.

18. Kayleigh McEnany,"Clinton and Trump Wrap Up Second Presidential Debate; Post Debate Analysis; Ohio Uncommitted Voters Weigh in on Debate; Interview with Kellyanne Conway; Fact-Checking the Candidates. Aired 10:36p–12a ET," CNN, Oct. 9, 2016, http://cnn.it/2wZOX1L.

19. Trump, "Full transcript: Second 2016 Presidential Debate."

20. Hillary Clinton, ibid.

21. Trump, ibid.

22. Dana Bash,"Clinton and Trump Wrap Up Second Presidential Debate; Post Debate Analysis; Ohio Uncommitted Voters Weigh in on Debate; Interview with Kellyanne Conway; Fact-Checking the Candidates. Aired 10:36p–12a ET," CNN, Oct. 9, 2016, http://cnn.it/2wZOX1L.

23. Jake Tapper, ibid.

24. Kayleigh McEnany, ibid.

25. "Clinton and Trump Wrap Up Second Presidential Debate; Post Debate Analysis; Ohio Uncommitted Voters Weigh in on Debate; Interview with Kellyanne Conway; Fact-Checking the Candidates. Aired 10:36p–12a ET."

26. McEnany, ibid.

27. Tapper, ibid.

28. "Clinton and Trump Wrap Up Second Presidential Debate; Post Debate Analysis; Ohio Uncommitted Voters Weigh in on Debate; Interview with Kellyanne Conway; Fact-Checking the Candidates. Aired 10:36p–12a ET."

29. Donald Trump, "Full Transcript: Third 2016 Presidential Debate," *Politico*, Oct. 20, 2016, http://politi.co/2dt5q1c.

30. Van Jones, "Debate Night in America, Third and Final Presidential Debate; Aired 11p–12a ET," CNN, Oct. 19, 2016, http://cnn.it/2xPbpfl.

31. Kayleigh McEnany, ibid.

32. Jones, ibid.

33. McEnany, ibid.

34. Jeff Lord, ibid.

35. Jones, ibid.

36. McEnany, ibid.

37. Ibid.

38. Jones, ibid.

39. Lord, ibid.

40. Solis Doyle, ibid.
41. Lord, ibid.
42. Solis Doyle, ibid.
43. Lord, ibid.
44. Nia-Malika Henderson, ibid.
45. Lord, ibid.
46. Henderson, ibid.
47. Lord, ibid.
48. Henderson, ibid.
49. Ibid.
50. Ibid.
51. Lord, ibid.
52. Borger, ibid.
53. Lord, ibid.
54. Borger, ibid.
55. Henderson, ibid.
56. Borger, ibid.
57. McEnany, ibid.
58. Lord, ibid.
59. Borger, ibid.
60. McEnany, ibid.
61. Solis Doyle, ibid.
62. Eric Lacy, "Excerpts from Detroit Native Dr. Benjamin Carson's Viral Speech That's Become a YouTube Sensation," MLive, Feb. 19, 2013, http://bit.ly/2ww kngc.
63. Ibid.
64. Jonathan Easley, "Poll: Voters grow weary of Russia probes," *Hill*, June 23, 2017, http://bit.ly/2rKpHY2; Rich Noyes, "Study: TV News Is Obsessed With Trump-Russia Probe," Newsbusters, June 27, 2017, http://bit.ly/2w6y7PF.
65. Thomas E. Patterson, "News Coverage of Donald Trump's First 100 Days," Harvard Kennedy School, May 18, 2017, http://bit.ly/2qAxzM4.
66. Donald Trump, "Full Transcript: Third 2016 Presidential Debate."
67. Hillary Clinton, ibid.
68. "Here's a List of Everyone & Everything Hillary Has Blamed for Her Loss," Fox News, June 1, 2017, http://bit.ly/2rovrHr.
69. "CNN Live Event/Special: Third and Final Presidential Debate," CNN, Oct. 19, 2016, http://cnn.it/2y3Z2sW.
70. Kayleigh McEnany, "Debate Night in America, Third and Final Presidential Debate; Aired 11p–12a ET," CNN, Oct. 19, 2016, http://cnn.it/2xPbpfl.
71. Gloria Borger, ibid.

72. McEnany, ibid.
73. David Axelrod, ibid.
74. McEnany, ibid.
75. Axelrod, ibid.

THE ELECTION

1. Herbert Kretzmer, lyrics for "Do You Hear the People Sing?" from *Les Miserables*.
2. Michael Edison Hayden, "Statistician Nate Silver Says Clinton Is a '2 to 1 Favorite to Win,'" *ABC News*, Nov. 7, 2016, http://abcn.ws/2fauzlE.
3. Post Opinion Writers Predict What Will Happen on Election Night," *Washington Post*, Nov. 8, 2016, http://wapo.st/2eUAx98.
4. John King, "Obamas Joins Clinton for Philadelphia Rally; Clinton, Trump Make Final Pitch in Battleground States; Clinton Speaking Now in Philadelphia. Aired 9–10p ET," *Anderson Cooper 360 Degrees*, CNN, Nov. 7, 2016, http://cnn.it/2xwFFM6.
5. David Axelrod, ibid.
6. "Trump says election will be 'Brexit plus, plus, plus,'" *Los Angeles Times*, Nov. 7, 2016, http://lat.ms/2h0h8rs.
7. Ibid.
8. Ibid.
9. Chad Livengood, "Clinton on Defense in Mich.; Trump Goes for 'Hail Mary,'" *Detroit News*, Nov. 5, 2016, http://detne.ws/2xdkMEW.
10. Anderson Cooper, "Obamas Joins Clinton for Philadelphia Rally; Clinton, Trump Make Final Pitch in Battleground States; Clinton Speaking Now in Philadelphia. Aired 9–10p ET," *Anderson Cooper 360*, CNN, Nov. 7, 2016, http://cnn.it/2xwFFM6.
11. David Axelrod, ibid.
12. Van Jones, ibid.
13. Kayleigh McEnany, ibid.
14. Axelrod, ibid.
15. "Poll: Trump Takes Wide Lead over Clinton with Independent Voters," Fox News, Sept. 6, 2016, http://bit.ly/2cpzewl; "Michigan Results," Exit Polls, CNN, http://cnn.it/2xjmbcU; "Wisconsin Results," Exit Polls, CNN, http://cnn.it/2y3CRmB; "North Carolina Results," Exit Polls, CNN, http://cnn.it/2f3bDYD; "Ohio Results," Exit Polls, CNN, http://cnn.it/2f4ARG9.
16. Lloyd Gruber, "How Political Scientists Got Trump Exactly Wrong," LSE, U.S. Centre, June 1, 2016, http://blogs.lse.ac.uk/usappblog/2016/06/01/how-political-scientists-got-trump-exactly-wrong/.
17. Ibid.

18. Jake Tapper, "Interview With Clinton Press Secretary Brian Fallon; Election Day Coverage. Aired 4–4:30p ET," *The Lead with Jake Tapper*, CNN, Nov. 8, 2016, http://cnn.it/2wWb5dO.

19. "Nevada: Trump vs. Clinton," Real Clear Politics, http://bit.ly/2yk5q2m; "Florida: Trump vs. Clinton," Real Clear Politics, http://bit.ly/2hGJyHn; "Ohio: Trump vs. Clinton," Real Clear Politics, http://bit.ly/2yl3lmU; "Iowa: Trump vs. Clinton," Real Clear Politics, http://bit.ly/2yjC98b.

20. Kayleigh McEnany, "Interview With Clinton."

21. Ibid.

22. "Pennsylvania: Trump vs. Clinton," Real Clear Politics, http://bit.ly/2f9Oujr; "Michigan: Trump vs. Clinton," Real Clear Politics, http://bit.ly/2xdB4h1; "Wisconsin: Trump vs. Clinton," Real Clear Politics, http://bit.ly/2xl8gTb; "Maine CD2: Trump vs. Clinton," Real Clear Politics, http://bit.ly/2w758Ho.

23. Brad Heath, Mitchell Thorson, and Jim Sergent, "How Trump Changed the Obama Landscape," *USA Today*, Nov. 15, 2016, https://usat.ly/2f3x4ce.

24. "Americans Cast Votes on Election Day; Trump Does Not Commit to Accepting Results. Aired 4:30–5p ET," *The Lead with Jake Tapper*, CNN, Nov. 8, 2016, http://www.cnn.com/TRANSCRIPTS/1611/08/cg.02.html.

25. "2016 Election Day: Live Updates," *Breitbart*, Nov. 8, 2016, http://bit.ly/2eKW PuG.

26. Ibid.

27. Clemence Michallon, "Supporter Who Painted a Trump 2016 Sign on the Side of His House Has His Home Egged, His Truck Damaged and One of His Walls Vandalized with Graffiti—Before His Front Yard Gets Set on FIRE," *Daily Mail*, May 22, 2016, http://dailym.ai/2xfp4cv.

28. Livengood, "Clinton on Defense in Mich.; Trump Goes for 'Hail Mary.'"

29. Michallon, "Supporter Who Painted a Trump 2016 Sign on the Side of His House Has His Home Egged, His Truck Damaged and One of His Walls Vandalized with Graffiti—Before His Front Yard Gets Set on FIRE."

30. "Clinton Campaign Cancels Election Night Fireworks: Official," *NBC News*, Nov. 7, 2016, http://bit.ly/2y3mHcO.

31. Jim Acosta, "CNN Live Event/Special: Standing by for Polls to Close in Three States. Aired 7–8p ET," CNN, Nov. 8, 2016, http://cnn.it/2y3nc6P.

32. Ibid.

33. Jeff Zeleny, ibid.

34. Wolf Blitzer, ibid.

35. Wolf Blitzer, "Election Night in America; FL, NC, NH, OH, PA, VA, Too Early to Call; Standing by for Polls to Close in 14 States. Aired 8–9p ET," CNN, Nov. 8, 2016, http://cnn.it/2xfCDJ9.

36. John King, ibid.

37. Wolf Blitzer, ibid.

38. Ibid.

39. Ibid.

40. Jim Acosta, "Clinton Wins Eight States & D.C., Trump wins 13 States; CO, FL, MI, NC, NH, OH, PA, VA Too Early to Call. Aired 9–10p ET," CNN, Nov. 8, 2016, http://cnn.it/2fAhjqf.

41. Ibid.

42. Brianna Keilar, ibid.

43. Jake Tapper, ibid.

44. Wolf Blitzer, "CNN Discusses a Very Tight Election; Trump Does Much Better Than Expected; Donald Trump Is Ahead with 167 Electoral Votes; 270 Needed to Win the White House. Aired 10–11p ET," CNN, Nov. 8, 2016, http://cnn.it/2eTBEFS.

45. Ibid.

46. David Axelrod, "Election Night in America: Clinton Carries California; Hidden Trump Voters. Aired 11p–12a ET," CNN, Nov. 8, 2016, http://cnn.it /2xlaS3r.

47. Gloria Borger, ibid.

48. Michael Smerconish, ibid.

49. Dana Bash, ibid.

50. Wolf Blitzer, ibid.

51. Jake Tapper, "Live Coverage of Election 2016; Donald Trump Leading Hillary Clinton in Electoral Votes. Aired 12–1a ET," CNN, Nov. 9, 2016, http:// cnn.it/2xuQ9KX.

52. Kayleigh McEnany, ibid.

53. Ibid.

54. Brianna Keilar, "Election Night in America: Clinton Carries California; Hidden Trump Voters. Aired 11p–12a ET," CNN, Nov. 8, 2016, http://cnn.it /2xlaS3r.

55. Jake Tapper, "Donald Trump Leading Presidential Race; Historic Revolution in American Election; Several States Too Close to Call. Aired 1–2a ET," CNN, Nov. 9, 2016, http://cnn.it/2xPd84C.

56. Jeff Zeleny, ibid.

57. Ibid.

58. John Podesta, "Election Night in America: Clinton Will Not Speak Tonight. Aired 2–3a ET," CNN, Nov. 9, 2016, http://cnn.it/2xYiR3Z.

59. Corey Lewandowski, ibid.

60. Anderson Cooper, ibid.

61. Ibid.

62. Dana Bash, ibid.

63. Wolf Blitzer, ibid.

64. Ibid.

65. Ibid.
66. Jim Acosta, ibid.
67. Donald Trump, ibid.
68. Ibid.
69. Ibid.
70. Ibid.
71. Ibid.

CONCLUSION

1. Patrick Marley and Jason Stein, "Foxconn Unveils $10 Billion Plan to Build LCD Display Plant in Wisconsin," *USA Today*, Aug. 8, 2017, https://usat.ly/2eOI8cJ.

2. Sean Higgins, "Unions Praise Trump Order on Keystone XL, Dakota Access Pipeline," *Washington Examiner*, Jan. 24, 2017, http://washex.am/2hgNSsY.

3. Paul Bedard, "University: Obama's TPP Trade Deal Will Whack 448,000 Jobs, Not Save Them as Promised," *Washington Examiner*, Jan. 28, 2016, http://washex.am/2ydmEd.

4. Martin Crutsinger, "U.S. Consumer Confidence at 16-Year High," Associated Press, July 25, 2017, https://usat.ly/2uxV6iA; David Jackson, "Trump Television Stalwart Kayleigh McEnany Named Republican Party Spokesperson," *USA Today*, Aug. 7, 2017, https://usat.ly/2wo3m5m; Christopher Rugaber, "The Median Household Income in the U.S. Is Rising," *Time*, Sept. 12, 2017, http://ti.me/2wXEceq.

5. Richard Sisk, "Trump Signs Bill to Speed Up VA Disability Appeals Process," Military.com, Aug. 23, 2017, http://bit.ly/2w6Q8JS.

6. Ibid.

7. "Top Military Officer Contradicts Obama, Says ISIS Not 'Contained,'" Fox News, Dec. 1, 2015, http://fxn.ws/1SvtzTU.

8. Carlo Muñoz, "Trump Sends Message in Terror Fight with Big Bomb Drop," *Washington Times*, April 13, 2017, http://bit.ly/2hgXRlQ.

9. "Trump's Executive Order: Who Does Travel Ban Affect?," BBC, Feb. 10, 2017, http://bbc.in/2jt2vsv.

10. David French, "Victory for Trump: SCOTUS Restores Vast Majority of Travel Ban," *National Review*, June 26, 2017, http://bit.ly/2xRZmOE.

11. Pete Kasperowicz, "House Sends $1.6 Billion Border Wall Request to the Senate . . . Again," *Washington Examiner*, Sept. 14, 2017, http://washex.am/2heLMxE.

12. President Donald Trump, "Remarks by President Trump to the 72nd Session of the United Nations General Assembly," White House, Sept. 19, 2017, http://bit.ly/2wEDdOx.

13. Ibid.

ACKNOWLEDGMENTS

I quickly realized that this project was more than writing a book; it was a faith journey, drawing me closer to my Lord and Savior Jesus Christ, whose spirit I hope comes through these pages. Truly remarkable men and women opened their hearts and, in some cases, their homes to me, and for that I am forever grateful to Kim Copeland, Donna Coates and Diane Catoe, Sabine Durden, Rob and Kelly Winebrenner and family, and Noah Patton. Though you all have suffered so much loss, Jesus' love shines through your tears and reinvigorated my faith walk.

To Stan Summers, Melissa Ackison, Brian Easton, T. J. Bray, Bill Barlow, and the First Liberty attorneys, I thank you for sharing your stories with readers. Your fight for the American Dream and our constitutional protections is to be commended.

David Larabell, my literary agent at CAA, believed in this project long before Election 2016, and I am so thankful for his efforts to find the perfect fit in the publisher Simon & Schuster, Threshold Editions. The guidance of my editor, Natasha Simons, and her assistant, Hannah Brown, was truly invaluable. Natasha believed in the *New American Revolution* early on, and her well-thought-out, spot-on edits undoubtedly made this book better. To Louise Burke, former publisher of Threshold Editions, and Mitchell Ivers, vice president and editorial director, your belief in this project means more to me than you will ever know.

Without a loving, supportive, and faith-filled family, this book would not have been possible. Your contribution to my career and to this book cannot be overstated. My husband as of November 2017, Sean Gilmartin, a self-described constitutional conservative and "Levinite," provided me with so much inspiration, fielding my ideas and helping to hone them. His love and support through my travels across the United States were indispensable to this work. My dad, Mike McEnany, raised me as a freedom-loving Republican and continues to be my intellectual sounding board along with my mom, Leanne McEnany, who raised me with dedication, heart, and self-sacrificing love. Together, their emphasis on faith was instrumental in my development and that of my remarkable siblings, Michael and Ryann McEnany. And to my grandmothers, Glenda Knight and Jean McEnany, you are the matriarchs of my family, and I love you very much, along with my grandfathers, the late Bill Knight and Pat McEnany.

I want to thank Dana Carpenter for allowing me to mention and dedicate this book to your sweet, beautiful angel, Megan Carpenter. Megan's valiant battle with cancer and faith in Jesus Christ every step of the way was awe-inspiring. I miss my sweet friend and still think of her every single time I see a feather.

And to my hero—Rachel Joy Scott. Just one day before I wrote these acknowledgments, Darrell Scott, Rachel's father, gave me his blessing in dedicating my book to his daughter. It was an honor to speak to the man who raised this beautiful young woman, whose life on this earth ended far too soon. As most of you know, seventeen-year-old Rachel Joy Scott was the first victim of the tragic Columbine High School shooting. I will never forget taking in those horrific images as a young eleven-year-old girl. It was the day that I saw evil and realized that it was alive in this world. On April 20, 1999—the day that thirteen innocents were gunned down—evil was at work, but it could not extinguish the good.

In the aftermath of the shooting, as we learned about the victims, the circumstances of Rachel Joy Scott's death came to light. The only surviving witness of Rachel's last moments told NBC that Rachel was asked if she believed in God before she died. She said yes and died a Christian martyr because of it. Rachel's funeral, aired on cable news, featured a white casket covered in the loving words and signatures of her peers. During the two-hour service, several of her friends spoke about her love for all, regardless of status or popularity. One young man said, "All my life, I prayed that someone would love me and make me feel wanted. God sent me an angel," he tearfully recounted. You see, Rachel's deeply held Christian faith gave her a deep-seated love for others, one that did not go unnoticed by her classmates.

I took a sincere interest in Rachel Joy Scott as a young girl and read several of her journals, oftentimes written directly to God, later published by her parents, Darrell Scott and Beth Nimmo. Those journal entries revealed a young woman with a remarkable connection to her savior and even a premonition of her own death. "This will be my last year, Lord. I have gotten what I can. Thank you," Rachel wrote less than one year before she died. And on the day of her passing, she drew a picture of a pair of eyes crying thirteen tears onto a rose. Moments later, thirteen bright lights on this earth would be extinguished by darkness.

Rachel's unwavering commitment to God and her profound bravery to die for her savior inspired me then and still to this day. Thank you, Rachel, for making the faith my parents had taught me real in my own life. It has always been my genuine hope that you would greet me one day at Heaven's pearly gates.

Last, and certainly not least, to my Savior, Jesus Christ. You died so I may live. You poured out your blood to save a humanity so undeserving of you. It is hard to fathom the debt that you paid on my behalf.

"For God so loved the world that he gave his one and only Son, that whoever believes in him shall not perish but have eternal life."
—JOHN 3:16